KT-210-682

Perception

From sense to object

WITHDRAWN

Hutchinson Psychology
Series editor Brian Foss

Already published

Personality
Measurement and theory
Paul Kline

Perception
From sense to object
John M. Wilding

In preparation

Thinking
C. Singleton

Perception
From sense to object

John M. Wilding
Lecturer in Psychology, Bedford College, University of London

Hutchinson
London Melbourne Sydney Auckland Johannesburg

Hutchinson & Co. (Publishers) Ltd

An imprint of the Hutchinson Publishing Group

17–21 Conway Street, London W1P 6JD

Hutchinson Group (Australia) Pty Ltd
30–32 Cremorne Street, Richmond South, Victoria 3121
PO Box 151, Broadway, New South Wales 2007

Hutchinson Group (NZ) Ltd
32–34 View Road, PO Box 40–086, Glenfield, Auckland 10

Hutchinson Group (SA) (Pty) Ltd
PO Box 337, Bergvlei 2012, South Africa

Photoset in 10 on 12 Times by Kelly Typesetting Limited
Bradford-on-Avon, Wiltshire

Printed in Great Britain by The Anchor Press Ltd
and bound by Wm Brendon & Son Ltd
both of Tiptree, Essex

British Library Cataloguing in Publication Data

Wilding, J. M.
Perception.
1. Perception – Psychological aspects
I. Title
153.7   QP441

ISBN 0 09 150720 1 cased
     0 09 150721 9 paper

To David, Martin and Jonathan for their patience and support

Contents

Acknowledgements

The author and the publishers would like to thank the following copyright holders for their kind permission to reproduce the following figures:

Figure 9 from *Explorations in Cognition* edited by Donald A. Norman, David E. Rumelhart and the LNR Research Group, W. H. Freeman and Company, copyright © 1975

Figure 10 from 'An example of a triple violation in detecting the unexpected in photointerpretation' by I. Biederman, R. J. Mezzanotte, *et al.*, in *Human Factors*, 1981, 23(2), pp. 153–64

Figure 11 from *Visual Perception* by T. N. Cornsweet, Academic Press Inc (London) Ltd, 1970, p. 314

Figure 18 from 'Organization of the primate retina' by J. E. Dowling and B. B. Boycott, in *Proceedings of the Royal Society London*, Series B, 1966, vol. 166, p. 104

Figure 19 from *Human Information Processing* (2nd edn) by P. H. Lindsay and D. A. Norman, Academic Press Inc (London) Ltd, 1977, p. 74

Figure 21 from 'Representation and recognition of the spatial organization of three-dimensional shapes' by D. Marr and H. K. Nishihara, in *Proceedings of the Royal Society London*, Series B, vol. 200, pp. 269–94

Figure 27 from *Signal Detection and Recognition by Human Observers: Contemporary Readings* by J. A. Swets, John Wiley & Sons, 1964, p. 69

Figure 31 from *Decision Processes in Visual Perception* by D. Vickers, Academic Press Inc (London) Ltd, 1979, p. 128

Figure 35 from 'Acoustic loci and transitional cues for consonants' by A. M. Liberman, *Journal of the Acoustical Society of America*, 1955, vol. 27, pp.

Figures

Tables

Preface

This is not meant to be a standard textbook on perception, in the sense of acting as a source for all the facts that a zealous undergraduate could desire. Rather, I have tried to define the goals of those who wish to understand perception and to provide a framework within which our knowledge about perception could be organized. In the course of trying to build this framework I have realized how complex the structure must be and how many of the pieces are missing and how inadequate many of our methods are for finding them. I have tried particularly to give readers a knowledge of the methods which researchers are using to try and fill in some of these gaps, so that they may themselves set about trying to supply some of the missing pieces or devising better methods where the present ones are inadequate. One exciting thing about studying psychology is that relative novices can, and do, make significant contributions to our understanding. My hope is that I may have clarified a few questions and encouraged my readers to set about finding answers.

Many people have aided the writing of this book. I should like to thank particularly Brian Foss who gave me the initial encouragement and has proved such a sympathetic editor, Naresh Mohindra for many discussions and suggestions, my colleagues for gifts of knowledge and loans of books, and students over the years for interest and scepticism.

1 Questions

As I look out of my window, I see grass and trees, gently swaying in the wind, with a lake beyond. The smell of new-mown grass drifts in through the open window and the warmth of the afternoon sun pours into the room. An asphalt path leads down through the trees to the lake and two squirrels are chasing each other to and fro across it, ignoring the woman coming up the path. A sudden screech of brakes calls my attention to the constant whirr of traffic on the road beyond the lake and now I hear geese honking, and a murmur of voices from the next room.

This is the scene I experience, a world of objects with background, acted upon and sometimes acting and interacting in events. I have no problem seeing and hearing and smelling and feeling all these things because they affect my senses directly and they make up the real world.

Or do they? I can look again and notice things I missed before, or see the scene in new ways. There is a white wall framing the window I am looking through and the window in fact fills less of my field of view than the wall, but I did not even notice the wall at first, and my impression was that the scene through the window was a panorama right across in front of me. There are metal bars dividing the window into squares and the glass is obscured with dust and spots, but for me the view seemed complete and unobscured. The 'grass' is patches of colour ranging from nearly white in the bright sun to nearly black in the shade, but I 'saw' green grass in light and shade. Other changing greenish shapes were for me permanent leafy branches moved by a wind I neither saw nor felt, and two constantly varying grey shapes were squirrels moving with a purpose. Another shape increasing in size and changing in position was an approaching woman. A particular pattern of sound frequencies was immediately linked to memories of geese, and another pattern to anxiety, sudden deceleration and images of a suddenly stopping car. A particular sensation of smell evoked memories of lawn-mowers and heaps of grass with children throwing them at each other.

Differences between experience and sensory information

What we experience, apparently directly, is actually very different from what is recorded by our sense organs. Yet it is very difficult to get away from the former and try to get back to the latter. Here is a list of some of the ways in which the information at the sense organs differs from the perceptual experience upon which it is based.

1   Perceptual experience is of a world of segregated objects and events (I will use the word 'object' in a broad sense to include such things as sounds, spoken words, and tunes, as well as visually defined objects like people, buildings and hills). But the sensory input is an unsegregated flux, which does not arrive ready for division like a bar of chocolate. We hear words separated by gaps, but physically there are as many gaps in the middle of words as there are between, and frequently there are none in between. Recall how a foreign language sounds.

   The situation is not very different for visual perception. Admittedly, visually presented words are usually printed with spaces in between, but most of the other input to our eyes is a patchwork of contours and colours which is far from being neatly organized to suit our needs. Occasionally we gain a glimpse of what the unorganized deluge of stimulation is like when we wake in a strange room or are confronted with a puzzle picture or a photo in which it is not clear which side is the top (Figure 1). Such situations are disturbing, and the sudden realization of where we are, or the sudden organization of the picture so that everything falls into place, produces relief and satisfaction, like we feel having solved a knotty problem. In fact the solution does often come by trying out a number of different possible guesses about the answer. Certain drugs and meditational methods are sometimes used to induce a similar state of non-organization, with the aim of experiencing the 'reality' behind normal experiencing. Our immediate visual experience is also of a three-dimensional world, with objects at different distances from us, while the eye receives only a two-dimensional pattern of excitation.

2   Second, the input to our senses is varying in many ways, while

Figure 1 *Sacks stacked in a warehouse*

our experience is of a stable world. Every time we move our eyes or our head, every time the sun goes in or comes out, the pattern delivered to our eyes changes. We move around in a room but do not believe the walls change shape and the objects in it move around, depending on the angle from which we see them. Sounds of cars or other voices come and go, mingling with the speaker's voice. The same word is uttered or written differently by different speakers and by the same speaker at different times. Faces change with emotion and age, tunes are played by different instruments and in different keys. Yet we can derive from the variation an underlying stability and disregard the change, or interpret it as having a significance of its own.

Another example of our ignoring variability is the grouping together or categorizing together of things which are physically different. In some cases the physical difference is actually un- noticed. Say to yourself 'keep calm and cool'. Three of the words begin with a 'k' sound, but in fact these three sounds differ considerably, You should be able to feel that they are produced differently. An Arab can hear the differences because in Arabic they are sometimes important for meaning, and a Spaniard confuses 'ice' and 'eyes', which are clearly different for an English speaker, because in Spanish this difference is never important. In other cases the differences can be perceived, but they do not stop us treating a class of objects as similar; the puzzle in these cases is often how we manage to select the similarity. Think of the difficulty of explaining to a Martian how to decide the thing in front of him was a dog or the sounds he could hear were Reggae. No simple clue is apparent and we cannot easily say how we do it.

3   Third, much that we experience is either not present in the input at all, or the basis for it is very different in form from our experience. I have already pointed out that gaps between spoken words are often not physically present; the same is true of stress and loudness in speech, which often depend far more on interpretation of the speaker's intentions than the physical characteristics of the sounds. Sound waves varying in frequency and amplitude are all that arrive at the ear, but the experience is rich and varied. In vision, fragmentary information, partly obscured, can provide experience of unfragmented objects. Contours may be seen where none exist (Figure 2) and one line may be seen as longer than another though they are really equal

Figure 2 *Phantom contours (after Kanizsa 1955)*

(Figure 3). We even claim to be able to judge hardness from appearance. The visual information at the eye consists of a two-dimensional pattern of points of light varying in location, intensity and wavelength, but our experience is of a three-dimensional world of solid objects, such as trees and squirrels. Even such an apparently simple matter as seeing straight lines need not be due to straight lines being projected on to the eye. It is possible to devise spectacles containing prisms which make all vertical straight lines project a curved line. At first these seem curved but after some experience of wearing the spectacles they seem straight again, and if the spectacles are removed they appear curved in the opposite direction for a time. This process of adapting can occur even if no such lines are actually experienced, but only a world of dots (Held and Rekosh 1963). In this environment, movement of the head up and down will produce not the usual 'flow' of the image in the opposite direction to the head movement, but a flow along the curved path produced by the spectacles. This unusual result of head movements can, it seems, give the necessary clue about the nature of the distortion, so that a correction to the sensory input can be made. Perception depends on interpreting the result of an action.

4   On the other hand, much of what arrives at the senses is disregarded – the wall and the window frame and the spots on the glass when I look out of my window at the scene beyond. The ticking of the clock, the pressure of our clothes, the nose in front

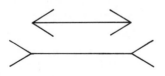

Figure 3 *The Mueller–Lyer illusion*
Although the line with outward pointing fins looks longer, both lines are really equal in length.

of our eyes are all there but we usually remain unaware of them. This does not, of course, mean that we cannot become aware of these things if we need to, nor that we take no account of them – indeed, when looking through the window I must avoid looking at the frame, but so long as it remains unchanging and irrelevant this can be done automatically without difficulty. It is change which causes attention to switch, when the automatic taking into account fails. It is obviously important to survival to respond to changes in the environment, and this is exactly how the nervous system reacts, with a burst of activity in response to changes, settling back to a steady state once monotony prevails. Indeed, when by special techniques the image on the eye is kept in exactly the same place, moving with the eye's movement, it soon disappears altogether, and in very uniform surroundings, such as smooth snow, a form of blindness can develop. Similarly,

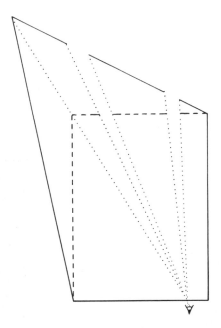

Figure 4   *Plan of a room giving the illusory perception shown in Figure 5*
The solid outline is that of the actual room, which projects the
same retinal image as a normal room, which is shown with broken
lines. The viewer interprets the walls and windows as if they were a
normal room and consequently does not correct for the smaller
retinal image of the more distant face.

once we are in the bath we can find we need to keep adding more hot water to maintain a pleasant feeling of warmth.

Minor irregularities or inconsistencies are also disregarded, such as misprints and a cough replacing a word in speech (Warren 1970), though this last experiment also showed that a silent gap was noticed; the cough was heard as a word, but the gap could not be so heard.

5 Sensory input is frequently ambiguous but perceptions are usually confident and correct. A given visual pattern at the eye could be produced by an infinite number of physical possibilities out in the world, but we are rarely in doubt or mistaken. For example, a large tree far away and a small one closer can project the same sized visual pattern on my eye. Nearly always we see the right-sized object at the right distance, though it is possible to devise situations which deceive us, such as the Ames room (Figures 4 and 5), which looks like an ordinary room viewed from an angle, but is really an odd-shaped room viewed from directly in front. Sometimes an unchanging input can be seen in more than one way (Figure 6).

6 Because our nervous systems respond mainly to changes and are therefore bad at recording exact copies, perceptions tend to be relative to recent experience or the prevailing context. If you

Figure 5   *The Ames room (from Ittelson and Kilpatrick 1951)*

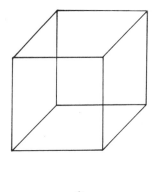

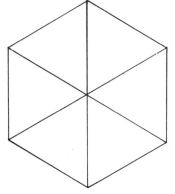

Figure 6   *Two Necker cubes*
The upper one can be seen in two different ways with different faces nearest to the observer, and the lower one is more likely to be seen as a regular two-dimensional pattern.

test the bath water after putting one hand under the cold tap and the other under the hot one, the first hand will tell you the bath is hot and the other will tell you it is cool. A kilogramme weight will feel light after lifting ten kilogrammes, but heavy after lifting a few grammes. The house seems dark when you come in out of the bright sunlight but not after a time indoors. The perceived size of objects depends on the company they are in (Figure 7). If you cover your eyes with halves of a table tennis ball and shine a coloured light on them, you soon cease to see any colour at all (Hochberg, Triebel and Seaman 1951).

Perhaps the most dramatic example is an experiment by Helson (1959, p. 577) who put people in a room papered with

Figure 7   *A size contrast illusion*
*Although the central dot looks larger when surrounded by the
smaller dots than when surrounded by the larger ones, it is the
same size in both cases.*

different shades of grey and illuminated with red light. You
might expect they would see greys or perhaps reds of different
brightnesses. Not at all. The lighter greys were seen as red, the
middle ones as grey and the dark ones as green; that is, any
paper reflecting less than the medium amount of light was seen
as the complementary colour. Perception was relative to the
mean or 'adaptation level' in the whole environment. Helson
also showed that estimates of weight depended on the series of
weights just experienced.

Perceptual achievements

In brief, our experience is of a selected and organized world of
separated, stable and identifiable objects and distinct events, and
this selection, organization and identification is achieved most of
the time without conscious effort or control or awareness of what we
are doing. No doubt it is because the process is so automatic that
people are often puzzled that there are any problems in understanding perception; they believe they are directly experiencing the
real world. Indeed, most of the time the experience is a highly
reliable guide to what is 'out there', and accurately guides subsequent action, even though it is not always obvious how the information could have been derived from what was available to the sense
organs. Of course we are sometimes deceived, as in visual illusions,
and such cases can provide clues about how the system functions
when it is not deceived. Nevertheless, the achievement is quite
remarkable in its speed and scope. An average adult knows some
50,000 words, several thousand faces (many of them recognizable

instantly from a few lines in a cartoon) and hundreds of tunes, butterflies or flowers, whatever the individual's particular interest happens to be.

A basic question which roughly sums up the achievements we are about to investigate is 'How do we know what this thing is?', to be taken in a broad sense which includes not just naming the thing but deriving knowledge about its nature, size, distance, position and so on. Appearance is often irrelevant, since unlike objects may be classed together (different founts of type, different views of the same object, different members of the same category and so on). It is what to do rather than what a thing looks like that is the important decision.

Approaches to explaining perception

In pursuit of the answer to this question there are several different steps by which we have to try to explain the phenomena of perception.*

1   The precise achievement must be specified, that is, what information we acquire about the world in a specific situation, whether everyone acquires similar knowledge or whether individual differences exist, and, if so, what type.
2   The nature of the effective input or stimulus, or how it can most usefully be described, must be isolated.
3   How the effective aspects of the input could be extracted by the senses and nervous system and additional information retrieved from memory, that is, the processes which relate the input to the achievement or output. This does not require a description of the working of parts of the nervous system, but a description of the mechanisms in abstract terms (for example, a store in which the raw input is held, then a second store which holds the results of operations such as extracting changes) and a description of the transformations carried out upon the input (such as the method of extracting changes in brightness level). In practice this goal and that of describing the effective stimulus are closely related, since the description of the effective stimulus has to select just those aspects of the input which are extracted by the analysing systems. However, it is quite possible to discover the

*The analysis owes a great deal to Marr (1976, 1980), but does not follow his views exactly.

effective aspects of the stimulus (such as the amount of light reflected by the grey papers in Helson's experiment described above) without having any theory about the processes by which it is extracted.

4   Ideally we also want to relate these postulated analysing processes to knowledge about the nervous system, both the way individual neurons behave and the larger scale organization in which different areas of the brain may carry out different operations. In some cases (but not many) existing knowledge about the nervous system may guide theories about the possible processes.

5   In practice, a fifth goal has also to be introduced; specification of processes in the observer such as motives and expectations (the so-called organismic factors) which affect the processes discussed above. There is even less possibility of describing how these are involved than there is of providing adequate theories about the processes themselves, so there tends to be a gap between the two types of investigation. Information processing models of the analysis of the input are devised which take little or no account of organismic processes, and accounts of the latter tend to be restricted to superficial demonstrations that such effects exist. Ultimately, however, the effects of culture, language, social pressure and all the rest will need to be included in the complete descriptions of what happens.

It will perhaps help to make these distinctions between different approaches to perception clear if I take a couple of examples of perceptual achievements from my opening scene; identification of squirrels and of the honking of geese. It is not too difficult to suggest some of the aspects of these stimuli which are critical, such as the shade of grey, size, shape and pattern of movement in the first case and a particular combination of frequencies and temporal pattern in the second (these ideas could then be tested by varying these aspects and discovering whether the identifications became more difficult or changed). Specifying the processes involved in these two achievements would require suggestions about how three-dimensional shape is derived from a two-dimensional input, and how displacement over time is converted into a type of movement which is labelled in my memory as typical of squirrels and compared with that memory. Obviously any characteristic which depends on changes over time requires a form of memory able to hold the previous shapes and positions for comparison with the present ones, as well as a memory that holds a description of the results of such comparisons and other associated information, such as that it is typical of squirrels. In the case of the goose noises, we need to explain how the frequencies making up the sound might be extracted and yet the sound is heard as one whole, and how the pattern over time could be extracted, which again would require a form of memory. Coming to the neural mechanisms, we would have available some information about how shades of grey are recorded and movement of simple kinds and also about frequency analysis of sounds, but little idea about how and where the more complex aspects of these identification processes might be carried out. Finally, it would be obvious that my previous knowledge of the scene from my window would predispose me to see small grey shapes as squirrels and identify honking sounds as geese, and that I might therefore be misled into identifying some escaped animals from the zoo or a car horn, while in other situations I might be less ready to identify squirrels or honking geese on the basis of the same physical information.

Some historical approaches

Classical perception

Different traditional approaches to perception have concentrated on different questions. Analysis of perceptual achievements and the nature of the stimulus have been the dominant concern of those studying 'classical' perceptual phenomena involved in the perception of objects in space, such as depth perception, constancy of size, shape, brightness, colour and location, the illusions and the perception of basic perceptual qualities such as brightness, colour, pitch, frequency and so on. The responses measured have typically been qualitative descriptions of what is experienced or comparisons or ratings of inputs on some dimension. Such investigations have attempted to isolate features of three-dimensional scenes (or representations of three-dimensional scenes) which convey information about size, distance and shape, and have also attempted to discover ways of measuring features of two-dimensional forms in such a way that they can be classified in an orderly way in terms of similarity, pleasingness and other psychological characteristics. Thus the features of the stimulus which serve as a basis for reported experiences are investigated, but usually the processes which intervene between the input and the experience or achievement are not pursued. However, this neglect of processes in relation to the above phenomena is beginning to change with the advent of computer simulation studies of how basic perceptual achievements might come about (see, for example, a recent book by Frisby 1979), though related studies of such processes in human perceivers are still rare.

Information processing

Studies which have tried to uncover intervening processes in perception (the third goal) have typically used a very different type of input; two-dimensional alphanumeric characters or geometric shapes varying in several ways. Accuracy and speed of identification have served as the main dependent variables. A related area of work, which uses simpler stimuli, often differing from each other in only one feature, such as position or size, has commonly been directed at a somewhat different goal; that of explaining the factors which affect choice reaction time.

It is not as yet clear how far the two disparate areas of study described above can eventually be combined, since the first is concerned with the perceptual mechanisms (which may or may not be learned) through which a three-dimensional world in depth is apprehended, and has as a result been particularly concerned with visual perception, while the second aims to derive principles common to all the senses for the operations involved in processing patterns with an arbitrary learned significance. Nevertheless, it seems highly likely that many of the mechanisms which developed to perform the first task are also heavily involved in the second, and that many of the processes employed in successful handling of patterned inputs devised by man are also relevant to perception of pattern in the natural environment.

Neurophysiology

The fourth line of investigation, neurophysiology, has often been pursued without direction from psychological evidence and tends to look at simple processes, though in the last fifteen years sophisticated techniques have identified some very complex processes which can be directly related to those derived from psychological investigation.

The 'New look'

The fifth area of investigation, the effects of organismic factors, was a very active area of research a few years ago by a movement which became known as the 'New look' in perception, but it has made little real progress in recent years and in most cases has barely progressed beyond demonstrating phenomena to be explained, such as the effects of hunger or personality or familiarity on perception.

Summary

In this introductory chapter I have indicated why perception is not as straightforward a matter as day-to-day experience might suggest and I have proposed a central question on which to concentrate. I have also identified the main lines of investigation which have been used in trying to understand perception. In Chapter 2 I shall consider in more detail why our explanations of perception should concentrate on processes and why neurophysiological investigations are not essential to this approach, and I shall also describe the main methods of investigation which can be used and some of the major problems.

Some questions of terminology

Before turning to these matters, however, a few commonly used terms and distinctions need some comment. Traditionally, distinctions have been drawn between sensation and perception and between perception and concept identification, but these distinctions are unclear and arbitrary and will not be maintained in this book. Sensation has been regarded as the recording of simple attributes of the environment such as intensity and frequency, without combination or segregation into objects (percepts). Sensation is to be studied, in this view, by considering the basic capabilities of the sense organs and by performance on very simple tasks. However, sense organs cannot be considered in isolation from the nervous system to which they are connected, and even the simplest tasks, as we shall see, cannot be separated from a complex tangle of comprehension, expectation and motivation.

2 Finding answers

In Chapter 1 a central question was proposed, 'How do I know what this thing is?' and the nature of an acceptable strategy in attempting to answer it was sketched, together with some of the different approaches which have been employed in psychological investigations of perception. Central to this strategy was the need to uncover the processes which mediate between the input to our senses and our ability to behave adequately in the environment from which this input originates. These processes also, we presume, are in some way responsible for the experiences which accompany or guide our behaviour.

In this chapter I will take up three issues arising from this sketch and consider them in more detail:

1   What are the achievements we are attempting to explain?
2   What are the different ways we might claim to offer an explanation of these achievements and why have I suggested that an explanation in terms of internal processes is the goal of an adequate perceptual theory?
3   Given that such an explanation is required, how can we go about uncovering these internal processes?

Achievements

Several of the main perceptual achievements we will wish to explain have already been indicated in Chapter 1. Obviously it would be possible to list an enormous number of specific types of information that an observer can extract from an input, such as colour, brightness, location, movement, shininess, pleasingness and so forth in the case of visual stimuli, and loudness, duration, temporal patterning, major frequency, timbre, soothingness and so forth in the case of acoustic stimuli. However, this book is primarily concerned with the identification of objects and I will therefore

Perception is commonly regarded as the extraction of information available in the input, as in distinguishing large from small objects or one shape from another, in which objects classed as similar appear similar and are not grouped by reference to some other characteristic such as biological relationships or function. These latter groupings are taken to be characteristic of conceptual or rule-based classifications and to involve prior learning about the world. Though this is sometimes a useful distinction, it is by no means a clear one. We can ignore differences between the appearance of objects which result from changes in distance or angle of regard because they do not indicate changes in the physical object; we can also ignore physical differences between (for example) different species of tree because we are only concerned to identify the objects as trees. These two situations are clearly different and we might choose to call the first a case of perception and the second a case of conceptual classification, but both are examples of identification and both will be considered in this book. Moreover, objects which are habitually classed together may come to look alike, making conceptual classifications more like perceptual ones.

Finally, no sharp distinction will be drawn here between perception and comprehension, since in most cases the former involves the latter, though I shall generally avoid any detailed discussion of complex issues like, for example, the comprehension of prose.

organize the achievements which will be our main concern with this end in mind.

Visual scene perception and object identification

Considering visual perception first, our concern is with two general achievements, the organization of the input into a set of objects in space (such as the scene from my window), through figure–ground segregation and depth perception, and the extraction of a description of specific objects (such as trees and squirrels), which can be manipulated in various ways, such as matching to stored representations and locating additional information in memory. Organizing in space, which will be discussed in Chapter 3, involves component skills needed to achieve depth perception, such as integration of the disparate images from the two eyes and use of changes in surface textures. The second achievement which is covered in Chapters 4–7, involves analysis of the physical input to extract the critical features of the object such as shape, size and colour. Since it is necessary to derive permanent characteristics of the object from an input in which position, size, orientation and other characteristics all vary, this extraction of critical features involves much more than simply sampling the input for physical features directly present in it. Subsequently the component features have to be combined into a whole, whether that be a single object or a whole scene composed of many objects.

In addition, we have to take account of the ability to select parts of the input for particular purposes (at any level from spots on a single leaf to the whole tree) and the possible limitations on the amount of information which can be handled (attention will be discussed in Chapter 5). We also need to consider the creation of the organized store of information about the world to which new information is continually being matched and added (learning processes will be discussed in Chapter 9).

Auditory perception

For auditory perception, most of our knowledge, for obvious reasons, concerns speech perception. Here too, though the organization of the input into separate objects does not involve any problems of depth perception, both object segregation and analysis must occur, together with the highly complex procedure of assembling the parts into a meaningful whole by using the relations between the parts signalled by grammar and word meanings. Obviously attention and learning processes are as important in auditory as in visual perception.

Basic perceptual operations

There are numerous operations we can carry out on the stored information and on the input, such as discriminating between two objects, naming an object, evaluating it on some scale, searching for a specified item in memory or in the input and so on. I shall not, however, treat these as distinct achievements to be examined separately but as component tasks to be used in investigating the nature of the operations carried out in identification; the relation between these different operations is discussed below.

Identifying objects

I have already admitted that I intend to use the term identification in a very broad sense, and not in a narrow sense, such as being able to produce a name. As pointed out above, perception has the function of guiding behaviour and appropriate behaviour implies that identification has occurred in the sense that the input has been classified as an obstacle to be avoided, a handle to be grasped, a friend to be greeted, a question to be answered and so on. We are here concerned with the processes which enable such appropriate behaviour to be selected, and in the majority of cases, unless some instinctive reflex-like response is available, this must involve contact between a representation of the input and stored information from past experience which can help to specify the appropriate actions. Ability to name an object is one relatively easily measured, but limited, piece of evidence that such contact has occurred. However, naming does not always imply that information about appropriate action is also available and inability to name does not imply that no contact with information in memory has occurred; in some cases of brain damage objects can be used but not named and no one would suggest that every time we open a door we say 'door' or 'handle' covertly to ourselves. In such cases the behaviour is automatic and does not require effort or diversion of attention from other ongoing behaviour such as conversation.

In general, automatic identification will occur at a level which is well practised and useful, such as identification of an individual in the case of familiar friends, or as male or female in the case of strangers in the street, or of birds as just birds if we are not ornithologists, and as Canada geese if we have a special interest.

Explanations

The different lines of investigation described in Chapter 1 are often regarded as offering different types of explanation, though the argument of Chapter 1 was that all these are necessary to understand perception properly.

Describing regularities in achievements

Explanations can be of various kinds. For example, faced with the question of why the Mueller–Lyer illusion (Figure 2) should make me see the line with the outgoing fins as longer, I can start by discovering that most people have the same experience; in other words I can establish that the achievement (in the sense the word has been used above) is a general one. I can also measure the degree of error as the angles and length of the fins are varied and perhaps even derive equations which relate these variables, thus establishing some of the critical stimulus features and enabling prediction to new situations. This is basically a gathering and ordering of the data, which clarifies the phenomenon to be explained and summarizes regularities in a mathematical form. A good example of a successful summarizing of this kind is Weber's Law, which states that the just noticeable difference between two stimuli which vary along a single dimension, such as the loudness of two sounds, is a constant proportion of the weaker stimulus. By thus identifying the key factors in the situation (the independent variables, or, in the terms used in Chapter 1, the proper stimulus description), causes of the experience or response are suggested but the method by which the variables produce the result they do is not elucidated. This form of explanation should be the first stage toward a fuller explanation specifying the intervening processes.

Describing critical features of stimuli

One problem in attempting to describe the stimulus adequately is that although 'stimulus' is used in psychology as though it were a precise term, this is quite untrue. Is the Mueller–Lyer figure the stimulus, or does the stimulus include the paper it is drawn on, the table underneath, the walls and window, and everything else affecting my senses at the time, like an itch in my foot or a voice next door? Or should the complex whole be divided into separate stimuli, and if so, how far should it be divided? Should the separate lines in the figure be regarded as separate stimuli, and how should a more complex total, like the scene from my window, be divided up into 'stimuli'? Whatever the decision on these problems, there still remain others. Is the stimulus the physical object, the light or sound waves emerging from it, the effects of these at the sense organs or later effects in the central nervous system?

Some psychologists distinguish the distal (external) stimulus and the proximal (sensory) one, but this twofold distinction is not adequate and more distinctions are forced on us. A 'squirrel stimulus' is an animal with particular characteristics, light of a certain wavelength and intensity reflected from the body of that animal, a pattern of activity in the light-sensitive cells of the retina of the eye, subsequent activity in the ganglion cells, the optic nerve, lateral geniculate bodies, visual cortex and then we know not where else in the brain. The output or response of one stage is the input or stimulus to the next and a full understanding requires each to be described and understood. Though the example is a visual one, the same of course applies to stimulation of the other senses.

The most useful description of the stimulus may have little connection with our intuitions derived from our direct experience, as has been illustrated already. Experiences may be due to aspects of the stimulus of which we are completely unaware and which are quite different from what we experience. We are not aware of frequencies in speech but of qualitatively different sounds. Perception of depth can depend on binocular disparity (differences in the images projected to the two eyes) or continuous changes in the texture density of a receding surface, attractiveness of a face can depend on pupil dilation in the eyes (Hess 1965), and hearing 'split' rather than 'slit' depends on the presence of a brief silent gap between the 's' and 'l' sounds in the first case which is absent in the second; there is no actual sound where 'p' is heard. We are not surprised that in the case of 'subjective' features, like shiftiness or intelligence or beauty, the important aspects of the stimulus are not immediately obvious to us, but only the end effect, which is the result of combining these important aspects unconsciously.

However, we tend to think that in the case of more basic physical features our perception must be direct and true, but all perception is indirect, a construction from clues provided to the senses. In attempting to describe the stimulus properly we are trying to uncover the nature of those clues.

Describing internal events: the contribution of physiology and neurophysiology

If we can devise such a description, we can then attempt to work out the sequence of internal events in more detail. In the case of perceptual phenomena it is often tempting to believe that investigation of the physiology and neurophysiology of the sensory system will provide most illumination. In the case of Weber's Law we do in fact find that the rate of firing in neurons increases more slowly, as the strength of the input is increased, in a manner approximately equivalent to that required to explain the law (of course it is still possible to ask why this should be the case and to search for a more basic explanation still in terms of the way neurons function). In the case of the Mueller–Lyer illusion, however, neurophysiological investigations are considerably less helpful. It seems likely that the phenomenon depends on events not open to current physiological techniques. Unfortunately, the majority of perceptual phenomena, like the Mueller–Lyer illusion, do not readily succumb to explanation in terms of physiological or neurophysiological findings and too ready a recourse to such evidence can be misleading. This is particularly true if the achievement to be explained has not been clearly defined by psychological methods first, so that it is unclear what neurophysiological evidence might be relevant.

For example, when early investigators found that an inverted image of the external scene can be viewed on the back surface of the eye, where the light-sensitive cells of the retina are situated, it encouraged them in the belief that perception was the creating of an internal copy of the external world. Here, it seemed, was direct evidence for the internal copy, though it was puzzling how the world could appear upright when the image was upside down. Because there was no clear understanding of what was involved in perceiving, and of the necessity for the input to be coded and classified rather than simply copied, the physiological evidence was misinterpreted as supporting an untenable position.

When later it was found that the excitation from the retina was passed on eventually to the visual cortex and that a square projected on the retina produced roughly a square pattern on the visual cortex, similar erroneous interpretations were made, but now transferred to the cortex. Of course this approach hardly advances our understanding at all, even if it were an accurate account of what happens (which it is not). How would the square on the cortex be related to other squares on a different part, or of a different size, or to the non-square shape produced by squares observed from an angle, or how could it 'find' the name in memory or 'choose' any other response? All the problems raised earlier about the relations between input and achievement still have to be solved and no relevant processes have been revealed. What is supposed to happen in the other areas of the brain which receive excitation from the visual cortex? These problems are not unique to vision; parallel problems arise for auditory inputs, which can produce the same experience following different physical stimulation, and different experiences following the same physical stimulation in a different context.

In fact the 'image' on the cortex is really a pattern of excitation in the neurons which happens to match the input's spatial characteristics roughly but need not have done so in order to preserve the information. The square pattern of excitation on the cortex is due to activity in a set of cells each signalling not activity at a single point, but a *feature* at a given point on the retina, such as a straight line or a corner. Thus the cortical activity is not a copy of the input but particular features have been extracted and the spatial correspondence between the input and the cortical excitation is only incidental. It is what the individual neurons do that is important and that depends on how they are connected to each other, not just their spatial proximity. It is easier to discover what they do by investigating what causes them to react, than by trying to trace the physical connections between them and deducing what they do from these.

However, neither of these types of investigation is sufficient without considering the associated experience or behaviour. Indeed, deductions from neurology and neurophysiology may be completely at variance with experience. Things which have no representation in the cortex can still be 'seen'. There is a small area on the retina, known as the blind spot, where the nerve fibres leave the eye, which cannot respond to light, but we have no corresponding experience of a hole in the world for we fill in the missing area from the context. Even more dramatically, areas of the visual cortex may be damaged, yet a regular figure, part of which stimulates such areas, may be seen as complete. Either completion again occurs from context or the visual cortex is not the key to experience. Whichever is the case, prediction from neurology would be quite wrong.

Neurophysiological studies in recent years have provided some exciting indications of how classifications of objects may occur by showing that different neurons in the brain respond to specific features of the input, such as straight lines or even monkey paws (Gross *et al.* 1972). It is tempting to see this type of research, which will be discussed in more detail later, as the main route to an adequate understanding of how identification occurs. However, these studies only probe one neuron at a time, so the information derived is very restricted and even the function of these line detectors is uncertain and may have been misinterpreted, as will be discussed below; we have no idea how a set of such neurons signalling a combination of contours could generate identification or experience of a unified square, especially as squares produce wide variations in the combinations of such contours they project on the retina. Still less can we conceive how a monkey's paw detector could be constructed or whether we could, with persistence, locate neurons responsive to each of the myriads of different objects we can identify. This uncertainty is sometimes jokingly referred to as the problem of 'grandmother cells'; is there a single neuron somewhere in your brain which is activated always and only by the sight of your grandmother? Even if such a cell were found, we would still need to know how it could achieve such a feat.

Since, therefore, the possibilities of advancing understanding of perception of any degree of complexity by neurophysiological investigation are quite limited, other ways are needed of getting a more general and comprehensive picture of the sequences of internal events and causal relations involved in analysing the sensory input. This has to be achieved by examining variables, processes and performance at a psychological level, deducing internal processes from relations between input, required achievement and actual achievement, such as seeing how quickly a decision can be reached that this is a bird, a goose, a Canada goose. Ideally, theorizing derived by such methods should advance ahead of neurophysiological research, clearly defining the possible processes which could mediate between input and achievement, and the order in which they are believed to occur. The neurophysiologists can then look for suitable structures to carry out the necessary operations. In practice, as in the examples already given, physiological and neurophysiological findings may be used prematurely to 'explain' a psychological phenomenon without the theorist asking whether they can really bear the burden cast upon them.

A simplified illustration may help to bring out some of the difficulties. Take the analogy of an electronic calculator. You press a series of buttons and answers are displayed. What is happening inside? We can open it up and look at the parts. Some years ago, in its predecessors, you could see the parts moving. Later you could still see separate components. Nowadays you can see very little internal structure because it is all inside an integrated circuit on a microchip and it requires very specialized equipment to examine this. However, even if we could map out the *structure* (the parts and their connections) it would give us little idea what the thing does. Of course the structure does limit the possible processes (a calculator without a memory cannot do some tasks and an animal with one ear has problems of determining the direction of sound sources) but knowledge of structure does not unambiguously determine what processes actually occur in the system. It might be possible for the knowledgeable to deduce from a machine's structure that if Button A, Button B and Button C are pressed in that order, then Component D is activated. It would, however, be much easier to discover this by actually measuring activity when these keys were pressed. Even that, however, would not really tell us what was happening, or what function the sequence fulfilled. It could take a long time to discover that there were special rules relating Buttons A and B to the consequences when Button C was pressed (causing addition, perhaps) and another set of rules when Button E was pressed (multiplication), these rules forming a network of consistent relations. In other words, starting with the physiology presents formidable problems, even if activity in all the relevant parts could be measured (which is not possible in the nervous system with current methods).

Describing internal events: the search for basic processes

What sort of explanation then will be satisfying? What is it we really want to know – surely not just a succession of neural activity patterns inside the head? What I have suggested in Chapter 1 is that it is the *processes* which produce the type of results I have been describing. Inside the calculator certain things happen when certain buttons are pressed, and produce a certain result. These things which happen also happen when other buttons are pressed, but they happen in different orders or they happen different numbers of times. If we can work out what these basic processes are and how they are combined, we will have made a good start. The description only needs to identify them in a way relevant to the goal or function of the machine and need not specify exactly how a particular machine carries them out; that is, it needs to refer to operations like adding or subtracting the contents of two stores, or storing a result for later use, and need not state exactly how this is done. It would be perfectly possible for the same operations to be carried out by a quite different machine working in a different way (with cog-wheels or marbles for that matter) without affecting our conclusions regarding the necessary operations. We need to use, in describing the possible ways in which the machine could carry out its task, a level of detail in which precise physical embodiments of the method of operation are not relevant. If there seem to be several such possibilities we can test between them by further observations.

For example, multiplication of A and C could be achieved by adding A to a counter C times or by adding C to a counter A times or it could be built in that the combination of A times C automatically activates a unit D which is the product. Certain tests between these possibilities could be devised, such as measuring the times to carry out this task when the size of A and C varies. Unless each combination automatically activates a built-in connection (which would be uneconomic unless the required number of different combinations were quite small) each task must require the combination in a certain order of some set of basic operations, depending on what information has been entered from the keyboard. In the case of the calculator, numbers plus an instruction as to what is to be done with them are entered. The number of operations which can be done on them is limited and they are activated directly by pressing certain keys. A sequence of such operations requires a sequence of instructions from the keyboard.

In the more complex case of a programmable calculator or a computer, there is still a limited number of basic operations available, such as comparison of two symbols, storing a symbol at a particular location, reading a symbol from a location, addition and subtraction. These built-in or *hardware* operations differ in different machines but must include a certain minimum number.

They can be combined into longer sequences to derive a required result by writing a program (the *software*), which is stored inside the machine or read in order from a tape. In more complex machines the program can be written in symbols which themselves specify whole strings of hardware operations and which have to be interpreted by another program in the machine before the sequence can be executed. Essentially the program sets the internal state of the machine so that, given a single instruction to start with, it will run through its basic operations in a certain order, though some steps can also be conditional on other new information arriving during the course of these events.

To understand what is happening we need to know not only the basic operations and the moment-to-moment changes, but the program which controls the whole sequence. Of course it is not possible to discover this simply by looking at the physical structure. This might be possible in the case of a simple calculator which can only do a very few operations that can be deduced by looking at connections between the parts, but it would probably be easier to examine the action of these parts, given certain inputs. In the case of the programmable calculator, however, this second solution too presents formidable problems, for any part which has been preset by the program to a certain state can determine what happens in any other part and the number of possibilities mushrooms beyond the capacity of ordinary observation. Moreover, simply to list a sequence of patterns of activity in the parts has no meaning for us. Inside the machine, the program, the inputs from the keyboard and the basic operations are all inextricably intermingled and defy our understanding.

It is for reasons like these that physiology and neurophysiology at present usually make only a very limited contribution to the understanding of complex psychological phenomena. Moreover, it is by no means obvious that detailed descriptions of the course of neurophysiological events would aid our understanding because they would themselves be too complex to understand. What we need, for example, when we find that people from different cultures are differentially able to identify different types of camel, is to discover what features they are using and whether the difference is removable by training. Then we have some understanding of how this identification has been achieved and can use the knowledge to build up a more complete picture of how the overall identification process might work. A record of differences in the patterns of neural activity inside the heads of the identifiers would have little to offer in advancing our understanding of the phenomenon.

Since such a picture of the identification process will most usefully consist of a specification of operations and a sequence in which they occur, it is conventional to describe it in terms of a flow diagram linking boxes (operations) into a sequence. Such boxes too readily become labelled with names as if they were elements or units in a brain which are activated in a fixed order. There is, however, no necessity for physically isolated bits of machinery inside the head to do a particular job, or for things to happen in a temporal sequence, one after another. The same neurons could be involved in many different tasks at different times under the control of different 'master units', just as physical parts like fingers can be applied to many different tasks. When we specify apparently physical structures we are merely encapsulating our understanding of the processes in a form we can readily comprehend and should not be seduced into thinking that we are necessarily referring to physical structures in the brain. Nor need the operations all occur one after the other in a fixed linear progression – lots of things may happen at once or be intertwined in complicated ways.

Methods

Introspection

Our task then is to try to map out what happens to the information delivered to the senses as it is passed through the brain and reorganized to make possible the location of information in memory and to control action. How can we get at this ongoing process if direct observation of activity in the brain is difficult and unlikely to be illuminating? From what has already been said it is clear that asking the observer to tell us what has happened is unlikely to prove very fruitful. There are some things people can report about in this way. Asking people to talk aloud as they solve problems has proved very illuminating (Newell and Simon 1972), though even in these cases there is some doubt as to how far the need to talk aloud may change what happens and how far it reflects the most important underlying processes. Moreover, this sort of method can only provide information about the behaviour at a rather gross level where it has already entered awareness. For example, chess players can tell us they are considering the conse-

quences of moving the knight, but often not how their attention
became focused the knight rather than another piece, and it is
precisely those processes which precede awareness that are
important for an understanding of perception. They are, for the
most part, not under our control, nor open to our introspection.
Effort often fails to reveal the nature of a puzzle picture (Figure 1),
striving for the name of a familiar face is often the worst way of
finding it, and knowledge of the truth does not make the two lines in
the Mueller–Lyer illusion (Figure 2) look equal. Ask someone how
they know a face is their mother's or a tune is 'Baa, baa, black
sheep' and they will be at a loss as to how to answer. The identification seems immediate and all they can say is 'I just do', though we
know that a great deal must go on to make the achievement
possible.

One final reason for the inadequacy of introspection in uncovering internal perceptual processes is that, as was shown in Chapter 1,
the reported experience is often qualitatively very different from
the physical basis on which it depends. The experience of straight
lines need not depend on physically straight lines, changes in perceived speech sounds such as 'slit' to 'split' and 'd' to 't' depend on
slight increases in time intervals between different elements of the
sound (Bastian *et al.* 1961), gradients in texture are normally
experienced as changes in distance, changes in the wavelength as
changes in colour and so on.

Experimental studies of perceptual performance

This is not to say that observers' reports are of no use. They tell us
what the observer experiences, given a particular input, enabling us
to map out the knowledge available about the environment. Of
course such reports are only guides, but more useful information is
gained from reports of changes in experience as the input is changed
and of which aspects change, enabling the critical features of the
input for different experiences to be isolated. Controlled reports,
asking for specific information (which line is longer, which patch is
brighter, which of these words did you hear) can be used to test the
efficiency with which different information can be obtained from
the input. Both the accuracy and speed of performance can be
measured in these cases. Use of these methods to try and separate
out the different transformations carried out on the input will be
discussed in detail in Chapter 6. Here I shall give a preliminary

sketch of some of the tasks in which they are employed. Ideally what we would like is to construct a model of the necessary sequence of processes for some achievement (identifying a tree perhaps) and then isolate particular operations within the sequence by devising tasks which require only some of the operations. Clearly this is very difficult (if not impossible) and in practice what has happened is that different tasks have been studied without any very systematic attempt to relate them to a general model, such as the one sketched very briefly above under 'Achievements'. However, there has been some improvement in this situation in recent years.

Varying the level of identification required and examining changes in performance can yield important evidence about the processes involved. What is the difference, for example, in the time required to identify something as a bird, a goose, a Canada goose? It is also possible to derive evidence from other widely used perceptual tasks, provided their relation to identification can be clarified. These are the tasks of *detecting* the presence of a stimulus, *discriminating* between two stimuli (or *matching* them for sameness), *searching* for a specific item or items in a current or recent display, and *evaluating* an item on some specified dimension.

Detection involves discriminating a given state from an immediately preceding state and therefore probably involves similar processes to those used in discriminating, as Vickers (1979) has argued in a recent book. Discrimination involves deciding which of two stimuli is longer or louder (for example) and matching two stimuli to decide if they are the same or different requires one response in the first case and another in the second. Presumably processes like discrimination and matching are required in identification in order to match the input to a set of possibilities in memory and to discover the correct name. Vickers's view is that there is a single basic type of decision mechanism to which different types of information can be fed, depending on whether the task is one of detection, discrimination or matching, so evidence from all three types of task is relevant to understanding identification. The processes which produce the input for the decision mechanism will vary in complexity in the different tasks. Whether the operations involved in detection also occur prior to more complex operations when discrimination is required is a further question to be considered. Evaluating (rating or scaling) is not considered by Vickers but could be included in his approach by assuming a series of matching operations to an ordered set of possibilities.

Many experiments have used special variations of matching tasks, requiring search for a given stimulus (usually a letter, digit or word) in a display (visual search or occasionally auditory search) or in a set committed to memory (memory search). In these cases the task is to compare a present input with a past one and give one response if a match is found and another (which may be no response) if it is not. In these tasks and same–different judgements, matches can be required at a physical level of representation or at some 'higher' level. For example, subjects may be asked to respond positively if two stimuli have the same name (A,a) even though they are physically different, or if both are vowels or both letters or if two words have the same meaning.

Clearly, the type of match required specifies the type of processing and representation which must be achieved, and valuable information can be acquired about which variables affect the process of achieving such a representation. What is not clear, however, is whether processes deduced from, say, physical matching, are components of the more complex identifying and name-matching tasks. Presumably to carry out the former a physical representation of the input (lines, curves and angles) has to be matched to a similar representation in memory (the target in visual search or the members of the memory set in memory search or the first letter presented in same–different judgements). These processes are the same as those assumed to occur in the first stages of naming where they are followed by retrieval and production of the associated name, or some other required identifying response, such as pressing a key. Hence it is tempting to assume that results from matching tasks are directly applicable to explaining identification processes. However, it is quite possible that the processes uncovered in a matching task are specific to matching, and identification bypasses some or all of them. Everyday identification clearly differs from such matching tasks since it cannot usually involve maintaining a specific target in a special memory store waiting for an input to be matched to it, as it is not known what input is about to arrive, nor may physical representations be constructed in detail or retained, since precise physical specification is usually of little value, due to variability in the environment.

Identification tasks themselves in a laboratory setting differ markedly from those in natural environments. In the day-to-day situation the only constraints on the possibilities which may occur are derived from context, and experience will usually be able to make use of these constraints to reduce the number of expected possibilities. In experimental tasks the total set of possibilities is often known to the perceiver and usually there will not be any natural variation in distance, angle, brightness, type face and so on, all of which can vary in the natural setting. Moreover, a long sequence of experimental trials is given with members of the limited set of possible stimuli appearing one after the other in random order at fairly brief intervals. Consequently, comparison with the preceding stimuli is possible in addition to comparison with representations of the possible stimuli stored in memory.

In investigations of these kinds, a stimulus or stimuli are presented and the observers (subjects) make an appropriate verbal or key press response. The difficulty is that this tells us nothing directly about intervening processes and inferences have to be drawn by varying the conditions and the task or by attempting to break into the process part way through by forcing premature responses or eliminating the input after a brief exposure (see Chapter 6). In all these cases performance is normally measured in two ways – accuracy and time. These need to be considered in conjunction, since faster responding is often correlated with less accurate responding, but often researchers have examined one without controlling the other. Time is in many ways the more useful, provided accuracy can be held constant, because it provides measurement of performance on a continuous scale. Measures of performance which discover the nature of what is and is not known about the input are much more valuable than simple records of whether the response was correct or not, but the latter measure is the one most commonly taken.

The major weakness of these methods of investigation is the artificial simplicity of the situations employed in order to obtain reliable data. These may be quite unlike the real situations in which sensory systems have evolved. The laboratory inputs are normally two-dimensional patterns, such as letters and numbers, which are highly familiar, or two-dimensional representations of three-dimensional objects, they are static instead of changing over time and the difficulty of the identification is commonly increased in some way such as by restricting the exposure time or reducing the illumination, in order to slow down or artificially curtail the normal processes. Separation of objects from background is no great problem in three-dimensional environments; head movements immediately locate the edges of objects since their images move across the retina at a different speed from the image of the background, covering the latter at one edge and uncovering it at the other. Such separation is more problematical in two-dimensional representations where no such cues are available and has generated much theorizing (see Chapter 3), which is partly at least a product of the restricted situations studied. J. J. Gibson (1950) has strongly criticized the concentration on artificial situations of this kind and argues that the normal input is rich in cues produced by movement and in relations which were neglected by most perceptual theorists. Gibson believed that the cues for depth, solidity, size and so forth are all immediately available in the input and automatically determine how a scene is seen.

In his second book, *The Senses Considered as Perceptual Systems* (1966), Gibson went further in criticizing much of the experimental work on perception, pointing out that normally integration of information from several senses occurs in organizing the experienced world and that the tendency to equate perception with vision is misleading. Faces have voices, birds flap their wings, dogs smell, velvet looks and feels smooth. This is indeed an important point. Though most of the evidence cited in this book will come from experiments on visual perception, because more research has been done on vision than on anything else, attempts will be made to draw parallels between processes in the different sensory modalities, in the belief that similar operations underlie the processing of information in the visual, acoustic, tactile and other sensory systems.

Psychophysiology

Another method of trying to discover internal processes is to record psychophysiological measures such as electrical activity in the brain as a whole (the electroencephalograph or EEG) or in muscles, electrodermal responses (changes in the electrical resistance of the skin), heart rate, breathing and pupil dilation. These measures sometimes provide useful auxiliary information, reflecting events both within awareness and outside it, as when subjects report unawareness of a stimulus, but one of these measures indicates a response to the input. In general, however, they are relatively crude indices of responses and give little indication of anything other than that some processing of the stimulus has occurred.

Artificial intelligence and computer simulation

Computer simulation provides one other method of trying to build models of intervening processes. Researchers either try to construct a feasible way of carrying out some perceptual task, irrespective of how human beings may do it, or try to match the way in which experimental evidence has suggested that human beings or animals might do it.

The first type of investigation, known as artificial intelligence, provides valuable insights into the logical structure of a task, the necessary component operations and the difficulty of carrying them out. The second, computer simulation of behaviour, provides a stringent test of the feasibility of a proposed model of the processes in an organism, showing whether or not they can produce the result which they attempt to explain. There are of course important differences between computers and living organisms which need to be taken into account (see Wilding 1978b, for a fuller account), but many important insights have come from this area of research, not least the whole notion of organisms as processors of information, transforming the input by a series of operations and using information already available in memory in combination with the input to derive new symbolic expressions or outputs.

The problem of variability: bottom-up and top-down processes in perception

Finally, in this discussion of methods of investigation I must cover some of the major difficulties. The main one can be summed up in one word – flexibility. In the discussion so far in this chapter it has been implied that there is some fixed standard process that can be uncovered with sufficient ingenuity, which is determined by the task and runs off automatically once the input arrives. In Chapter 1, however, I pointed out that studies of processes could not ignore the influences of organismic factors, such as expectation and motivation. There is a continual debate on the issue of whether the input automatically evokes responses or experiences of distance and size owing to the way the nervous system is pre-set to process it, or whether there is a constant process of predicting and testing based on previous experience. Some theorists such as Gibson, and recently Turvey (1977), have argued for the former position. Gibson writes: 'For every aspect or property of the phenomenal world of an individual in contact with his environment, however subtle, there is a variable in the energy flux at his receptors, however complex, with which the phenomenal property would correspond if a psychological experiment could be performed' (1959, p. 465). He believed that these variables directly and automatically evoke the corresponding experiences, rather in the way the red belly of a male stickleback evokes attack by a rival, and regarded any further discussion of mechanisms and processes as unnecessary, though it is difficult to see why, even if there were innate reflex-like responses, no further explanation should be needed of their method of operation.

A related but less extreme view is taken by Marr (1976, 1980) in his artificial intelligence models of perceptual processes. He argues that a great deal more information than is commonly assumed can be derived from a visual input by 'bottom-up' processes without invoking 'top-down' processes (like expectations) to prime certain possibilities.

The contrary view is exemplified strongly in the writings of Richard Gregory (1969, 1970), who insists that perception is based on hypothesis testing to a much greater degree than is commonly appreciated. Gregory argues that perception would be impossible without a model of the world inside our heads to guide the way the input is processed, which is in turn revised and updated by the incoming information. In a sense, for theorists of this persuasion, we see the model in the head rather than the world outside, filling in gaps and using inadequate data to trigger a more adequate internal representation guided by expectation. It is, of course, very easy to demonstrate the importance of pre-existing knowledge. I pointed out in Chapter 1 that my familiarity with the scene from my window aids the identification of running squirrels and honking geese. If you meet your milkman in Paris you may have problems remembering who he is. Handwritten words which are illegible out of context may be perfectly easy to decipher in sentences. Expectations can also cause errors and create comedy. I recall once when I had been looking for hours on a hot day for a shop where I could buy veneer and at last saw 'VENEER' in large letters over a shop across the road. However a moment later some gremlin had changed it to 'VINER – Florist'!

One problem is how these organismic factors operate. Do they affect the way the input is processed (the 'real' perception) or only the willingness to make a particular decision (the threshold or criterion for the decision)? Can we even separate these two possibilities – or are there others? Certainly we cannot answer the question until we have devised an adequate model of how the identification may occur.

Once we concede that processes vary with people and situations we admit the possibility of different ways of tackling the same task, much as strategies in solving problems can vary between times and people. There is no guarantee that, given a simple perceptual task to perform, all observers are operating in the same way or even consistently within a series of observations, particularly if the task is a novel one and they are trying to discover the best way of going about it. Such variations in strategy are, of course, equivalent to changes in the software while inbuilt processes remain constant and automatic; however, the reverse does not follow, and if something seems to be carried out in a fixed way, it can be either because it is inbuilt or because it has been strongly overlearned. Considerable effort is expended in trying to separate a built-in, fixed core of perceptual processing from variable, learned or invented strategies and biases which the observer brings to the task.

A good deal of this effort is also devoted to studying the learning process itself. Which skills are present at birth or learned very early and which improve with prolonged experience? Exactly what is learned – specific skills or a much more general model of the word or mode of operating? How is the model of the world stored – as images (visual, acoustic, tactual) to which the input is matched, or is the description in some more abstract form, usually called a propositional form, in which 'boy', for example, is represented as 'human, male, immature, noisy' etc.?

3 Stimuli: scenes

In this chapter I return again to the scene I described in the opening paragraph of Chapter 1 and consider ways of trying to explain how it is perceived. To do this I shall look at a number of different historical approaches to perception, beginning with theories which attempted to explain perception in terms of simple sensations plus 'top-down' inferences or previous experience. The inadequacy of such explanations will lead us to consider more complex bases of perceptual experience, such as relations between elements in the scene, and to views of perception which emphasize the importance in determining our perceptual experience of automatic processes which handle complex 'wholes'. However, merely postulating automatic production of wholes is equally unsatisfactory as an explanation of our perception since we need to know how it could occur, and influences of past experience and expectation are readily discernible, so both these automatic bottom-up processes and the top-down influences need to be analysed for an adequate understanding of what happens.

Achievements of scene perception: figure–ground segregation and the constancies

The first step in any investigation, as given in Chapters 1 and 2, is to describe the achievement which needs to be explained. In the case we are considering, this is a formidable task and all I shall do is to pick out some aspects of what we know about such a scene. Psychologists often restrict themselves to much more specific perceptual achievements than these.

1   We separate the scene into objects in a background, though what counts as object or figure and what as ground can vary as attention switches from one object to another.
2   We see a scene in depth with moving objects remaining constant

in size and shape, even though the size and shape projected on the retina change with distance and angle of viewing. These two pervading characteristics of perception are known as size constancy and shape constancy.

3 We see grass or trees staying the same colour in shadow rather than changing to a different one (colour and brightness constancy).

4 We build a complete and stable scene out of a sequence of looks at it, ignoring intrusions like window bars. Sounds, smells and sights are related to each other. If we move our eyes or our head the scene does not appear to move. The maintenance of a stable world despite changes in the view due to our movements is called position constancy.

Of course this list is incomplete and has been drawn up without any systematic observations to guide it. Such observations will normally require observers to describe what they see or to demonstrate ability to judge distance, size, brightness and so on by estimation or by matching to some standard. For example, I could present a set of green patches and ask an observer to select the one most like the colour of another patch in the shadow (obviously it is unsatisfactory to ask for a match to the grass in shadow because the observer can use past experience rather than sensory information). Or I could present a shape fifty yards away and ask an observer to tell me which of a selection of shapes twenty yards away is nearest to it in size. By such methods we can work out systematically exactly what is and is not known about the input.

Once this is clear, the next task is to discover what aspects of the stimulus are important in conveying this knowledge, or, putting it in other ways, what is the effective stimulus or the most meaningful way of describing the stimulus. Rather than discussing these questions in relation to each of the above achievements in turn, I will in this chapter consider some different historical approaches to perception which illustrate different ways of trying to describe the stimulus in order to pick out the features which are critical for the perceptual achievements. One way of looking at the differences between theories is in the simplicity or complexity of the basic unit they use in describing the stimulus. Some start with the assumption that the appropriate units are very simple ones, such as points of light in the case of vision, and that what has to be explained is how the wholes of experience are created out of these. Other theories assume that much larger and more complex units should be the starting point, such as shapes or areas or relations between more basic elements, and do not concern themselves with questions of how these units are created by the nervous system. Both agree that the visual input can be described in either way; the difference seems to lie in the type of information which they think is extracted automatically by bottom-up processing and at what level we have to start involving expectations, hypotheses and past experience (top-down processing).

Structuralist theories: simple sensations

I shall look first at the structuralist theories, as they are called, which tried to explain perception on a basis of elementary sensations, and then at several different approaches which assume that more global aspects of the input are the real bases of perception. The structuralist approach tends to invoke top-down processing to solve its difficulties and the other theories make much less use of such a solution.

The visual distal stimulus can be completely described as a set of points defined by their location, the mixture of wavelengths of light which they reflect or emit, and the intensity of that light. The acoustic stimulus can be described in terms of the amplitude and frequency of the movement of the air molecules which is produced. Stimulation of the eye, even by poking it, produces sensations of light and stimulation of the ear produces sensations of sound, so each type of nerve must evoke a specific experience when stimulated. Hence it was not unreasonably assumed that there must also be specific receptors in the eye for each position, wavelength and intensity, and in the ear for each amplitude and frequency, which are activated by a specific type of event and produce a specific experience.

There is, of course, quite detailed knowledge about how the simple sensations of colour, intensity, location, frequency and amplitude are signalled in the sensory organs and connected nerve cells (see, for example, Lindsay and Norman 1977, for more detail).

Colour

The eye contains two types of photoreceptor; cones in the central area and rods in the periphery, both containing light-sensitive substances which absorb light and initiate neural activity. Rods are for vision in dim light (nocturnal animals have only rods) and do not distinguish different wavelengths of light (i.e. colours). Cones function in daylight and three different types have been identified, with maximum sensitivity at different wavelengths. However they are sensitive to quite a wide range of wavelengths and DeValois and DeValois (1975) suggest that neural units exist which receive combinations of inputs from different cone types. They suggest three pairs of complementary neural units (blue and yellow, red and green, black and white). Mixtures of colours will of course be signalled by combinations of activity in these units, though we do not know how such combinations are signalled as a single different experience. Perhaps there are other neurons collecting the combined outputs of the six types of cell.

Visual intensity

The more energy in the light falling on the eye, the faster the rate of firing in the neurons. However, the light-sensitive substances in the rods and cones will regenerate less rapidly if the stimulation continues and the frequency of firing will decline as a result; this adaptation process has already been mentioned in Chapter 1.

Visual location and direction

Direction may be judged relative to the body, irrespective of where the eye and head are pointed, or relative to the eyes or head. Since the world does not appear to move around as our eyes or head or body move, a compensatory mechanism must operate, which allows for the input changes consequent on our movements. This mechanism can be bypassed by moving the eye with the finger. The world then appears to move in the opposite direction to the eye, because no movement across the retina has been predicted. In amphibians the direction appears to be innately computed. Rotation of the eye causes frogs to strike for flies in the wrong direction for the rest of their lives. Humans on the other hand can adapt to inverting spectacles and learn to reach in the right direction automatically after practice and to see the world as normal.

Acoustic frequency and amplitude

It is now widely accepted that different frequencies (experienced as different pitches) of sounds stimulate different positions in the cochlea in the inner ear. The cochlea is a spiral organ containing the basilar membrane. When the ear is stimulated by a sound a wave travels up the basilar membrane reaching its maximum amplitude at a point which depends on the frequency of the stimulating sound. If the sound contains a mixture of frequencies, more than one peak will be produced. The peak of the wave causes nerve cells connected to the corresponding parts of the basilar membrane to fire, so that a pattern of neural activity is created reflecting the pattern of frequencies in the sound. The other attribute of sound waves, their amplitude, is probably signalled by the number of activated cells, since cells with different sensitivities or thresholds have been found. It has sometimes been suggested that frequency of firing in the nerve cells signals frequency of the sound and sometimes that it signals amplitude. There is also a third possibility, that in the human ear it signals the rate of pulsing in human speech (that is the rate at which bursts of air are forced through the vocal cords) which is characteristic of an individual speaker and determines the perceived pitch of the voice; this characteristic thus enables the combination of frequencies originating from a single speaker to be combined into speech sounds (Broadbent 1962). Recently, however, Darwin (1981) has shown that such grouping is not as strongly determined by the fundamental frequency as was once thought.

Structuralist theories: additions to simple sensations

The scene from my window must stimulate an enormous and changing set of visual receptors, different from any other scene, which signal the characteristics of each point. So far, so good, since the retina certainly does consist of a vast number of light-sensitive elements which react individually to points in the environment, though of course the eye is continually moving, which creates some problems for the theory. The main problem, however, is to explain how more complex experiences arise, rather than experience of points of light and pure tones. The structuralist approach assumed that the elementary sensations which are the basic building blocks of perception could, with training and effort, be experienced and reported. Since it was difficult to argue for points as being thus available, they accepted larger units such as lines, edges and patches of colour (acoustic perception did not receive much consideration), which could conceivably be reported as being things of which we can be aware. Thus it was argued that we can decompose the trees into patches of grey, brown and green, a human figure into patches of pink, black and blue, the sound of car brakes into a compound of pitches and so on and become aware of these component elements.

There are several problems with this approach. First, experience is of wholes, not collections of elementary sensations bundled together, and in fact the so-called elementary sensations of the structuralists are themselves already combinations of more elementary units, as already pointed out, and this combining was not properly explained. More recent knowledge of brain functions, as we have seen, shows how complex combining occurs throughout the sensory systems, so that single neurons detect spots or edges or even more complex patterns. Second, the wholes are not just the sums of more elementary parts, but the relations between the parts are important. Perception of vowel sounds depends on the relations between the main frequencies present, not on the absolute frequencies; T, L and + are all different and a blind Venetian is not a venetian blind. Third, the structuralists showed little concern over the problems of object segregation or the integration of information obtained by sampling a scene over time. Fourth, their theory could not explain how, when looking out of my window, I perceive the distance of the squirrel, the size of the human being, the uniform width of the path and the uniform colour of the grass, or indeed any separate objects at all. Fifth, illusions cause difficulties: if the lines and fins in the Mueller–Lyer illusion are separate sensations, why do the latter affect the former, and why does a large object feel lighter than a smaller one of the same weight (the size–weight illusion)?

It was on the achievements of depth and distance perception and the constancies that the structuralists' explanatory efforts were concentrated, because these provided the most pointed challenge to their theory, involving as they do achievements for which no obvious information is available in the input as conceived by the structuralist theory. A two-dimensional pattern on the retina could be produced by an infinite number of physical inputs. A square pattern could be produced by a large square far away, a smaller one close up, or a variety of trapezoids inclined at appropriate angles. Movement of the observer can remove some of the ambiguities, because different combinations will produce different patterns of transformation as movement occurs, but this does not solve all the problems and in any case was not considered as a possible solution by the structuralists.

Three main types of solution were offered. Helmholz (1850) suggested that unconscious inferences occurred which took into account the illumination falling on a surface or the distance of an object from the observer when determining brightness or colour and size or shape. The theory therefore claims that correct judgements of some features depend on combining other kinds of information; it is not clear whether this is a learned skill and whether the latter type of information is only available at an unconscious level. The theory is imprecise and difficult to test, both as an explanation for the constancies and as a more general view about how perception operates. It has difficulty in suggesting how the necessary information about illumination or distance is available, why we are not readily aware of it if it is available as a sensation, and why, if we are asked to judge the illumination or the distance, we often make mistakes which would lead to false estimates of brightness or size, while direct judgements of these are usually accurate. Of course it is possible that the unconscious inferences are more accurate because they are well practised and the conscious reports are not, or that the inferencing is an automatic process so that we cannot become aware of its basis at an incomplete stage, but this assumption would leave the notion of the availability of sensations in some disarray. Still more difficult for the theory to explain is that children show good brightness constancy very early and also good size constancy over shorter distances.

A second possibility is to look for other sensations which might provide the necessary information. Sensations which were invoked to explain perception of distance were convergence of the eyes to fixate on an object (greater convergence being necessary for nearer objects) and accommodation of the eye (greater curvature of the lens being needed to produce a sharp image of nearer objects on the retina). However, accommodation could only be effective over distances of between 0.2 and 3 m, since the lens is fully relaxed when looking at objects further away, and Leibowitz *et al.* (1972) found that in practice it was only effective as a distance cue for objects up to 100 cm away. Convergence could not be effective for objects at distances of more than 6 m since the eyes are effectively parallel when looking at objects further away than this. In the case of brightness and colour, variation in the size of the pupil and adaptation in the nervous system (reduced activity once a change has produced a response) would tend to counteract the effect of changes in illumination, but if brightness constancy depended only on these it would not be as stable as it is.

A third approach was to invoke information in memory. Knowledge of the correct size or brightness or shape or colour (squirrels are about 30 cm long, grass is a particular shade of green) could, it was argued, be used to correct the sensory information, or memories of sensations associated with walking towards an object or reaching for it could allow its distance to be estimated. What was never explained was how the sensations of the moment, which by definition did not provide the necessary information and could have arisen from a vast number of possible objects, could somehow evoke the right set of sensations in memory. Such an ability would imply pre-existing perception of distance, which again would seem to depend on familiarity with the object, and situations in which a given retinal size of image has in the past been matched with a certain reaching or moving experience. Though such a process might explain my learning of the distance of the book on my desk in front of me, it is difficult to conceive how I ever managed to calibrate the retinal size of an image of a squirrel 30 m away with the sensation of walking 30 m. Conceivably I could have learned a rule for the rate of change in the size of the retinal image as I move, and use that to calculate the size when the object is close to me, but it is not at all clear how structuralists could cope with the learning of rules. Nor is it clear how our generally correct perceptions of the size of novel objects could be explained. Thus none of these three approaches offers a satisfactory solution to the problem of explaining the constancies.

Relational cues for perception

With further investigation, however, many possible sources of the necessary information about size and distance have been discovered which make unconscious inferences from distance to size unnecessary. The slight differences in the views received by the two eyes (binocular disparity) were shown to be a powerful cue for distance perception with the invention of the stereoscope, which presents separately to the two eyes pictures giving slightly different views of an object. The most remarkable demonstrations of the effectiveness of this cue have been provided by Julesz (1964) using pairs of dot patterns which when viewed singly appear identical and random. Displacing an area in one of these laterally causes the displaced, and therefore binocularly disparate area, to appear floating in front of or behind the rest of the pattern when they are viewed in a stereoscope (see Frisby 1979, for some delightful examples). Some other cues for distance which do not require binocular vision are the relative blueness of objects (more distant ones appear bluer due to absorption by particles in the air of the longer wavelengths of the light they reflect), relative elevation in the field (more distant objects being higher if on the ground and lower if in the sky), overlap of more distant objects by nearer ones, and the casting of shadows. These cues are obviously different from and not readily reducible to simple sensations. They all depend on relations between different areas of the visual field. Other cues of more complex relational kinds which were later identified by James Gibson will be discussed below. Briefly, Gibson suggests that *gradients of change* in a number of variables can signal distance (for example, texture gets finer as the ground recedes) and the angle of inclination of a surface and that perceived size depends on the relation of an object to its surrounding field. Rock and Ebenholz (1959) have shown that the relative size of an object to its frame determines perceived size when the perceived distance remains constant. Obviously the relative size of the objects on my desk to each other remains constant as I advance towards it, unlike the size of the images they project on my retina, so this could provide a basis for size constancy.

Brightness relations also remain constant as the light falling on a scene changes; for example, when the sun goes in everything reflects less light but the lighter objects still reflect more than the darker ones. Such relational cues could be the main determinants of perceived brightness and colour. Wallach (1963) presented a central grey spot with a surround of different brightness and found that the perceived brightness of the central disc depended on its relation to the surround rather than the absolute amount of light reflected (Figure 8). Helson's (1959) experiment on colour perception described in Chapter 1 provides a more striking example of relative perception.

Even in Helmholz's own day Hering (1877) had countered the theory of unconscious inference by suggesting that a more automatic process of brightness contrast occurring at a retinal level could explain brightness constancy. Evidence from the horseshoe crab (*Limulus*) establishes a possible neural basis for such effects

Figure 8   *A lightness contrast illusion*
Although the central grey patch looks lighter when surrounded by
black than when surrounded by light grey, it is the same lightness
in both cases.

(Ratliff 1961). When activity is recorded in the nerve fibre from a single ommatidium (receptor unit) in the eye of the crab, activity is maximal when no neighbouring ommatidium is illuminated; illumination of such a neighbouring ommatidium reduces the activity in the first unit by means of *lateral inhibition* (in subjective terms it makes the light look dimmer). However, it seems unlikely that this could explain all brightness constancy which occurs over a whole field, since contrast effects depend on close proximity. Moreover, Gilchrist (1977) has shown that contrast does not occur if two surfaces are seen as being at different *distances* even if they are adjacent to each other on the retina. This implies that contrast effects depend on processes occurring after a representation in depth has been constructed which must be at a much later processing stage than the retina.

Helson's Adaptation Level Theory, which he devised to explain the colour perception experiment referred to above and other findings, provides a more promising approach to explaining brightness constancy. He argues that a running average (the Adaptation Level) of the level of stimulation is kept and used as a reference to judge new inputs. The theory applies to a number of different types of perception, though it obviously could not easily be applied to size and shape constancy. Heavier weights or stronger illumination raise the Adaptation Level, making a new weight seem lighter or a new patch seem less bright than they would have done previously.

Top-down influences on perception

Can we then explain these phenomena by automatic processes of adjustment and comparison, without invoking expectations and biases derived from past experience? Helson seems to imply that adaptation is an automatic process, but an interesting experiment by D. Brown (1953) suggests that this is not necessarily true. Brown got his subjects to estimate weights one after another and obtained the usual result that heavy preceding weights made later ones in the sequence seem lighter and light preceding weights had the reverse effects. However, when he asked a subject to pass over the tray on which the weights normally stood this had no effect on subsequent judgements, even though it weighed the same as a 'real' weight which did have an effect. It seems that only something seen as related to the task influenced the Adaptation Level.

Some other experiments also suggest that the physical input on its own is not the sole determinant of what is perceived. I have already mentioned Gilchrist's experiment. Several experiments have shown that the identity of a shape affects its perceived colour. Shapes associated with red, such as hearts, look redder than those not normally associated with red (Harper 1953), though there are some uncertainties in interpreting the results (see Chapter 8). Changes in the perceived relation between an object and the source of the illumination affect perceived brightness, even though the physical relations remain unchanged. Hochberg and Beck (1954) got observers to look through a hole in a screen at what appeared to be a grey rectangle lying on a black surface with some white cubes to show the direction of the light from above. When they revealed by waving a stick about behind it that the 'rectangle' was in fact a trapezium standing vertically, it suddenly looked brighter, presumably because it would now be seen as receiving less direct light from above than when it was lying flat and hence had to be brighter in order to reflect the same amount of light to the eye as before. Hochberg (1972, p. 421), admits that attention might, for example, be redirected to the vertical rather than the horizontal faces of the white cubes when making the new judgement, so it could not be certain that the physical input remained completely unchanged. Nevertheless, even if this were the explanation for the change, it would still be evidence that factors within the observer and not just the physical input were determining the perceived brightness. It seems clear, therefore, that at least in some situations the physical input on its own does not determine what is perceived. The argument has therefore led us back to a view resembling that of Helmholz, except that the judgements of size, brightness and so on are now assumed to be based on relations between elements of the whole scene. The necessary inferences or computations may sometimes be quite automatic (or even innately programmed) and at other times require more flexible 'top-down' processing based on past experience.

The legacy of structuralism

Thus the attempt to describe stimuli in terms of elementary sensations has proved inadequate; more complex descriptions involving relations between elements and observers' biases are needed. A development from speculation to empirical investigations of the effectiveness of different cues has also been illustrated. These investigations, by controlling aspects of the input and finding out what observers reported, aimed to find the effective cues (or an adequate description of the stimulus) but did not generally go into the internal processes which abstract the cues. Even in the case of a clear-cut cue, like binocular disparity, the internal processes remained obscure. Neurons have since been located which respond to specific degrees of binocular disparity, corresponding to different distances from the fixation point (Blakemore 1970) and Marr and Poggio (1979) and Mayhew, Frisby and Gale (1977) have been devising a detailed model of the extraction of depth through disparity, using artificial intelligence methods.

Another development was the realization that a variety of different types of evidence may be used toward a single achievement such as constancy, rather than one single cue being responsible. Different cues may be used at different times so that the achievement can be maintained in many different situations, and combinations of individually unreliable cues may produce usually reliable conclusions. However, this obviously makes the task of defining the effective stimulus an extremely difficult one.

The difference between a view like that of Helmholz and the *Gestalt* and Gibsonian theories, which we are about to examine, is partly about the nature of the cues for distance, but more importantly about the automaticity of the processing which extracts such cues. The structuralist view as outlined seems to be fixated on the very early stages of the perceptual processes and unwilling to admit that any organization of the elementary input can occur automatically, while the alternative theories to be discussed below are fixated on the results of such organization without asking how the organization occurred. For Gibson, the higher order relational cues are the immediate basis of perception, not the material of unconscious inferences.

Gestalt views of perception

The most concerted theoretical attack on structuralist assumptions was launched by the *Gestalt* psychologists in the 1920s (Koffka 1935, discusses perception). They rejected the assumption that objects could be decomposed into elementary units, and provided hundreds of demonstrations that the perception of wholes is not always predictable from the perceptions of the parts, that figures and patterns are perceived as wholes or *Gestalts*, and that relations between parts or between parts and the background context are crucial to perception, affecting perceived brightness, colour, size and so on and producing illusions, hidden figures and grouping in the field. This last effect is one example of figure–ground segmentation, a topic which much concerned the *Gestalt* psychologists and which had previously been ignored.

In a two-dimensional representation the figure is seen as separated from the background, usually as positioned in front of it; it is treated as a unity or whole and is the focus of attention. It is arguable that some of these characteristics are in fact transfers from experience of three-dimensional scenes where they really are the case, but of course the clues used for separating figure and ground in the latter also need elucidation. The *Gestalt* psychologists and others (for example, Hebb 1949) believed that the differentiation of the visual field into figure and ground is an automatic, innate process, and listed the most important features responsible: proximity, similarity, common fate, continuity, and closure. Elements in the field which are close, similar, move together, enclose an area and are easily connected will be grouped together and form a whole. In the *Gestalt* theory there are forces in the field, rather like magnetic attraction between objects, which pull the parts together to form a whole or *Gestalt*, the simplest and most consistent form possible, given the nature of the input. They cited the analogy of soap bubbles which form a sphere because this is the shape resulting from the combination of the pressure of the air and the attraction between the molecules in the soap solution. A sphere gives the maximum thickness which can surround the volume of air enclosed. Similarly, the Gestaltists argued, lines attract each other but are kept apart by the space between and tend toward the simplest form consistent with the physical pattern. These forces, in the most specific statement of the theory, were supposed to operate across the surface of the cortex. According to Wertheimer's principle of *isomorphism* there was a direct relation between physiological events at a molar level and behavioural events, so that molar events in the brain corresponded to experience. This principle was designed also to bridge the gap (which gave the structuralists such problems) between the molar (whole) nature of experience and the molecular (fragmentary) nature of physiological (neural) events. Stimuli were believed to produce excitation on the surface of the cortex similar in form to their physical shape, and electrical forces of attraction between these areas were supposed to produce structures of the same kind as (isomorphic with) experience. These forces were assumed to be present in all cortical tissue, so the resulting experiences were innately determined.

The principle of isomorphism is clearly false. The correspondence between perceived shape in three-dimensional space and cortical projection is very weak, and I have already indicated that later neurophysiological studies of the relation between neural excitation and input have revealed that the gross similarities are merely incidental to the important processes going on. Moreover, the principle of isomorphism obviously cannot apply to aspects of stimuli other than the shape of two-dimensional figures (the brain does not vibrate when we listen to most music!) yet we obviously experience sound and three-dimensional objects and colour and touch patterns. Likewise, modern neurophysiological knowledge indicates that the *Gestalt* notion of forces operating across the surface of the cortex is unacceptable. Nevertheless, interactions between different parts of the input, such as those which the principle attempts to explain, are a reality and indicate that no straightforward picture of large numbers of neurons each going its own way is adequate to explain how aspects of the input are combined to produce whole, separated objects to which attention can be paid. These problems still remain unsolved.

Simplicity and information

According to the *Gestalt* view, the forces operate to produce the simplest organization. However, the *Gestalt* theorists were unable to suggest any method of measuring simplicity, even for the relatively simple situations which they studied, with a two-dimensional figure on a background. It is even more difficult to see how the notion can be applied to complex scenes or other inputs. Later theorists have, however, devised a method of measuring simplicity in terms of *information*. Information theory developed in the 1940s as a response to the need to quantify the load on communication channels in telephone systems. The information in an event is related to the number of possibilities which might have occurred. Clearly if more possibilities are open, the occurrence of one of them is more informative and a communication system such as a telephone line has to be capable of signalling more distinct events, thus becoming more complex and expensive. More specifically, one *bit* of information resolves the uncertainty between two *equally likely* alternatives. If one is more probable than the other, its occurrence is naturally less unexpected and less informative; conversely, a rare event is more informative. With four equally possible events, occurrence of one of them provides two bits of information (one bit to divide the set into two subsets of two, the other to divide one of these subsets into the occurring and non-occurring event within it). Occurrence of an event from eight equally likely possibilities provides three bits of information and so on. Each doubling of the number of possibilities adds one bit of information; as a result, the information in n equally likely events is h bits where $2^h = n$. To get h when n is known we can find $\log_2$ (the logarithm to the base 2) of n from special tables. Logarithmic tables are more usually taken to base 10 or base e; the logarithm is the power to which the base number must be raised to get the required number. If the events we are concerned with are not equally probable, the calculations get more complex, but this need not concern us here (see Attneave 1959 for a detailed treatment).

Now figures which are predictable, because they have few angles and straight rather than irregular lines, contain less information than those with many angles and irregular lines, and are psychologically simpler. A circle is predictable from any part, a symmetrical figure is predictable from half of it, geometric shapes are quite predictable, doodles are not. Information in figures is high at points where the direction of edges changes. Experimenters using this approach found that simple figures were rated as more pleasing, seen at lower exposures and remembered more easily. However, this leaves to be tested the *Gestalt* suggestion that there is a tendency for perception to simplify complex figures by 'ironing out' changes, closing gaps and so on. Attempts to identify such processes have proved rather unsuccessful, and if there are such processes they seem to operate in memory rather than in perception.

However, one way in which simplicity might be important is in the perception of ambiguous scenes and figures, where the simpler possibility, containing less information, should be preferred if the *Gestalt* view is correct. Hochberg and McAlister (1953) have suggested that the organization which entails the minimum number of lines and angles will be preferred, so that Figure 6b is usually seen as a two-dimensional shape and Figure 6a as a two-dimensional representation of a three-dimensional shape. If the idea is to be more than an attractive intuition some suggestion is needed as to how the lines and angles are combined to form possible wholes and how the simplest of these possibilities is selected. Moreover, the theory ignores the importance of context in most situations in determining the preferred interpretation, so other factors need to be considered as well as the simplicity of the figure itself.

Automatic processing or controlled hypotheses in the perception of wholes

According to the *Gestalt* view and Gibson, the combining into wholes is an automatic achievement of the nervous system and therefore no question arises as to how the simplest possibility is selected. However, there are various arguments which might be advanced against this view. Palmer (1975) has pointed out that elements of a cartoon face are not easily recognized unless they are interpreted as parts of a face, so knowledge of the context is needed to interpret the parts, as well as the reverse. Similarly, Biederman and his co-workers (Biederman *et al.* 1981, 1982) have shown that an object displaced in a scene, so that it violates expectations about the need for support, or about its size or so that is improbable in the scene or position it occupies, is more difficult to identify (Figures 9 and 10). Second, figure and ground are not invariable in any given field. A group of patterns can become a figure against the page on which they are printed, or one pattern can become the figure with other figures as the background, or one part of that figure can stand out against the background of the rest of it; in other words, attention can be switched just as level of identification can be changed. Direction of attention and method of grouping are strongly affected by factors in the observer. Rewarding one aspect of an ambiguous

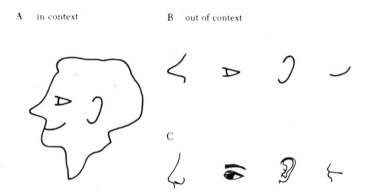

Figure 9   *Facial features which are recognizable in the context of a profile are less easily recognized out of context. When the internal structure of the features is added they become recognizable out of context (from Palmer 1975, Figure 11.6).*

Figure 10   *An object which violates expectations about probability, support and size takes longer to see in a scene (from Biederman et al. 1981, Figure 3)*

figure induces a tendency to see that aspect as the figure. Experience with puzzle pictures facilitates seeing the concealed figures. Medical students learning to interpret X-rays report seeing them as an undifferentiated whole at first, but with experience the lesion or other departure from normality comes to stand out like a separate entity (Abercrombie 1960). Similar reports come from factory inspectors who have to reject faulty products coming off a production line (Thomas 1962). Deregowski (1980) has described the problems posed to peoples unfamiliar with pictorial representation when they attempt to see an animal in a picture or photograph.

These examples suggest that, when automatic bottom-up processing is unsuccessful in segregating the input into separate objects and into a focal figure against the background, a top-down hypothesis or plan has to be used to look for a particular type of entity. The efficiency of the top-down process depends on experience in using the features which indicate the sought-for pattern. After long experience it seems that the process can run off without the need for conscious control, but even in cases where bottom-up processing is normally successful it seems likely that knowledge about the probable type of input is important. In simple cases of a single figure on a plain background, only contours need to be found which are spatially contiguous and/or processed close together in time. This, of course, is exactly the type of input which has been used in very many psychological experiments and it has been suggested from the results of such experiments that there is an early level of processing, the iconic store, which holds visual information in a form in which units have been spatially segregated but not yet identified. However, this conclusion is derived from experiments in which the input consisted of a matrix of letters against a plain background and segregation would be easy, especially as the observers knew what to expect. It is highly debatable how far we should generalize from these experiments to less artificial situations, such as natural visual scenes. It seems likely that segregation of the field of complex overlapping objects into separate entities must require longer and more detailed processing and hypothesis testing to determine which lines and angles should be combined together to form objects. Such processing, even if automatic, is unlikely to take place in the very brief intervals which have been suggested for the formation and decay of the representation in the iconic store.

While the *Gestalt* examples illustrate that stimulus description has to be complex, including relations and quite complex psychological elements rather than mere points and patches, the emphasis on ill-defined forces and the pseudo-neurophysiology still offers little progress toward understanding the *processes* which extract the relevant information from the stimulus or even precisely what features of the stimulus such processes are designed to abstract. The *Gestalt* insights into the importance of relations within the visual field are further emphasized by James Gibson's efforts to uncover complex cues for depth and distance perception which are available in any normal three-dimensional scene.

Higher order features: the contribution of James Gibson

Gibson identified 'higher order' features as immediate cues for depth, such as linear perspective and changes in texture density, displacement of the input as the head or eye moved and changes in the disparity of the images to the two eyes. The rate of gradient of change in texture indicates the angle of inclination of a receding surface, more horizontal surfaces showing a faster rate of change. Perceived size is a function of the number of the texture elements covered by an object (which is a particular case of the relative size cue mentioned earlier). As the eye moves, projected images move across it, images of nearer objects moving faster. If the head moves, eye movements to maintain objects within fixation have to be longer for nearer objects. Forward movement produces an expansion of the visual field around the point of fixation, expansion being faster further away from the fixation point. Lateral movement produces changes in the parts of the object which can be seen. As the observer moves bodily, objects nearer than the fixation point move across the retina in a direction opposite to the direction of movement, objects further away move in the same direction and the speed of movement is faster further away from the fixation point.

Gibson believed not only that gradients of change in a static scene were immediately abstracted by the nervous system, but that changes over time also yielded an immediate unified experience. He argued that visual transformations consequent on the movement of the observer are distinctive and give immediate perception of relative distance, once again making the point that early theorists were simply wrong to assert that information about distance is not available in the normal input, and that the artificiality of test situations with a single stationary eye makes conclusions irrelevant to normal perception. In his last book (Gibson 1979) he attempted a systematic examination of the characteristics and events in a natural environment which a seeing organism needs to identify, and the visual features which are typical of these.

Gibson's demonstrations once again emphasize that relations between separate elements are critical to perception (though demonstrations that these are the cues used by actual rather than theoretical observers are rather rare). He claims that the perceptual experience dependent on these is immediate and does not regard discussion of the processes involved in abstracting the cues as important, nor does he clearly opt for innate or highly learned processes. Clearly, however, a full understanding of these perceptual achievements requires a detailed analysis of the mechanisms involved, showing the sequence of processes by which the critical information is abstracted from the input. Moreover, segregating a complex jumble of overlapping surfaces into separate objects can be achieved even in photographs where neither motion parallax nor adequate texture gradients are available, which suggests that other information may also be used. Gibson's insistence on the automaticity of processing is short of supporting evidence and inadequate as an explanation of what happens. Moreover, it leaves unexplained large parts of perception which are clearly not automatic. These will be considered in the next chapter.

Frequency analysis of scenes

A recent development in theories about visual perception has been the application of frequency analysis (for a review see Georgeson 1979). A complex visual pattern can be analysed into a combination of regular frequency patterns in a similar way to the analysis of any sound into its pure tone components. Figure 11 shows how the combination of two sine waves produces a compound pattern. As higher frequency components are added, more sharply differentiated contours are produced. Of course, in complex patterns such analysis has to be carried out along at least two axes at once. Several investigations have produced evidence that spatial frequency detectors exist in the human visual system, by exposing observers to a grating of a single frequency for a time then testing the degree of contrast required in order to see a grating of this and similar frequencies. Lower sensitivity is found for the satiated frequency.

This approach presents a possibility of an all-purpose automatic

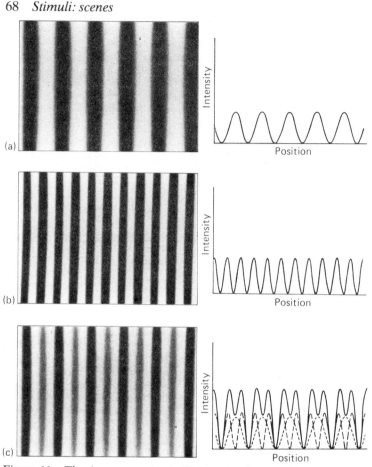

Figure 11   *The sinewave grating in (b) has twice the spatial frequency of the one in (a). When the two are added the pattern shown in (c) results. The intensity at each point in (c) is simply the sum of the intensities of the corresponding points in (a) and (b) (from Cornsweet 1970, Figure 12.2).*

global analysis of the visual field which would generate unique combinations of frequency patterns. It has been suggested that texture gradients could be extracted by this type of process. However, the evidence for single units responsive to a frequency over the whole visual field is inconclusive, since the satiation findings could simply be due to units responsive to a given bar width and it is unclear how such globally responsive units could evolve. Nor is it clear how separate objects could be isolated in the complex frequency description of the field or how the important common characteristics of different inputs could be matched. What seems more likely is that units do exist which respond to bars of different widths, that is, to a single stripe or bar of a given visual angle (see the description of Hubel and Wiesel's work in Chapter 4). These are repeated all over the visual field and each one detects any inputs with the appropriate characteristics in the area to which it is responsive. Finely tuned units (narrow stripe detectors) will only respond if the input is in exactly the right position and thus give very precise signals about contour location but will also pick up random 'noise', while the less finely tuned units are responsive to contours over a wider area and ignore noise.

Artificial intelligence in scene analysis

Marr (see Chapter 6 for a detailed description) has used this approach in his artificial intelligence research to achieve the first step of segregating figure and ground. Units of the type just described scan the input and pick out the changes in brightness in the field. By using a combination of finely and less finely tuned units, the important contours can be isolated, being the ones picked up by both types of unit. Subsequent processes look for continuities of contour and build up a figure segregated from the ground by using combinations of the types of cue identified by the *Gestalt* psychologists. A three-dimensional representation is subsequently constructed using cues for distance such as texture gradients.

However, Marr's program handles just one object on a background, and obviously this is the simplest situation to handle. Other artificial intelligence theorists such as Guzman (1969) have programmed computers to segment drawings of overlapping three-dimensional forms (Figure 12). In this case, with only overlap cues

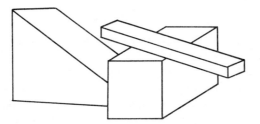

Figure 12   *Example of the type of scene used by Guzman for analysis by computer*

available as to relative distance from the observer, the program has to start from its knowledge about the type of input it will receive and some quite complex rules for separating out objects from each other. Different types of contour junction signalled different types of relation between two adjacent surfaces.

Arrows → indicated a junction of two surfaces of the same object and forks Y indicated a junction of three surfaces of the same object. Tees ⊣ usually indicated one object in front of another and angles ⌞ indicated a single surface in front of another. After a preliminary assignment of surfaces to objects on the basis of these cues, tests for consistency of the assignments were made. Hochberg (1968) has shown that this type of feature is important by presenting a sequence of views from drawings of three-dimensional objects so that either each successive view contained a contour junction or so that the picture was split at the junctions so that half was seen in one exposure and the other half in the next. The former condition produced perception of three-dimensional objects, but the latter did not.

Auditory figure–ground relations

There are, of course, analogous auditory phenomena to those I have been considering, in that sounds are segregated from background, as a musical instrument is segregated from the rest of the orchestra. Segmentation of speech into words depends on knowing the language, that is, on top-down processing, not on the physical gaps, and on satiation – if you repeat 'Monday, Monday . . .' to yourself, you will soon hear 'Demon, demon . . .'.

Conclusions

It has been argued that, though some segregation processes are automatic, segregation of a complex input into separate objects against a background must be carried out by beginning with automatic processes, followed by a hypothesis or expectation about the nature of the input and the relevant features which can be used to assign different areas to the same object. Sometimes these features may be very simple ones, such as an enclosed area surrounded by a uniform background, such as letters or shapes on a page, or they may be the *Gestalt* features of proximity, similarity, common fate and so on, but in other situations quite complex relations have to be extracted. In speech, perception segregation depends on fitting the input to known units (words). Some puzzles and jokes depend on inducing the wrong expectations about units (for example, 'Pas de lieu, Rhone que nous', which as French is nonsense, but when heard as English makes sense). Unfortunately the evidence on which theories about the necessary processes have been based is drawn from presenting human beings with relatively easily segregated inputs; where more complex inputs have been presented, as with concealed figures, no attempt has been made to study the processes, but only the overall time or success rate.

None of the theories I have discussed so far considers the problem of integration into a unitary whole of the samples of a scene as the eyes move. Studies of eye movements in examining pictures show that the main points of information are sampled many times, but experience is of a single whole rather than a series of very partial snapshots. Parks (1965) has shown that this ability to combine discrete samples can operate quite automatically. He moved pictures rapidly behind a narrow slit so that only a succession of very thin slices was presented to the eye. Provided that the rate of movement was fairly fast, a single picture was seen. Film makers too provide us with a succession of views out of which we are able to construct a total picture. Hochberg (1968, 1978) has discussed these issues in some detail and suggested that an integrative schematic map is used to organize the input from successive glances, so that what is 'seen' is actually the confirmed map rather than the input. This however leaves unexplained where the integrative map comes from in cases where we have no expectation about the input to guide us.

In summary, I have now examined some theoretical approaches to the problems of object segregation and the construction of a three-dimensional scene consisting of objects of different shapes and sizes at different distances. What now has to be considered is the notion of 'object'. Are the wholes into which we divide the world unavoidable and unambiguous or are there many different ways of perceiving and identifying open to the observer which are selected depending on other contextual factors? Moreover, are these segregated objects to be regarded as indissoluble wholes or should they be defined in terms of component features?

4 Stimuli: objects

Variability in object descriptions

In this chapter I shall consider other questions about the nature of the stimulus which further call into question the assumption that the input is the overriding or only factor we have to consider when explaining perceptual achievements. The chapter is divided into three main parts. The first considers the varying ways in which a single object may be described or identified, depending on how precise or general an identification is needed. The second looks at whether complex objects are treated as indivisible wholes by the perceptual system or whether they are decomposed into component parts or features. The third section considers the notion of stimulus features and some of the features used in perception. A prevailing theme throughout will be that there is great flexibility in perception and any attempt to lay down inviolable rules is doomed to failure.

In the last two chapters the importance was noted of context, expectation and task demands in determining which aspects of the input are processed and how they are processed (the milkman in Paris phenomenon). Taking an experimental example, in the context of numbers O will receive one identification and in the context of letters another. More remarkably, searching for letter O in numbers is faster than searching for it in letters, while the reverse holds for figure O, even though the physical shape is the same and the only change between the two situations is the shapes it has to be distinguished from (Ionides and Gleitman 1972).

Note how difficult this makes the goal of finding an adequate stimulus description. It means that the description needed differs with the task; that there is no single, neutral description for all purposes. What we would like is to be able to spell out a description of a scene or a sentence which predicts that a view of the same scene from a different angle would be recognized as the same scene, because both contain the same features, or which predicts that another sentence will be interpreted in the same way, but this only seems to be possible if the set of variations which are to be distinguished from all other possibilities is somehow specified so that the common features are indicated which characterize that set and distinguish its members from non-members. In other words, the stimuli have to be defined with reference to the total set of possibilities in that situation. It has been pointed out already in Chapter 2 that identification may be carried out to different levels or degrees of precision, ranging from just a 'thing', through animal, human, young female to Jane Smith, or from sound, through animal sound, bird sound, goose sound to Greylag goose alarm call. More information is required to make a more precise classification and in some cases the aspects of the input which are relevant will change depending on the level or type of identification required. There are a number of distinctions involved here and different researchers have highlighted different ones of these or picked out the same one in different ways. I shall discuss four such distinctions.

Rosch: levels of categorization

The work of Eleanor Rosch (Rosch *et al.* 1976, Rosch 1975) is concerned with the way in which human beings divide up the variety of objects they experience into categories and how these categories are organized. This will be discussed further when I come to consider how the models of the world we carry about in our heads are constructed. The findings relevant to our current concern are that the common categories of Western culture exhibit, according to Rosch, three main levels of organization, and hence of naming. The *basic* level is that most commonly evoked when encountering an object, such as 'chair' or 'hammer'; at this level objects with the same name are usually perceptually similar and users have little difficulty in offering a list of characteristic perceptual features. The *superordinate* level ('furniture' or 'tool') embraces a variety of objects with minimal perceptual similarity but with a common biological origin or function, or as some might say a group of objects linked by conceptual rather than perceptual common attributes. *Subordinate* names ('Chippendale chair' or 'claw hammer') require minor distinctions to be drawn within the basic level, involving a few additional perceptual features. However, in the case of biological categories (which is why I avoided using geese and trees as examples) Rosch found that the superordinate name ('fish' or 'bird' or 'tree') tended to be evoked by pictures of examples rather than the basic object name ('salmon' or 'robin' or 'oak'). Presumably it is not the case that 'animal' is the true superordinate and 'fish', 'bird' and so on are really the basic names, since 'rodent' or 'reptile' would probably not be the normally evoked name though they are of similar generality. Rather, it must be that the structures are not rigid and much depends on familiarity and usefulness. In an unconstrained situation, therefore, there do seem to be general preferences for a certain level of identification, probably one which is sufficiently precise for most day-to-day purposes and which is based on readily available cues. However, more precise identification is feasible, given that the observer has the defining features and name available in memory, and assignment to the more general superordinate category is also feasible provided that the relations between the names are known.

Garner: inferred sets

Garner (1974) made a similar distinction to that of Rosch, though based on a very different line of research. He pointed out that identification of an object (a two-dimensional visual pattern in his experiments) depends on the set from which it is assumed to be drawn. Thus ○ will be named 'circle' in most cases, selecting among a set of varied shapes, but if ○ is added to the set of possibilities the description has to become more precise to identify the first shape unambiguously, and if ● and ◎ are further added the description has to become more and more detailed, adding still more aspects of the original figure in order to name or identify it. Not only will the description change but the features of the stimulus which are attended to or perceived or used to achieve the description will also change.

Garner argued that any object is assigned to an inferred set and that the description or name selected depends on this inferred set. This set will normally depend on familiarity, and the current goal of the perceiver, but Garner also showed that certain types of pattern seem to imply their own inferred sets more or less automatically. He used a rather artificial set of stimuli to illustrate this. They were patterns of five dots placed in a matrix of three squares wide by three squares high (Figure 13). Some of the patterns remained identical when rotated in steps of 90° or reflected around the vertical or horizontal axis, while others produced a set of four different

Figure 13   *Examples of dot patterns used by Garner*
            Rotating and reflecting the patterns will produce 1, 4 or 8
            different patterns, respectively, for the left, centre and right hand
            figures.

patterns when transformed in these ways, and yet others a set of eight different patterns. Garner showed that the first type, with a rotation and reflection (R & R) subset of one, was identified more quickly, rated more aesthetically pleasing and recalled better than those from larger R & R subsets. It seems likely, therefore, that objects will be identified by reference to the smallest set consistent with the current goal.

Craik and Lockhart: depth of processing

Another related notion is that of 'depth of processing' (Craik and Lockhart 1972). From research into memory for lists of words has come the idea that material may be processed in the perceptual system to different 'depths' or 'levels', with deeper processing leading to more stable memory traces. The sequence was naturally conceived as beginning with the analysis of simple physical features (lines, curves and corners) and their relations, proceeding through combinations of these to letters, words and word naming which gives acoustic and articulatory features, then to meaning, associations and categorizations of the word on a wide range of semantic features (pleasantness, part of speech, etc.). Similar hypothetical sequences of processing have been postulated for faces and pictures. However, while the general principle that different features may be processed on different occasions is unobjectionable, there seems to be rather little evidence that any orderly fixed progression through all these features must occur when proceeding to the deeper levels of processing, apart from the rather broad distinction between physical and semantic (meaningful) cues, which is reasonably clear-cut for words but rather less so for other types of material. Even in the case of these two levels, the evidence that the two levels of processing occur in strict temporal sequence seems as yet debatable. More likely is that a variety of analysing processes goes on simultaneously or in a continually switching and interacting sequence. The normal level of processing certainly involves semantic processing, since words are read for meaning and irrelevant physical characteristics are not generally part of conscious experience. Single letter misprints go unnoticed and the well-practised skill of reading runs off without control. A striking example of this is the Stroop effect. Words which name colours are presented in ink of a different colour which has to be named. It is virtually impossible to prevent the word name (or even the names of words associated with a conflicting colour such as 'grass' printed in red ink which has to be named) from causing interference.

Artificial intelligence: domains

The fourth area from which we can gain some insights into different levels of identification is artificial intelligence. As mentioned briefly in Chapter 2, it has proved necessary to define a series of levels of perception or *domains* which determine how the input is classified and what features will be looked for in the input. The two visual patterns in Figure 14 can be interpreted as equivalent to each other and to many other possible two-dimensional representations which can be related to them by systematic rules. This identification involves assigning the patterns to the domain of three-dimensional objects and the features which define these objects are two-dimensional surfaces at different angles to the observer in certain spatial relations to each other, which remain unaltered when the objects move in space. This is the highest domain to which a relatively simple pattern of this type can be assigned and is the natural and immediate assignment, at least in cultures which are familiar with representation of solid objects on a two-dimensional surface. However, the pattern could equally well be assigned to a domain of

Figure 14   *Two visual patterns which can be taken as representing the same object if they are assigned to the domain of three-dimensional objects*

two-dimensional shapes and so on down to the lowest domain of points varying only in brightness.

Different domains are distinct from each other and require not just different degrees of analysis of the input but a different kind of analysis. When assigning an input to the domain of three-dimensional objects, retinal shapes are corrected for the position of the viewer, not treated as two-dimensional projections in the frontal plane, so additional processing has to be carried out to determine their angle of inclination relative to the viewer. In a three-dimensional scene, information from movement probably triggers off these corrective processes and this normal mode of operation is carried over into processing two-dimensional representations of three-dimensional scenes, but a computer has to be specifically directed whether or not to treat two-dimensional representations in this way.

Although these distinctions were coined for coping with visual representations of geometrical objects, analogies can be seen in other types of perception. In reading, the visual pattern can be treated as just that, or as a representation of an auditory pattern, which in its turn can be treated as just that or as representing an object or idea. In turn, strings of words can be assigned to a domain of propositions. Again the natural and immediate assignment in the practised performer is to the highest domain, but learners pass through stages where they can only assign the input to lower domains. Assignment to higher domains requires more complex processing but enables a more economic categorization of the input, treating much variation as irrelevant to the nature of the objects or the meanings of the sentences. There are also higher possible domains of scenes composed of combinations of objects or paragraphs composed of propositions, but these are not generally treated as unified entities but rather as combinations of the objects or propositions which occur at the next level down, since the number of possible variations becomes enormous and infrequently repeated if the units become too large and complex.

Levels of identification: an attempted synthesis

This concept of domains is not concerned with the same kind of difference as Rosch's and Garner's distinctions between levels of identification. In those two distinctions it is mainly the number of features used in identifying the object, and not the type of features, which is important in determining the level, and that level varies within a single domain of objects (three-dimensional in Rosch's case and two-dimensional in Garner's). For Garner, the broader the inferred set from which an object comes, the fewer the perceptual features needed to identify it. As the number of features identified is increased, the inferred subset is narrowed from geometric shapes to types of circle to outline circles and so on. This is parallel to Rosch's distinction between basic names and subordinate names, circle being basic and more complex distinctions being subordinate. Thus in Garner's terms, use of the basic name selects within the inferred subset indicated by the superordinate name.

The levels of processing approach is concerned with a broad domain-like distinction between assigning words to the domain of visual or auditory patterns characterized by appropriate features, and assigning them to a domain of meanings, characterized by a different kind of feature, and is also concerned with the amount of detail abstracted within each of these domains, such as the visual appearance of the word in the first case and the pleasantness in the second.

Hence it provides a vaguer but more inclusive approach, probably because it has been devised from considering symbolic material where there is an obvious distinction between the object itself (physical level) and what it stands for (semantic level) and a variety of features available within each of these domains. We might wish to regard the notion of domains and the distinctions between different levels of identification as special cases, therefore, of the more general depth of processing approach. However, the subordinate, basic and superordinate levels of identification clearly do not correspond to a change from shallow to deeper processing since more features are needed to identify at the subordinate level than at the basic level and a different type of feature is needed to identify at the superordinate level compared with the basic level. The difference between the first two is better characterized as one of greater breadth of processing within the same level in order to make subordinate distinctions, while the superordinate level seems to require use of a previously learned system of classification and hence is similar to processing at a semantic rather than a physical level.

Hence, though a complete reconciliation of the different distinctions within one comprehensive scheme is not immediately obvious, there does seem to be a strong possibility of building such a scheme around the notions of, first, type of distinction (physical- or stimulus-based versus representational- or memory-based) and second, the fineness of discrimination or amount of detail abstracted within each of these.

Summarizing the argument of this section, we can conclude that the appropriate description for a given input is highly dependent on the way the perceiver chooses to process it, which may vary qualitatively in the way information is interpreted and the degree to which information in memory is tapped, and quantitatively in the number of features extracted from the stimulus and from information in memory associated with it. Though this greatly complicates any attempt to derive regularities relating input and response or experience, the situation is fortunately less formidable than appears, because in normal unconstrained situations there are strong preferences for processing inputs in particular ways, such as the preference for treating two-dimensional displays as three-dimensional representations or for extracting meaning in linguistic processing or for identifying at the basic level in Rosch's sense, so much so that it is difficult to prevent these levels of analysis from being carried out automatically. It is very compelling to see outline drawings in three dimensions rather than in two dimensions and to analyse word meaning even when this is maladaptive, as in the Stroop effect described above. Hence attempts to describe the stimulus in appropriate ways can, in the first instance, proceed on the assumption that there are preferred modes of processing.

Describing stimuli: wholes and parts

I now turn to a consideration of the validity of describing the stimulus, at whatever level, in terms of features. This approach is contrasted with describing the stimulus as a simple, indivisible whole, stemming from the *Gestalt* tradition, in which the forces inherent in the input are assumed to generate the simplest unitary percept compatible with the total pattern. In theories attempting to explicate the processes leading to identification, these two opposed traditions most commonly appear as feature-testing and template-matching models, respectively. There is, however, a tangled cluster of distinctions involved in this issue which we need to consider. First I will outline these different distinctions and then consider their validity in the light of experimental evidence.

Template versus feature matching

The former assumes that a complete representation of the whole stimulus (for example the letter 'A') is matched to stored patterns of the possible inputs. These templates seem to be thought of as simply large 'collections' of neural activity evoked directly by the input. The theory encounters severe difficulties in handling variability in size, orientation, typeface, handwriting, speech differences and so on, so that it seems essential to include some processes for extracting the significant aspects and ignoring the irrelevant. The feature testing approach assumes that lists of component features such as lines and angles (in effect miniature templates) are extracted and matched to lists defining the possible inputs. This theory encounters difficulties over its neglect of relations between features (for example L and T both consist of one vertical and one horizontal line so more information is needed to distinguish them) and modifications have been proposed to deal with this, which are discussed later in the chapter.

In both these models the matching processes may be assumed to occur either serially (to one possibility at a time, one after another) or in parallel (to all possibilities simultaneously). Also, in the feature-matching model the features may be processed serially or in parallel, but the latter possibility is not equivalent to a template-matching model, since the different features are still treated separately. Matching processes may also either continue until all comparisons have been made (exhaustive processing) or only until sufficient evidence has been acquired (self-terminating processing). Chapter 5 discusses the issue of serial versus parallel processing in more detail.

Holistic versus analytic processing

This often seems to be an alternative way of stating the same distinction as that above. Lockhead (1972) has referred to holistic processing as 'blob' processing. However, the terms are so imprecisely defined by their users that it is difficult to reach an unequivocal decision on whether they are equivalent or not. Templates strictly should include all detail of a shape so that a letter A made of up dots ⠢ requires a different template from one composed of lines A, whereas holistic processing of these patterns would ignore the internal details and treat them as equivalent. In this case, obviously, template matching and holistic processing are not equivalent.

Global versus local processing

This is used less equivocally to distinguish processing of the overall structure of a stimulus from processing internal detail or structure. The difference between this distinction and the two preceding ones is that it regards these two processes as independent; sometimes local processing will be unnecessary, as in the dots versus lines example above, at others it will be necessary in combination with global processing, as for example when distinguishing words with the same overall shape but composed of different letters, and sometimes global processing will not be important, as when searching for a word containing a particular letter. There are of course no hard and fast rules for deciding what is to count as local and what as global, since this depends on the type of stimulus and the task.

Prototypes or iconic concepts versus symbolic or rule-defined concepts

'Prototype' has been used in connection with two different distinctions which have not been explicitly separated. Posner (1973) distinguishes groupings of objects which depend on deriving a prototype from a varied selection and groupings which depend on a precise rule. A prototype is a mean of all the variations experienced, and Posner demonstrated the ability to derive such prototypes in experiments where he presented a series of dot patterns which had been created by taking one pattern and distorting it by some rule, such as moving each point five places horizontally with some random probability. A series of the resulting distortions was shown to observers, who had to learn one name for the set of distortions produced from each prototype. They never saw the prototype during this learning but subsequently showed excellent ability to classify it correctly and often claimed they had seen it before. Because he assumed, without investigation, that no feature description of these patterns was possible, Posner believed that the prototypes were 'iconic concepts' or unanalysed representations, presumably like templates. He did not discuss how they might be derived, but some early theories about concept learning drew an analogy with a composite photograph in which the exemplars were 'superimposed' until the common features stood out; it is possible to imagine a neural process of this type.

A second sense of prototype can be derived from studies by Reed (1972), Rosch and her co-workers (for example, Rosch *et al.* 1976) and others, which assumes analysis of the object into separate features, but no definite rule which unambiguously identifies members of the category by their possession of certain defining features (dictionaries have the unenviable problem of defining such indefinables; the *Shorter Oxford Dictionary*, for example, defines a bird as 'any feathered vertebrate animal', which would exclude plucked chickens!). The prototype is the typical member of the class defined by the mean on each feature over all the members, and objects are categorized in terms of their similarity to this prototype on the features, some features being given more weight than others. This distinction, therefore, depends on the nature of the rule rather than the nature of the representation, since both prototypes and rule-defined concepts are here defined in terms of features.

Reed (1972) used pictures of faces which could vary in different ways. He showed his subjects two sets of five faces each, chosen so that neither set could be defined in any simple way (such as all with long noses and high foreheads) and then asked them to assign new patterns to the correct set. He tested several possible ways they might do this and found that the best explanation of their behaviour was that they constructed a prototype face for each set and then judged the similarity between the test face and these prototypes. The subjects' reports suggested that the prototypes were like visual images.

Rosch *et al.* (1976) have also argued that many concepts do not have clear boundaries and therefore that some exemplars are more typical than others (a robin is more bird-like than a penguin). More characteristic exemplars are characterized (identified as a bird) more quickly, produced earlier in lists of exemplars of the category and learned at a younger age. Rosch and Mervis (1975) showed that the degree of prototypicality depends on two things:

1   the cue validity of the features possessed by an exemplar, measured by counting the number of such features which also occur in exemplars of contrasted categories, a low score indicating high cue validity;
2   the degree of family resemblance of an exemplar to its fellow category members, measured by counting the number of

exemplars in which each attribute occurs and adding these totals together over all the attributes of a given exemplar, a high score indicating high family resemblance.

These two factors affected speed of learning, speed of identifying and ratings of prototypicality. However, the authors emphasize that prototypes can depend on other factors as well, such as frequency of occurrence, salience of attributes or exemplars and as yet undefined *Gestalt* properties, since separate defining features are not essential. Another implication of this approach is that features vary continuously rather than being simply present or absent as a rule-based definition requires, and the degree to which an exemplar possesses a feature is also likely to be important.

It should be emphasized that experience and internal processes may be very different. Experience of a unified whole or an image does not prove that a stimulus is processed as a unified whole or as a visual image, nor does an analysis in terms of features imply that no unified whole is experienced, though we have little idea how the synthesis could occur. Hence the fact that 'bird' or 'triangle' evokes a visual image does not mean that is what is inside our heads (how could it be?), but that information is in our heads which can produce such an experience. It is the logical nature and neural representation of that information which we want to discover. An image could be derived from an unanalysed template-like representation or from an abstracted list of features; reports of images do not differentiate the possibilities, though other aspects of behaviour might. Nor indeed does the fact that some concepts can be defined by a precise rule prove that everybody's representation is in that form rather than in the form of a prototype.

A final point is that representations or definitions are not the same things as categorizing processes. Ability to produce an image does not prove that identification is done by matching images, nor does ability to offer a precise definition prove that identification is made by matching such definitions rather than a less precise process. Observers will use a method which works well enough for their purpose.

Analogue versus propositional representations

An analogue representation is a direct representation, though not necessarily in the same form as the input. Length of lines, for example, might be represented by the number of neurons activated and contrast might be represented by the rate of firing. A propositional representation is an abstracted classification, such as having one neuron activated if a line of a given length occurs and a different neuron for a different length. The *Gestalt* idea of 'squares on the brain' is an analogue theory of representation, while if four separate units each detected one side and then fed into a special square detector, this would be a propositional representation. Though much of our experience and behaviour implies analogue representation, such as the ability to scale stimuli in terms of more and less of an attribute and to rotate mental images of objects continuously (Shepard and Metzler 1971), the problem is to decide how complex stimuli could be represented in this way and compared with other complex stimuli. Templates would be analogue representations of the input and lists of features would be propositional ones.

Integral versus separable combinations of feature

This distinction is more carefully worked out than the others. It has been made by Garner (1974), who points out that quite often a combination of two simple features is not treated as such, but forms a new and different feature. Length and height can vary independently but shape or size change is the immediately experienced feature. Likewise, it is virtually impossible for observers to disentangle changes in hue (wavelength) from changes in saturation (amount of grey or mixture of opponent wavelengths) in colours, and they are treated alike as changes in colour. Combinations of this kind are called *integral* by Garner.

Other types of combination where separate physical changes remain psychologically separate are called *separable* by Garner. Examples would be changes in size and colour or in roughness and temperature. Garner does not in fact suggest a simple dichotomy between the two types of combination, but accepts that there must be a continuum of degrees of combination with the integral and separable types being at the extremes. He does not discuss possible causes of the variation. Two obvious possibilities suggest themselves – innate combination due to the way the nervous system is designed to process some combinations (such as speech sounds), and learning to simplify the task demands by processing combinations in a new way (such as in the child's learning of letter names for complex shapes).

Several differences have been demonstrated between the way in which these two kinds of stimulus combination affect behaviour. If subjects are asked to rate the differences between pairs of integral stimuli composed of combinations of features the results are predictable from ratings of the differences between pairs differing only on one of the component features in the following way. If α is the difference estimated between a pair of stimuli a_1 and a_2 differing only on Feature A and β is the difference between a pair b_1 and b_2 differing on Feature B only, then when the two features are combined to form pairs which differ on both at once (a_1b_1 versus a_2b_2 or a_1b_2 versus a_2b_1) the difference is $\sqrt{(\alpha^2 + \beta^2)}$. Putting this another way, in what I hope may be a familiar geometric context, it is as if the stimuli form the four corners of a rectangle in a 'difference space' (see Figure 15), so that the distance along the diagonal can be calculated from the differences along the sides by Pythagoras's theorem. Taking an example, if subjects rate the difference between two rectangles differing only in height as three units on some scale, and that between two others differing only in length as four units, then the difference between a pair differing in both height and length will be $\sqrt{(3^2 + 4^2)} = 5$ units.

If on the other hand a similar exercise is carried out on pairs of stimuli composed of combinations of separable dimensions, subjects find the task less easy to carry out and give responses in which the combined difference is the sum of the two components. This is called a city-block metric (as opposed to the Euclidean metric illustrated below) because it is as if you have to go round the

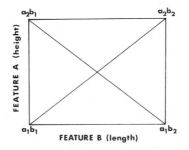

Figure 15   *Differences between four objects in a Euclidean space*
Objects separated on the horizontal axis differ in length, while those separated on the vertical axis differ in height. Objects separated by the diagonals differ on both dimensions and the degree of difference is found by calculating the length of the diagonal from the length of the sides.

sides to get from one corner to the diagonally opposite one in Figure
15. Thus, if two triangles differing only in size are rated as three
units apart and two others differing only in redness are rated as four
units apart, a pair differing on both features will be rated as seven
units apart. The two dimensions of difference are not combined but
treated separately (Attneave 1950).

The second way in which differences between integral and separable features can be shown is in the effects of variation in an
irrelevant dimension on the speed of discriminating the stimuli on a
relevant dimension. This irrelevant dimension can either remain
constant (unidimensional variation) or vary in a random way such
that either value on the irrelevant dimension can occur with either
value of the relevant one (orthogonal variation) or it may vary in
such a way that the same value of the irrelevant dimension always
occurs with the same value of the relevant one (correlated variation). With separable dimensions these different types of relation
do not affect the speed of sorting packs of cards into two sets
differing on the relevant feature, which suggests that the relevant
dimension is processed and the other one ignored. With integral
dimensions, however, orthogonal variation slows down sorting
compared with unidimensional variation, while correlated variation
speeds it up. This speeding up is known as *redundancy gain* because
the correlated information in the second dimension is redundant,
but nevertheless aids performance. This suggests that the combination is treated as a single type of variation, making the stimuli
more discriminable from each other in the correlated case and less
discriminable in the orthogonal case. However, the average discriminability would still be greater in the orthogonal case; assuming
rectangle height in the above example is the relevant feature and
length the irrelevant one, with length held constant the two sets
differ by three units, but with length varying the average distance
between the two sets is the average of three and five units or four
units. The theorists have some difficulty with this and Lockhead
(1979) argues that the task is no longer a straightforward identification one, but requires 'condensing' two different stimuli on to
one response and this causes the problems.

The implication of the distinction between integral and separable
combinations is that some types of stimuli may be treated holistically and others analytically. The problem is that theories of holistic
or blob processing offer no specification of the processes or mechanisms by which this could be carried out. Analytic processing theories

on the other hand do attempt to grapple with this problem of how the input could be matched to the possible inputs represented in memory.

Automatic versus effortful processing

This distinction, which is discussed in detail in the next chapter, is also relevant. Automatic processing, as will be shown, seems to occur with well-learned identifications, and to depend on direct access to information in long term memory. Several inputs can be processed at once and several possibilities can be tested at once. Effortful processing, on the other hand, involves a slower sequential matching of one input at a time to one possibility at a time. Though the distinction was made in experiments involving letters as units (Schneider and Shiffrin 1977), it can equally well be applied to feature components of patterns, which may be dealt with simultaneously when the pattern is well known, but have to be processed one after another when it is an unfamiliar one or when the rule is a complex unpractised one, such as assigning large red stars to one category and all other patterns to another. Thus automatic processing could be holistic processing or parallel processing of independent features, while effortful processing seems to be analytic and sequential.

Wholes and parts: some general principles

Most of the seven distinctions I have discussed are concerned in some degree with the extent to which the original input remains in a relatively unanalysed form or is decomposed into separate elements. Obviously some features, such as colour or movement, are registered separately by specialized receptors, but it does not follow necessarily that they are experienced separately. Combinations of features may be treated as unanalysed wholes either because combination occurs at some later level of analysis or because separate analysis of the different features never occurs or because some relation between the features is used. On the other hand, separation of features may occur either through problems in synthesizing elements into a whole or through the development of more sophisticated perceptual analysis.

The importance of practice and level of cognitive development in determining the nature of stimulus processing has not been carefully investigated. Posner argued that iconic concepts are a less developed type than rule-based ones. This could mean either that the degree and precision of feature analysis increases with age and experience, so that a global unanalysed representation develops into a listing of features, or that the definition develops from a prototype to a precise rule. Some evidence bearing on these questions will be discussed in Chapter 9, suggesting the first possibility (see also Fletcher's experiment described in the next chapter). Rosch's work of course indicates that even adult concepts are not always defined by precise rules.

Intuitively it seems necessary that development of more precise ways of categorizing the world requires development of more analytical processing. In fact simpler organisms do extract fewer features, the simplest of them responding only to light or dark, and more complex organisms, such as frogs, extract only features which are important for survival (see page 97). These are not, however, examples of unprocessed wholes but of inbuilt and inflexible selective devices. More complex organisms still must be able to acquire a basis from which different features can be extracted for different purposes. Hence they have an elaborate system for recording the input in detail and for then selecting from it a wide variety of features according to the situation. In this sense both global, template-like representations and feature lists are available. In some cases, however, the sensory systems are not designed to differentiate features which are distinguishable by other measuring devices; these are some of the cases of integral dimensions such as hue and saturation in colours and different dimensions of speech sounds.

Also, it seems necessary to be able to learn to extract higher-order features of complex patterns to reduce the increasing complexity inherent in the first type of development. Some of these higher-order features, such as texture and parallax gradients, which signal universally important aspects of the environment, like distance, may be innately processed, but there also seems to be an ability to develop by experience analysis of emergent or higher-order features such as shape or size rather than length combined with height, or regularity in a pattern.

These two trends can be confused and may seem to be opposed, the one toward more precise analysis and the other toward more efficient synthesis. The first is shown in the development of the ability to extract features, and analytic processing of detail, the latter in the development of ability to use emergent features in processing complex patterns.

A third trend also enables more to be done by processing several features in parallel, especially when the joint presence of specific combinations is identified by a specific label or response (a word for example). This combining is often referred to as 'chunking'. Parallel processing of distinct features is different from treating them as integral or using an emergent feature. A fourth trend is toward more precise definition of category boundaries of proto-typically defined concepts and toward rules instead of prototypical definitions. In fact much scientific and philosophical activity is directed at this goal.

Thus I have suggested several ways in which inputs may be treated, depending on innate processing systems, task demands and practice level. These distinctions as yet remain somewhat imprecise and difficult to define and identify by experimental methods. However, I will describe some examples of the processing of wholes, even if the precise basis of these is as yet unclear.

Processing patterns as wholes: some examples

Faces seem to be processed as wholes, since presenting separate features in sequence destroys identification of faces but not of geometric shapes (Klatzky and Thompson 1975). Since babies will accept jumbled features and, at a later age, concentrate on eyes, this is apparently a case of integration through learning. Reicher (1969) and Wheeler (1970) have shown that letters are more easily identified in the context of a word than in isolation and it will be argued in Chapter 10 that this is due to parallel processing of the letters combined with the need for only some features of each letter to be extracted in order to define a word. Weisstein and Harris (1974) have shown superior perception of lines presented as parts of figures compared with lines presented on their own, where con-straints of this type could not apply since the different lines could combine with the rest of the pattern to form equally plausible total figures, which suggests that the whole or emergent features (rela-tions between lines) were being processed. Pomerantz and Garner (1973) and Pomerantz and Schwaitzberg (1975) have shown that even spatially discrete elements may be treated as forming a single whole pattern. Pomerantz argued that if a discrimination between two elements is aided by the addition of the same element to both (which of course provides no further help on its own in distinguishing them) this must imply that the combinations are more easily discriminated than the originals because they are being treated as new whole forms (as the *Gestalt* psychologists put it, the whole is greater than the sum of the parts). He demonstrated such a phenomenon using the two bracket shapes, (versus) as his first discrimination; a pack of cards had to be sorted into two piles, one for each shape. Adding another bracket to each to give ((versus () or)(speeded up performance even though the extra identical elements might have been expected to cause more confusion. The combinations certainly look more different from each other than the originals and this seems to be because they form unified wholes. When they are presented with a bigger space between the parts or when a different pair of elements which do not group well is used, such as (⌢, the effect vanishes.

Lockhead has reached a similar conclusion from an experiment showing that the *way* in which two features are combined affects the ease of identification. Suppose we have four different lengths and four different heights; they can be combined so that as length increases, height also increases, giving a series of squares or rectangles increasing in size. Lockhead called this type of combination linear for obvious reasons; if the combinations are plotted on a graph with height on one axis and length on the other, a straight line will result (see Figure 16). However, there are other ways of combining the two, including what Lockhead (1979) called a sawtooth correlation in which Length 1 is combined with Height 3, Length 2 with Height 1, Length 3 with Height 4 and Length 4 with Height 2 (the plot of these on the graph goes up and down like the teeth of a saw). This produces four differently shaped rectangles. Speed of sorting is faster in this case than in the first case. If the task is done by using the two dimensions separately there should be no differences because the differences between the four values are exactly the same in both cases; in fact we might expect the first to be easier as the pattern of changes is the same for both features and the responses. However, if the shapes are treated as wholes the figures differ more from each other in the second case, as can be shown by getting ratings of similarity. This finding is not just restricted to the type of example I have given, which, it could be argued, is special because it creates two different sorts of difference, size and shape.

It has from time to time been suggested that the right and left hemispheres of the brain are differentially designed to do holistic or

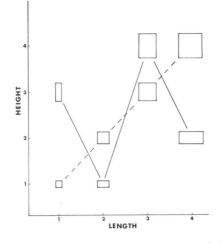

Figure 16   *Examples of two sets of four patterns in one of which differences of length and height are correlated in a linear way (connected by broken lines) and in the other of which they are correlated in a sawtooth pattern (connected by continuous lines)*

global processing (right hemisphere) and analytic or local processing (left hemisphere). Martin (1979) and Alivisatos and Wilding (1982) tested this theory by using large letters composed of smaller letters. The small letters were either the same as the large letter (congruent conditions) or conflicting with it (incongruent). Martin used speed of naming and Alivisatos and Wilding used speed of same–different judgements, and both presented the stimuli to one or other side of a fixation point so that they initially activated one hemisphere only. Both experiments showed that when the required match involved attending to the large letters the left hemisphere showed interference from the small letters and the right showed very little such interference, suggesting local processing in the first case and not in the second. However, Alivisatos and Wilding also showed that when the task required attending to the small letters to match the two stimuli, the right hemisphere performed as well as the left, so there was no inability to carry out local processing when needed, only a greater ability to exclude it when it was not needed.

Descriptions of stimuli as combinations of features

Speech

We must now look more carefully at this notion of 'feature' which has so far been taken for granted. What is a feature and what evidence is there for the existence of specific feature processors? Most of the examples given so far have been visual ones. We will look now at a different area – that of speech perception.

Phonetic analysis divides speech sounds according to a limited set of linguistic features – vowel (unchecked) versus consonant (checked); voiced versus unvoiced; position in the vocal system (front, middle or back); type of check (stop, fricative, nasal, liquid). The possible number of combinations of these features gives a very large number of sounds (phones) but within a particular language only some subset of the possibilities is used in speech and these variations convey meaning because substitution of one for another in some combination will either produce a nonsense word or a different word in the language. For example, replacing /b/ by /p/ can change boat to poat (non-word) or bin to pin (a different word). However, in some cases speakers may use different phones in different words, which are heard as the same. In English the difference between /k/ (hard) and /q/ (soft) is undetected as in the sentence 'keep calm and cool', and the difference between aspirated and non-aspirated /p/ as in 'pin' and 'spin' is ignored.

Such variations of similar sounds which are treated as identical within a particular language are called allophones of a single phoneme. Phonemes are the sounds in a given language which convey meaning; different languages have different numbers of these; in English there are about forty-four different phonemes and they are written between slashes, as in the examples above, to distinguish them from phones which are written between square brackets.

Hence certain combinations of phonetically defined features of the external stimulus are related to certain perceived differences which are important for word identification and hence for meaning. Miller and Nicely (1955) showed that confusions in perceiving consonants could be related to such features. The task then was to discover how these features were related to physical differences in the sound arriving at the ear and how such differences were distinguished by the sensory system. This task proved relatively easy for vowel sounds; each vowel is characterized by a particular combination of frequency bands. The ear seems to be designed to extract the frequency pattern in the input at each moment in time, so the physics and the physiology fit neatly together. In the case of consonants, however, it has proved very difficult to discover physical differences consistently related to the apparently convincing linguistic analysis of the input. The problems arose because the physical characteristics of a sound perceived as /t/ or /p/ or /k/ are heavily dependent on the vowel sound with which the consonant is linked. We have already seen that the /k/ in 'keep calm and cool' varies in where it is produced, depending on the vowel which follows. It is hardly surprising that the physical nature of these differently produced /k/ sounds changes with the way they are produced. But if it does, how do we identify the variations as the same sound? Certainly not by any simple search for the presence of a certain number of key features, but rather by treating consonant plus vowel as a single unit, that is, a syllable. Clipping of speech sounds at syllable intervals is particularly damaging for perception. In this case identifying the features used depends on making the right type of segmentation into units which are the ones dealt with by the perceiving system. Thus the unit for perception need not be the same as the unit which is most useful in analysing meaning.

Some theorists have suggested that there are innate detectors in the human brain for specific features of speech. The physical difference between voiced consonants (like /b/ and /d/) and unvoiced ones (like /p/ and /t/) is the length of the delay (known as voice onset time) between the mouth opening and the voicing in the following vowel rather than presence or absence of voicing. Sounds with a short voice onset time give perception of voiced sounds, but repeated exposure to such short delays causes adaptation and increased probability of reporting an unvoiced sound, suggesting a specific voice onset time detector has been affected (Eimas and Corbit 1973). However, Diehl (1981) has criticized this kind of argument and pointed out that if the context of the phoneme is important, fixed feature detectors of this kind cannot be useful (Chapter 10 considers speech perception in more detail).

Visual stimuli

Analyses of features for visually presented language have been much less sophisticated, but Geyer and Dewald (1973) have devised a feature list to describe upper case letters and confusions between them.

We have already encountered the use of features in computer programs designed to segment a scene into component parts, in which the features consisted of different kinds of contour junction. Another example of research attempting to discover perceptual features to explain behaviour comes from extensive research on the octopus by Sutherland (1961). He trained them to choose one of two shapes to obtain food rewards, such as a square presented with a non-rewarded circle, then varied the positive shape to discover which shapes would continue to evoke the response. By comparing the group of shapes which elicited the same response against those which did not, hypotheses could be devised about the critical features being used by the animals to guide behaviour. Sutherland originally deduced that many of his findings could be explained by just two features being extracted – the horizontal extent and the vertical extent. Pairs of shapes such as $\square$ and $\square$ were easy to distinguish and pairs such as $\diagdown$ and $\diagup$ were impossible (they are identical on both the above features). These two features were also related to some neurophysiological data on the visual system of the octopus, which appeared to be designed for the type of analysis proposed. Sutherland went on, however, to find that quite abstract 'features' seemed to be used in treating some shapes as alike. Some groupings were best explained by similarities in contour irregularity or the ratio of contour to the square root of the area, so clearly more complex processes would be needed to produce such results.

Word meaning

A very different application of feature analysis is to the meaning of words. A complex treatment of this topic has been provided by Miller and Johnson-Laird (1975) who developed into a full-blown theory their earlier work investigating the main dimensions of meaning of words related to a particular semantic area, such as movement or emotion. By getting subjects to specify the differences in meaning between pairs of verbs within one of these areas (for example, walk and run differ in the speed component) they were able to uncover about twelve dimensions of meaning within each conceptual field. They related these dimensions to perceivable correlates, thus attempting to connect perception with semantics.

Neurophysiological evidence concerning feature analysis

Direct neurophysiological evidence can be cited in support of both analytic and holistic processing. The work of Hubel and Wiesel (1962, 1968) and others which demonstrated line and corner detectors in the cat and monkey brains has already been referred to and must now be expanded on. Hubel and Wiesel, by recording the activity in a single neuron in response to different inputs, showed that different aspects of the input were abstracted at different levels of the visual system. In the optic nerve and lateral geniculate, cells were found which responded to a dark spot on a light ground (off centre and on surround) or the reverse. A uniform light or dark area had no effect. The implication is that a cluster of retinal units responsive to the onset of light (on units) surrounded by a ring of units responsive to the offset of light (off units) combine to activate the optic nerve and lateral geniculate units. The receptor neuron could fire when the combined input reached a certain level. To reduce the possibility of false responses, inactive receptors of either type could reduce the activity of the other type and active receptors of either type could increase the sensitivity of those of the other type.

In the visual cortex, cells were found which responded to edges or contours (light on dark or dark on light) at specific points on the retina, or in some cases over a wide area of the retina. In another part of the visual cortex, units were found responding to corners or edges of a specific length (that is, edges with two corners). Each type of unit was arranged in an orderly fashion in columns in the brain, with all the units responding to a particular retinal area grouped together, covering all the possible orientations and types of input, and with adjacent columns responsive to adjacent retinal areas (this, of course, is why a square on the retina produces a roughly square pattern of excitation on the cortex).

It is tempting to regard such units as the basic feature detectors, and as linked in a hierarchy, with lateral geniculate circular units combined into contour detectors at a specific location, and several of these detectors of contours at a specific location combined to produce a contour detector sensitive over a wider area, and then presumably patterns of contour detectors feeding into square detectors, triangle detectors and so on. However, we have no evidence on whether or how these contour detectors combine to form even simple shape detectors, and in fact the different types of unit seem to be derived from independent combinations of inputs from the lateral geniculate bodies (Blakemore 1975). Clearly, records from one unit at a time provide very little evidence about the overall structure of the system. Furthermore, some theorists have strongly questioned the earlier inclination to treat these units as straightforward feature detectors.

Uttal, Bunnell and Corwin (1970) showed that lines of dots in a random array can be seen as lines, longer sequences and those containing more dots being easier to detect. Such perception could not depend on activation of cells like those found by Hubel and Wiesel, so at least some line detection must depend on more complex processes of locating regularities. Some have argued that Hubel and Wiesel's units are spatial frequency detectors responsive to bars repeated at specific frequencies, which carry out the type of frequency analysis discussed in Chapter 3, but it was argued there that the evidence for this interpretation rather than for detectors of single contours is inconclusive. Marr, from his attempts to achieve object recognition on computers, has argued that several such units would respond to any single input, since the units are not sharply tuned to a particular orientation but will respond over a range, though less strongly the more the input differs from the preferred orientation. Moreover, since these units require a number of conditions to be jointly fulfilled to produce a maximum response (for example, location, orientation and width), and variation on any of these will still produce some response, the number of different inputs which will evoke some response in any unit and the number of units responding to any input is quite large and varied. Therefore 'the identification of visual stimuli must rely on some comparison between the activities of the multichannel neurons' (Blakemore 1975, p. 265). That is, tests must be made to decide which receptor neuron is responding most strongly. Marr found it necessary to include these extra stages in his simulations before a single feature could be signalled unambiguously to higher analysing processes. He suggested that Hubel and Wiesel's units are probably concerned with a preliminary process of identifying contours in the ambiguous and distorted input, that is, with segmentation and figure–ground discrimination processes rather than the final identification. There is also evidence that other features, such as colour (Zeki 1973) and brightness and texture, are recorded at separate sites in the visual cortex, but we know nothing of how these separately analysed aspects of the input are synthesized again into a whole. Nor for that matter has any physiological evidence been provided for the processing of curves.

One study has demonstrated similar units in the human cortex (Marg, Adams and Rutkin 1968) and there is some indirect behavioural evidence that there are probably units in our visual systems responsive to straight lines and curves. If an image is stabilized on the retina so that it does not shift relative to the retina when the eye moves, it tends to fragment and disappear, probably because neurons habituate to steady stimulation and respond mainly to changes. Parts of the image disappear in quite orderly ways, straight lines or curves vanishing then reappearing as wholes as if they are handled by a single neural element which has habituated, then recovered. However, Schuck (1973) has shown that subjects may simply be more ready to report such changes than less easily described ones. Another technique for discovering special feature receptors is to satiate an assumed type of receptor by prolonged viewing of a stimulus containing it, then to test sensitivity to it and similar features. Gilinsky and Cohen (1972) found that reaction times to lines of specific orientations were increased by prolonged viewing of that orientation, and Blakemore and Campbell (1969) found that prolonged viewing of a grating of alternating black and white stripes reduced sensitivity to such gratings, as measured by the level of illumination required to see the bars, but did not affect sensitivity to gratings of a different frequency (that is stripes of a different width) or orientation.

Other evidence from direct neurophysiological recordings indicates that in lower animals more complex combinations are abstracted quite early in the processing, rather than simple features being abstracted and then (presumably) recombined. In the frog's optic nerve, neurons respond to four types of stimulation – a round dot, a dimming of the ambient light, a moving edge, and steady contrast between two areas (Lettvin, Maturana, Pitts and McCulloch, 1959). The significance of these in the frog's life is obvious. Other types of stimulation are ineffective. To record round dots would require combinations like those already described for the lateral geniculate receptors in cats, and movement and shadow receptors can be designed by appropriate combinations. These combinations must of course occur very early in the frog's visual system since they are already functioning at the level of the optic nerve. In the bullfrog's auditory system are units responsive to a very precise combination of frequencies typical of the mating call

(Diehl 1981). Other complex receptors which have been isolated are the monkeys' paw detector and units responsive to three-dimensional objects in the superior colliculus of monkeys (Updyke 1974), though it is not known whether experience was needed for developing these. However, no critical features could be discovered for the latter and Updyke suggests that these units may have been responding to the significance of already identified objects rather than being involved in the identification process.

Behavioural evidence concerning complex feature analysis

Behavioural evidence for inbuilt complex pattern detectors for shapes of particular significance in a species' environment can also be derived from studies of instinctive behaviour. Goslings have been reported to respond to a moving hawk shape by running for shelter, while the same shape moved in the reverse direction so that it resembled a goose had no effect. The young of many species which are mobile at birth avoid going on to a glass covering a deep drop, tsetse flies approach a black stripe moving at a certain speed (*Guardian*, 25 September 1980).

Some difficulties of the feature analysis approach to stimulus description

Finally in this chapter, some difficulties of the feature analysis approach to stimulus definition must be noted. First, at the risk of stating the obvious again, it is extremely difficult to isolate the relevant features in any stimulus and no general principles seem to be available as to what might count. This is particularly difficult in the case of the many rough and ready categories we use all the time – dogs, jokes, cups and so on. Second, there are major difficulties in how the features might be combined. A simple addition, in a list, will not do. For.example, specifying a vertical line and a circle as the two features of a letter will not distinguish p, b, d, q, nor will a vertical plus a horizontal line distinguish T and L. Moreover, the absence of other possible features must be indicated, rather than failure to notice them, if L is to be distinguished from E, and which features need to be absent depends on the possibilities which may appear; if a 4 might occur another feature must also be signalled as absent. This problem is of course related to the first one of deciding what to count as a feature, but suggests that relations between

features (or more complex features) need to be specified. This
further implies that, unless all possible relations are to be specified,
the features tested will be restricted according to the expected set of
stimuli. Indeed, it is quite easy to demonstrate that the same
physical input will be identified differently depending on the
company it keeps or current goal of the perceiver, for example, 12,
13, 14 and A, 13, C. This of course makes it virtually impossible to
devise a single all-embracing description of any stimulus which will
cover any set it might be drawn from.

A more striking example comes from an experiment by Tversky
(1977), who asked people to judge the similarity of pairs of
countries. Actually the task was a little more complex in that they
were given two pairs of country names and asked to say which pair
was more similar. Thus, given the pairs East Germany and West
Germany on the one hand and Ceylon and Nepal on the other, 67
per cent said the former pair was more similar. Another group was
then given the same pairs and asked to say which pair was more
different. 70 per cent said the former pair was more different. Thus
the same pair was judged both more similar and more different.
What features were used in the judgement clearly depended on
which judgement was required, and two apparently closely related
judgements elicited the use of different features.

Structural descriptions: variability with precision

An approach to stimulus description which attempts to take account
of variation in the way the stimulus is analysed is known as
structural description theory (Reed 1972). He argues that a
complex pattern, such as that in Figure 17, can be described in a
variety of ways: two parallelograms, a diamond surrounded by four
triangles, two large triangles and so on. Or it could be stored as an
unanalysed image. The task of identifying whether parts of the

Figure 17   *A figure used by Reed (1972) which can be given several different
structural descriptions*

figure such as a parallelogram or triangle were present in it will vary in difficulty depending on how the input was described. Using a variety of complex patterns of this kind and testing with parts which might or might not have been contained in the figure, Reed found that certain components were generally more easily recognized as having been present than others. This suggested that particular structural descriptions were preferred. An attempt to distinguish elements directly available as components of the description and those retrieved from searching the representation of the whole pattern in memory by looking at decision times proved unsuccessful. There seems to be no evidence in the data as to whether the preferred descriptions were due to the nature of the pattern, based on simplicity or some such criterion, or due to previous experience with the components or the patterns themselves.

Psychologically defined features and physical correlates

A further problem which has been illustrated in some of the examples given, is that of relating plausible psychological feature analyses to physical correlates in the input. Analysis of speech sounds in terms of phonemic distinctions makes sense, but no unambiguous correlates of these distinctions have been found in many cases. Another striking example of this problem is perception of weight. One might suppose this to be a relatively straightforward problem, once the adaptation phenomena already discussed have been taken into account. However, the size of the object has an effect in that larger objects feel lighter than smaller ones of the same weight (the size–weight illusion). It seems that something like density rather than weight is judged. This is a good example in support of Gibson's claim that single senses should not be considered in isolation, because perception is an integration of a variety of sensory information. Given the difficulties of establishing reliable feature analyses within one sensory modality, it is not surprising that the interaction of modalities is only taken into account when it becomes particularly striking, as in a case like the size–weight illusion.

In conclusion, the assumption that complex stimuli are analysed into component features has proved a very useful one and increased our understanding of many areas of perception. However, it is quite clear that no simple version of such an approach is adequate, which postulates simply sets of independent detectors each looking for one easily defined aspect of the input. More sophisticated versions are needed incorporating complex features and sensitivity to task demands, current context and past experience in the type of features used and the level of identification achieved.

5 Attention

Different meanings of 'attention'

Clearly not all the stimulation arriving at the senses affects behaviour, at least in any obvious way. Some of it is ignored and difficulties ensue if too many things have to be kept track of simultaneously. Furthermore, we are not aware of all the information which has behavioural consequences; though some theorists have argued strongly against the possibility of perception without awareness, in the view of the present author the evidence is now irrefutable. In the present chapter I consider the processes involved in selecting some information and ignoring other and the factors limiting how much can be coped with at the same time. This involves the notion of attention, which has commonly been used in two main senses:

1 selective attention, the mechanisms which reject some information and take in other (whether the latter enters awareness or not);
2 capacity, an ill-defined reference to the idea that the amount of processing that can be carried out on incoming information has some upper limit.

Clearly this can be true in the fairly obvious sense that if there were only one detector for a square or the vowel in 'thought' it would be impossible to perceive two squares or two speakers saying the word simultaneously. The implication would be that several different things could be perceived at the same time but not several identical, or even similar, things. However, the limited capacity theory has commonly made the additional assumption that there is some general purpose processor used in handling all input from the senses which can only do a limited amount of work at a time and hence inputs to this processor need to be sorted beforehand so that it is not overloaded. It is assumed that important (selected) inputs undergo more complete processing and also that more processing can be done when the perceiver is functioning more efficiently, as when wide awake for example. The notion of capacity has been used both to refer to the amount of which a perceiver can be aware, in which case the general processor is equivalent to consciousness, and to the amount of input at any one time which can affect behaviour, whether it enters awareness or not.

The notion of capacity owes a good deal to the measurement of the power and efficiency of man-made information processing systems with memory stores of defined sizes and a definable processing speed. The notion of a single general processor also finds a parallel in these devices. However, theorists using the notion of attentional capacity in psychological study of humans and other animals have been reluctant to specify this any more precisely in terms of factors such as the number of neurons, processing speed, precision of operation and so on, largely because of our uncertainty about exactly how the nervous system functions and therefore which of the possible factors are the relevant ones.

'Attention' is also sometimes used in a third sense of vigilance or lasting concentration, but this is not directly relevant to our current concerns.

Clearly, if capacity is limited, then some selection process is necessary if behaviour is to be adaptive, responding to the important aspects of the environment and ignoring the unimportant ones, and these two assumptions of limited capacity and selection have dominated theorizing about attention for the past twenty years, together with the additional assumption of a single general purpose limited capacity processor. However, some theorists have recently begun to take issue with the last assumption, arguing that processing is distributed throughout many special purpose systems and unavoidable limitations in capacity only occur when two inputs both require the same specific type of processing. Other limitations, it is suggested, are simply due to lack of a learned connection between an input and the required response, and no active top-down selection process needs to be postulated since selection is an automatic consequence of these learned connections. This view is parallel to the *Gestalt* and Gibsonian view of automatic structuring of inputs without any top-down processes, such as hypothesis testing and directed analysis. This position seems to be too extreme. Although there are clearly stimuli which automatically attract attention (intense or novel or biologically significant ones) it is equally clear that in many cases attention can be voluntarily directed to different parts or aspects of the input, or biased toward them by instructions, motives or expectancies.

The questions

I shall begin with a description and discussion of the limited capacity approach and consider the alternative view afterwards, since this reflects historical precedence. First we need to clarify the questions which will need answering. It is a general experience that it is frequently very difficult to attend to two things at once, particularly when they are not well practised. Thus, when learning to drive a car or play the piano, listening to conversation usually disrupts performance. In skilled performers, however, both tasks can be done at once, though if the driving conditions or the musical score become demanding, the difficulty can reappear. Even walkers can sometimes be seen to stop when considering a difficult question. Hence it is taken as self-evident that selection of inputs or actions does sometimes occur, but of course proper experimental evidence is needed to determine the conditions in which this occurs and whether it is simply overt actions which cease or the processing of the relevant input, and to discover just what is and is not known about non-selected inputs, such as when we listen to one person talking and ignore someone else in the background. Does the background speech affect perception and understanding of the main input (that is, how efficient is selection and exclusion)? And how much is still known about the background speech (that is, how much extra is still taken in while concentrating on a main input)? And third, how far is it possible to handle both speech inputs at once (how much extra can be taken in when this is necessary)?

Experimental approaches

These questions correspond to the main experimental paradigms used in the study of attention. In all cases two or more inputs are available. The task may be to attend to one and exclude the other (selection paradigm), though often additional measures are taken without warning the subject beforehand to see how much of the ignored input was in fact perceived, or the task may be to try and attend to both inputs (dual task paradigm). In each case performance should be compared with performance when no second input is present or with a condition in which the interfering input differs in some way, if the main concern is with the effect of variations in the interfering input. Variations in the nature of the inputs and the required responses are used to discover whether the limitations are in processing the inputs or producing the responses simultaneously, and to demonstrate what aids selection and exclusion in the selection paradigm, or performance on the two inputs in the dual task paradigm. This type of evidence is relevant to the issue of whether interference between tasks is due to quite specific similarities of the two inputs, which would imply competition for specific processing systems, or whether it can occur between any pair of tasks, which would imply competition for a single general processing system.

Broadbent (1971, p. 177) has suggested a distinction within selection tasks between stimulus set and response set. In the first, selection depends on some physical property of the input (left ear, black letters) while in the latter it depends on some property which necessitates prior categorization (English words, digits). Hence in the latter case the selection paradigm becomes similar to a dual task, in that considerable processing of all inputs is required to determine whether they fulfil the selection criterion or not.

Search tasks, also frequently used in investigating attentional limitations, can be seen as variants on the selection paradigm, often involving response set rather than stimulus set. In such tasks multiple inputs have to be examined for the presence of a specified target. Thus, for rapid performance, divided attention is required between the inputs (which may be, for example, spatially distributed letters or two sequences of letters to the two ears), though no overt response is required to most of them. By requiring search for any one of several targets it is also possible to demand that each input be compared with more than one possibility, with a view to discovering whether only one or more than one such comparison can be carried out simultaneously.

Apart from the search tasks, so far I have used examples of what might be called 'large scale' or 'macro' attention, whether input to one sense rather than that to another has to be selected (car driving against listening to speech) or of one sequence of input within a sense modality (one speaker rather than another). However, obviously we will also need to consider 'smaller scale' or 'micro' attention, such as attending to some object or some aspects of a visual scene rather than others. The same issues arise as have been discussed already – how efficient is selection, what is known about the non-attended inputs, what sorts of information can be processed simultaneously, if any? Furthermore, if differences were to emerge in the findings at these different levels of attention, further questions would arise as to whether these differences were due to the amount of processing required (more for prose than for letters), the quality or type of processing (physical identification of letters and semantic processing of the meaning of prose), the degree of similarity of the two inputs or the level of practice. In fact we have to develop a model of the type and sequence of processes involved in identifying the input. As a result, models of attention have gone some way toward providing models of the sequence of process occurring in identification, which I have suggested is the type of explanation we need to pursue.

Single-channel models

Most work on attention stems from Broadbent's *Perception and Communication* (1958); previous to that date attention had been ignored as a construct unworthy of a serious scientific psychology, being neither a stimulus nor a response. Broadbent's model of attention was derived from study of a number of tasks in which auditory information was delivered from two or more sources, such as two loudspeakers or two earphones. He found that spatial differences enabled two simultaneous messages to be dealt with one after the other, such as instructions being followed, but if both messages came from a single spatial location, separating the two was difficult. You have probably experienced this problem yourself when listening to a tape recording in which several voices are mingled; it is quite easy in the original situation where the voices are spatially separated, but not when they are all coming from one loudspeaker. Broadbent also found that if sequences of digits were given, alternate digits coming from different sources such as right and left loudspeakers or earphones, there was a preference for reporting them back 'channel by channel' rather than in the order of arrival. Thus all items arriving at the right ear would be recalled, then all arriving at the left ear. Broadbent suggested a very simple 'filtering' device which selected input from one source or *channel* distinguished by a simple physical characteristic; this selected input was processed in full, while the other was held briefly in a simple relatively unprocessed form until the filter switched over and allowed it through for further analysis. Broadbent's concept of channel did not necessarily need to be related to the sense organs, because presentation of three messages, one in the left ear, one in the right and one in both which was heard as if it were central (Treisman 1964a), also enabled any one of these to be selected. Hence channels can be distinguished by differences other than the sense organ stimulated.

However, Gray and Wedderburn (1960) showed that this simple notion of channel selection could not be sustained; if digits and words were mixed, recall tended to follow the sequence of words even if this meant switching ears; the same happened if digits and letters were mixed (Yntema and Trask 1963), so it was not just due to word sequence but to grouping all the items of one type. Clearly selection was not just made by physical characteristics since meaning could be used, so at least some analysis of meaning must have occurred before selection. Broadbent's idea that the unselected input was held in a fairly unanalysed form was therefore wrong.

A series of similar experiments to those of Broadbent carried out by A. Treisman (1964a, b, c) supported these conclusions. Instead of short strings of items, she used continuous prose and asked listeners to repeat back (*shadow*) the prose coming from one loud-speaker or one earphone as it occurred. This task had first been used by Cherry (1953). Treisman found that physical differences between the passages, such as voice, pitch, loudness, spatial position of the source, aided the task, while meaningful differences, like the language, did not, and people recalled only physical details or noticed only physical changes in the unshadowed passage. Even changes from one language to another were not noticed. However, like Gray and Wedderburn, Treisman also found that meaningful information in the rejected (unshadowed) ear could have indirect effects. If the shadowed passage switched to the other ear, shadowing tended to switch too. Cherry had previously shown that listeners heard their own name in the unshadowed passage about a third of the times it occurred. Later results, discussed in more detail below, supported these findings, which suggest two things. First, even when a continuous input has to come through the filter, the rejected input is not totally lost, as Broadbent's filter model would imply. Second, the rejected input is not just known by its physical characteristics as it should be if not yet fully analysed. To account for these findings Treisman introduced one modification and two new ideas. She suggested that physical features were analysed first and any one of these could be used to select a subset of the total input for more detailed semantic analysis. The first new idea was that the rejected input was not excluded from further analysis but only 'attenuated'. Exactly what this meant was not clearly explained. Treisman denied that it was to be interpreted as a reduction in signal amplitude so that, for example, a message might sound quieter. A more plausible possibility is that it is the analysis rather than the information that is attenuated, so that fewer features are tested or fewer distinctions made on any one feature. The second component of Treisman's theory was to specify the information in memory to which the incoming information was to be matched. She proposed a store of 'dictionary units' representing words, the sensitivity or threshold of which could be adjusted according to such factors as importance and likelihood of occurrence. Hence the unit responsive to one's own name would be especially sensitive, and as phrases from one input are shadowed they would lead to a lowering of the thresholds of units representing likely continuations, which would make them responsive even to the attenuated information available from the rejected input. Obviously this could also account for a result like Gray and Wedderburn's in that if the first item identified is a digit it will increase the likelihood of other digits being identified. However, it is no longer clear where the inputs representing the delayed letters are supposed to be held before they are recalled in an experiment like Broadbent's. Treisman (1964b) did find that if the same message was played to both ears, with one lagging behind the other, subjects noticed the identity at a lag of 5 s when the rejected message was lagging, but at only 1.2 s lag when the rejected message was leading, implying a very short survival time for the rejected message. Norman (1969) obtained rather longer estimates of around 20 s for the survival time by stopping subjects in the middle of shadowing and asking them to recall as much as possible of the preceding rejected message. Summarizing, Treisman's theory incorporates the following claims:

1   There is one channel or processor through which all inputs have to pass.
2   The capacity of this device is limited and fixed.
3   Analysis proceeds from physical to semantic characteristics and a fixed selection device operates after the physical features have been analysed.

4 Several inputs can be analysed at once on some physical dimensions, but only one selected input receives full semantic analysis. Others may be partially analysed and evoke responses if the response threshold is low.

These claims embody the notion of an inflexible and sharply restricted system and subsequent research and theory has questioned these assumptions. One of the problems is in determining how far differences in the conclusions about the nature of the attentional mechanisms are due to differences in the type of task on which the conclusions are based, but this issue will be discussed once the various alternative views have been outlined.

Criticisms of single-channel models

Position of the filter

The first disputes arose about the location of the filter. Deutsch and Deutsch (1967) and Norman (1968) argued that selection occurred late in the processing sequence, thus explaining how semantic information in a non-attended input could affect behaviour. Treisman attempted to counter this attack in a complex series of experiments (Treisman and Geffen 1967). They used shadowing again, but subjects also had to tap to target words which might occur in either the shadowed or the unshadowed message. Detection of these was nearly perfect for words in the former and nearly zero for words in the latter, supporting the view that the selection device operates early in the process. Deutsch and Deutsch, however, replied that the shadowed input required two responses so it was given high priority, and cited an experiment by Lawson in which tones instead of words had to be detected, all else being as in the Treisman and Geffen experiment. Performance was about the same on both ears. However, tone detection would precede the filter in Treisman's model so this result would be expected, and in any case, Broadbent (1971, p. 152) later showed that responses to the tone on the unshadowed ear were slower than to tones on the shadowed ear, indicating some impairment and casting doubt on any idea of a strict parallel processing even of such simple stimuli. Treisman and Geffen also argued in support of their case that homonyms (words sounding the same as each other, like 'wails' and 'whales') were not distinguished on the unshadowed ear, so no semantic analysis could be taking place, but Wilding and Farrell (1970) showed this was not strictly true and criticized the comparisons on which Treisman and Geffen had based their conclusion. Discrimination of homonyms, of course, requires use of context and therefore quite complex analysis of the unshadowed input, which could not occur in Treisman's model if only important or probable information triggers dictionary units. Subsequently a variety of experiments has shown that semantic analysis of the unshadowed input can occur. Lewis (1970) showed that related words on the unshadowed ear delayed shadowing responses, Corteen and Wood (1972) showed that city names on the unshadowed ear evoked Galvanic Skin Responses when some city names had previously been associated with electric shock, and Mackay (1973) showed that interpretation of certain types of ambiguous sentences was affected by information on the unshadowed ear (though Newstead and Dennis (1979) have suggested that Mackay's result was due to rapid switching of attention).

The debate about the position of the filter, therefore, reached no firm conclusions. The evidence suggests that a good deal is known about unattended material (against Broadbent and Treisman) but not enough to support the view that complete analysis is possible (against Deutsch and Deutsch and Norman). Maybe the type and degree of selection depends on the task requirements. This view was advocated by Neisser (1966), who used a search task in which subjects had to look for one or more letters in a series of rows of random letters (or in some cases they had to find a row without a specified letter in it). Neisser found that search was very rapid and that with relatively little practice several targets could be searched for as rapidly as one, suggesting comparison of the input with several possibilities simultaneously; the error rate remained relatively high in this latter case but no extended practice was given and this might have reduced errors. Subjects reported that the non-target letters were not identified but remained as a blur from which the target stood out like a figure from a background. Neisser argued that full identification requires a constructive process which synthesizes the whole from its component features, and that this synthesizing process requires focused attention. The non-target letters were assumed to be handled by a preattentive process which searched for one or two critical features, then if these were found the full synthesis process took over. Subjects sometimes claimed that they responded to the presence of a target without knowing which one it was until after the response if they were searching for several simultaneously. The results are, however, equally compatible with focused search for one or a few features followed by analysis of all features when one is detected, and Neisser gives no particular reason for preferring his own account in terms of preattentive processing. That account is of course very similar to the Broadbent and Treisman models, though the materials being processed in Neisser's experiments were much simpler and the selection process was assumed to be operating on particular items rather than a whole continuous input, and there is no clear evidence on whether several items are searched simultaneously or not. Increased number of items per line did slow the search but not by a large amount, implying at least some parallel processing. However, Neisser believed that the selection process is more flexible than did the other theorists, and that it can be set according to the demands of the task, so for him there was no problem about the differences in materials. It has subsequently been shown by Ionides and Gleitman (1972) that Neisser's conclusion about preattentive analysis is not necessarily true. They found that searching for letter O in digits or a zero in letters was faster than searching for letter O in letters or zero in digits, so category information was available. This tallies with the evidence already described in connection with shadowing studies that information about meaning is available from inputs not receiving full attention and illustrates that information outside awareness (or outside what subjects reported about the background letters in a search task) may yet affect performance.

Flexibility and shared attentions

Kahneman (1973) argues for still more flexibility, in his case in the allocation of processing capacity to different concurrent inputs, the controlling factor in the amount of capacity deployed being the task difficulty. This approach was taken up more systematically by Norman and Bobrow (1975) who argue that processing can be concentrated on one task or distributed between several, so performance on, for example, the unshadowed ear in a dichotic listening task depends on the difficulty of the main task (data limitation) and the amount of processing capacity devoted to the unshadowed input (process limitation). Data limitations include such factors as contrast, signal-to-noise ratio and speed of input, and can prevent correct decisions however much effort (that is, capacity) is deployed. Process limitations are such factors as speed of operation, capacity of short-term memory, alertness and strategy. Norman and Bobrow proceed to demonstrate how, in dual tasks, depending on the data and process limitations involved, interference may occur compared with performance on a single task, or no interference or even facilitation.

Controlled and automatic processes

All the theorists whose views have been outlined so far accept the first two of the four claims of the Broadbent–Treisman model (a single processor of limited capacity), though Kahneman and Norman and Bobrow believe the capacity deployed is quite variable. Schneider and Shiffrin (1977) and Shiffrin and Schneider (1977), however, in two lengthy papers, argue for qualifications about both these claims. They too used a search task in which a set of one, two, three or four items was specified as the target set, then a series of search arrays (also one to four items) was presented, in one of which one of the targets might be present. Speed or accuracy of locating the target was measured. They showed that when the target sets were drawn from the same set (memory set) of items throughout and these items never served as non-targets in the search arrays (though of course the actual target sets varied from trial to trial), neither the size of the target set nor the size of the search arrays had any effect on performance, provided the distinction between the memory set of targets and the non-targets was well practised, either by using sets already highly familiar, such as letters (with digits as the non-target set), or by giving prolonged practice on a new distinction between two arbitrarily chosen sets of letters, one as targets, the other as non-targets (GMFP versus CHND). However if the items used in the target set were sometimes targets and sometimes non-targets in the search arrays, then an increase in the size of either the target set or the search array impaired speed and accuracy.

Shiffrin and Schneider argued that in the first case, when stimuli are consistently mapped on to responses, *automatic* processing operates. In this mode stimuli 'attract attention and initiate responses automatically, immediately and regardless of other inputs or the memory load', by triggering existing sequences of operations in long-term memory (this description is reminiscent of the older notion of stimulus-response compatibility discussed later in connection with choice reaction tasks). *Controlled* processing, on the other hand, occurs in working or short-term memory and is a 'temporary activation of . . . a sequence that is not yet learned' which 'requires attention, uses up short-term capacity and is often serial'. The advantage of this latter type of processing is that new situations can be dealt with by switching in or recombining existing skills.

Though Shiffrin and Schneider clearly succeeded in demonstrating a difference between the behaviour in their two situations, their specification of exactly what they assume to have happened is far from precise. How can a limited capacity system bypass its own limitations? The authors imply a dichotomy between the two types of processing but clearly a learning process is involved and the change is unlikely to occur in one all-or-none step. And what exactly is this learning process? The distinction they draw is between inputs which have to be routed through a short-term store to match them to the target set in memory and inputs which locate this target set directly in long-term memory, but this tells us nothing about how the pattern recognition process is supposed to occur in either case. How are inputs directed to long-term or short-term stores? Do they go to both and only require handling in the STS if no result eventuates in the LTS? If so, what then happens in the STS? Somewhere the information must be available as to which items are targets and which are not, and that can only be in some form of long-term store, so how is it located if it was not directly available for matching to the input? I ask these questions to illustrate the need for precise statements and to point out the danger of too readily accepting that words like 'automatically' have solved anything. No doubt they identify differences which can be experimentally supported, but as has been stressed so many times already, this is only a first step toward specifying possible processes.

One possible specification of Shiffrin and Schneider's distinction is that, with practice, continuous control of processing is suspended. Suppose the system learns fixed ways of processing stimuli which always require the same response, but when several responses are possible a control system can modify these in the light of instructions, or take over when novel combinations occur. This control system can call up sequences of operations or analysis in the light of task demands and will include methods of dealing with new situations rather like solving a problem in the sort of way described by Newell and Simon (1972). This system will be brought into play (attention will be attracted) when automatic processes fail. Allport (1980) has made a similar proposal and an experiment by LaBerge (1975) illustrates the difference and the effect of practice in producing automatic processing. He gave one symbol followed by another, which had to be judged as same or different. The symbols were either letters, such as b, d, or novel symbols such as ⌊ ⌋ and responses were equally fast in both cases. However, sometimes instead of the second single symbol, a pair was given to be judged such as pp or ⌈ ⌈ . When this pair was of an unexpected type (novel symbols following a letter or vice versa), the novel symbols were handled more slowly than letters, suggesting that switching of processing was required in the first case, but letters were processed automatically even when unexpected. This difference vanished after practice.

Attention unlimited

In a radical attack on the whole conception of a general purpose, limited capacity central processor, Allport points out that many examples are now available demonstrating that two quite complex tasks can be carried out simultaneously even after quite short periods of practice, provided the tasks are sufficiently different not to demand the use of the same specific processes, though even this qualification seems not to hold in some of the data, as we shall see.

In the shadowing tasks, or Broadbent's digits on two channels, both inputs were linguistic and the difficulty of handling them simultaneously may have been due to competition for specifically linguistic analysing systems. Furthermore, the shadowing task at least, and to a lesser extent the split-span task, are unfamiliar and unnatural ways of responding to such inputs, which may conflict with well-practised habits. Allport quotes many examples of ability to handle two inputs simultaneously, some of them quite astonishing. In an experiment of his own (Allport, Antonis and Reynolds 1972), he found musicians of reasonable competence could shadow prose while sight-reading music. Peterson (1969) found that reading letters aloud and adding digits presented auditorily, while not as efficient as either task alone, was possible, and each was unaffected by the difficulty of the other. Hatano *et al.* (1977) showed that Japanese abacus operators could answer general knowledge questions while calculating. Tierney (1973) found copy-typing and shadowing were possible but not audio-typing and reading aloud, and Shaffer (1975) reported very similar findings. Finally, Spelke, Hirst and Neisser (1976) were even able, after extended practice, to produce an ability to read silently while writing to dictation or while writing category names in response to the dictated words. Thus, even two tasks involving derivation of linguistic meaning can apparently be carried out simultaneously. Furthermore, the shadowing task itself becomes much less restrictive with practice. Underwood (1974) tested the performance of Moray, who had carried out many shadowing experiments and practised the task over many years, and found that his knowledge of the non-shadowed input was at a much higher level than that of the unpractised subject.

Quite clearly, therefore, it is by no means necessary that the simultaneous performance of two tasks should be impossible, even when the inputs intuitively appear to demand fairly similar forms of analysis. Allport concludes that there is no general purpose limited capacity central processor, and that where interference arises it is due to other causes, of which he identifies two main possibilities:

1 incompatibilities of simultaneously required actions, whether of limbs, speech system or other neural subsystems; in other words, response conflicts may occur even when simultaneous stimulus processing is possible;
2 maintaining more than one goal so that each input evokes the response required and not one of the many other possibilities it might evoke.

This seems to embody the same notion as was discussed above in connection with Shiffrin and Schneider's theory, of continuous control when several responses are possible.

These suggestions of Allport's, however, seem inadequate. They do not explain why spatial separation of the sources should make selection relatively easy as in Broadbent's experiments; nor why ear-by-ear recall is preferred in split-span tasks, nor why little is known about unshadowed inputs (but see below for Allport's attempted explanation of the latter). Once incompatibilities of subsystems inside the head are entertained, almost anything can be included, since we have little idea about what subsystems exist and are required in any pair of tasks. One is very soon back with something very like a general purpose limited capacity processor. Second, it is not at all clear what maintaining a goal involves. The implication is that there is some central executive for activating specific responses when inputs arrive, according to rules established by the nature of the task, rather than stimuli automatically evoking responses, and that this executive has to handle all inputs and therefore has difficulties when several are arriving together. This, as Allport half admits, is very reminiscent of his rejected central processor and would help to answer a major question which Allport does not answer – what exactly happens with practice to enable more than one thing to be done at once? It could be assumed that the decision process is bypassed and a direct connection established without any competing responses. If so, then not only is a theory of attention still required to explain the behaviour of unpractised subjects (surely the majority of behaviour in the case of humans whose ability to deal with new situations is the reason for the success of the species) but also a theory of automatic processes to explain skilled behaviour. Allport makes an inadequate effort to cope with these needs. In the shadowing situations, he argues, the un-shadowed input has to be 'decoupled' from speech output so that only the shadowed input controls output, so little is known about the former. However, speech input very rarely controls output directly in the way which would require such decoupling, so this explanation is unconvincing, and in any case there is no reason to suppose that decoupling from control of *output* would require loss of comprehension (this would be a very inefficient device). In the case of automatic processing, Allport suggests that the 'calling pattern' (which seems to mean no more than 'stimulus') evokes the response directly. He does not, however, explain how calling patterns are extracted from the input and why such processes do not interfere with each other when several inputs occur at once in cases of automatic processing.

Processing several objects or features simultaneously

So much for the evidence from macro-attention studies, as I have called them. What now of micro-attention – identifying several simultaneously present objects or the several features of one object? One example of the former, namely search tasks, has already been introduced, and the discussion of features in the last chapter was closely related to the second issue; in fact, the flexibility of feature processing which was emphasized must involve variation in attention.

Handling several objects simultaneously usually involves processing the same features, such as colour and shape for each object, and sometimes the same values of these, such as red or square, in several spatial positions, while handling one object involves processing several different features in one spatial position. Treisman (1969) suggested that the second may be much easier than the first and she quoted an experiment by Lappin (1967) who found that it was easier to report three different features of one object than the same feature of three objects and this was in turn easier than reporting a different feature of each of three different objects. However, if multiple use of one feature analyser is difficult, the second ranked condition should have proved the most difficult, so the multiple spatial positions and unfamiliar combinations may be the main causes of the difficulty in the second two cases. The result suggests that separate objects tend to be processed one after another. Obviously if two objects have a shape and a colour the correct colour must be somehow kept linked with the correct shape, either by processing them at the same time or labelling each by (for example) its position, unless higher order features can be used which are different for the two objects, or unless the combination of the two objects can be treated as a unified whole. Words are an example of the second possibility and treating a pair of faces as two distinct combined patterns instead of two collections of parts would be an example of the first.

An experiment by Treisman (1977) illustrates what happens when two fairly novel combinations have to be handled together. She presented a pair of coloured letters (items), then a second pair, and subjects had to decide whether either of the first two matched either of the second two letters. The response times implied serial matching both of items and of dimensions forming the items, and Treisman suggests that this was necessary to tie the shape and colour into a spatial-temporally segregated package to avoid confusions (this does not explain, however, why the features had to be processed serially within the items). Evidence that this tying together can go wrong is provided by experiments by Snyder (1972) and Studdert-Kennedy and Shankweiler (1970). The first presented twelve letters in a circle, all black and normally oriented except one, which was either red or fragmented or inverted. Subjects had to report the odd letter and often reported an adjacent one. The second experiment reported a similar phenomenon with pairs of consonants delivered separately to the two ears. Features such as voicing and place of articulation were sometimes interchanged between the two ears. The implication of these results is that parallel processing can be done but has disadvantages when the items to be processed are composed of different values of the same features.

Reaction-time measures in the investigation of serial versus parallel processing: problems of interpretation

The other evidence that I shall consider supports this view, but before describing it some difficulties of drawing conclusions from these micro-attention tasks must be discussed. In the previously discussed experiments the tasks were sufficiently difficult for errors of identification or recall to occur. However, obviously few errors occur when just a pair of objects or a single object defined by just a few features has to be identified, and consequently speed of response is an attractive and more sensitive alternative measure. Many studies have been done using a dual task paradigm to investigate the issue of serial or parallel processing of items and features, using time to identify or carry out some closely related task as a measure of performance. There are, however, considerable difficulties in interpreting the data from studies using response latency as a dependent measure for several reasons. First, the choice cannot be a straightforward one between completely serial and completely parallel processing. An unlimited capacity parallel processing device would handle ten features as easily as one, but a limited capacity parallel processing device would have to spread capacity more thinly as the number of features increased, causing slowing and/or decreased accuracy. Whether processing is serial or parallel, the different processes may carry on independently of each other (be *functionally* parallel) until all the results are combined, or they may affect each other (be functionally interacting). Second, the distinction between integral and separable dimensions described in the previous chapter implies that the distinction between serial and parallel processing is meaningless in cases where two dimensions form a new integral dimension.

In his experiments on integral and separable combinations, Garner was concerned with the ability to exclude the irrelevant conflicting evidence in the orthogonal combinations (a selection paradigm) but not necessarily with the ability to process two features in parallel in the correlated combinations, since the correlated dimension was not necessary for correct performance. Moreover, separability was achieved by spatial separation and this may tend to induce serial processing of the spatially separated objects, as we have seen. The studies we are now to consider are concerned with ability to exclude information which is not spatially separated and to process such information in parallel when it is required (selection and dual task paradigms, respectively).

A third problem in such investigations is that of controlling the number and similarity of the possible stimuli. If two sizes and two brightnesses are combined there are, of course, four possibilities, so direct comparison with a two-choice situation is impossible. If the number of responses is reduced to two by requiring the same response to two of the combinations, as in an orthogonal combination, performance may slow down simply because of the difficulty in assigning stimuli to responses rather than in processing the input, especially in the early stages of practice. As mentioned earlier, Lockhead considers these not to be true identification tasks because they involve condensing more than one stimulus on to one response, even when one dimension can be disregarded (though it is difficult to conceive of a pure identification task in his sense!).

A fourth problem lies in locating the exact source of any delay that is observed in experiments attempting to decide between serial and parallel processing. Methods of attempting to locate at which stage in the processing sequence an effect occurs will be described in the next chapter and all that is needed here is to note that experimenters have often not attempted to discover this.

A fifth major difficulty has been raised by Townsend (1974), who demonstrated that any pattern of results can be produced equally well by a serial or a parallel processing model, because each can be translated into the other by appropriate mathematical transformations. For example, suppose two features are extracted in parallel by totally independent analysing systems, each unaffected by the other. If the time to carry out the operation varies from trial to trial, as seems likely, then the time to complete both operations must on average be greater than that to complete one, so an increase in latency does not prove that one feature has been processed after the other. In addition, two features may be processed in parallel, but owing to limited capacity each may take longer than it would on its own. Furthermore, increased time can also result from increased caution as well as slower processing, which might produce increased accuracy with increased latency.

These qualifications all suggest that an increase in time to process two features compared with one cannot be regarded as unambiguous evidence for serial processing, but implies either that or a limited capacity parallel system. What of the other possible result, that two dimensions are processed as quickly as one? Is this unambiguous support for parallel processing? Unfortunately not. Errors may increase when two dimensions have to be processed, while speed is unaffected, which implies that accuracy has been sacrificed for speed in a system which does not have unlimited parallel capacity. Even if this is not the case, Townsend's argument that either possibility can be translated into the other still holds. To explain such a result in a serial processing system, it has to be assumed that extra effort or capacity can be deployed to speed up the operation and compensate for the extra load in the more difficult task. That may seem unlikely (after all, why not use this extra capacity to do the simpler task more quickly?) but in fact Kahneman (1973) argued for just such a system in which the amount of effort available for an easy task is never sufficient to guarantee perfect performance and increased difficulty does not always produce more errors, because more effort is deployed. We can therefore conclude that when two dimensions are processed as quickly as one the single-channel limited capacity model can be rejected, and that either extra demands are handled by more efficient processing of each in turn or that additional dimensions can be processed in parallel with the original one.

Finally we should note again that parallel processing of distinct dimensions is not the only possible way of handling combinations simultaneously. Use of a higher order or integral feature are other possibilities discussed earlier, and perhaps holistic processing is another, but since the definition of this possibility is unclear, this is difficult to decide.

Serial versus parallel processing of features and objects

Evidence from selection tasks

Now for the evidence, first from selection paradigms then from dual tasks, search tasks and choice reaction tasks. Garner's results have already been dealt with; selection was possible of one spatially separate colour patch, since orthogonal variation in another one had no effect. Spatial separation is not in fact necessary, since Smith and Kemler (1978), for example, obtained a similar result using squares varying in size and brightness. One feature could be selected without interference from the other. Fletcher (1981) showed that experience is sometimes needed before selection is possible. Letters to be identified in some cases had dot patterns superimposed. Repetition of exactly the same stimulus (letter + same dot pattern) speeded response early in practice, responses to repetition of dots only were slower, and to repetition of letter alone were no faster than to non-repeated stimuli. Thus the letter was not selected from the whole pattern. After practice, responses to repetition of the letter alone were as fast as to repetition of the whole pattern, and responses to repeated dots alone were no slower than to non-repeated stimuli. Hence the letter had been selected and the interfering dots ignored. However, the Stroop effect demonstrates inability to select one type of information from a single spatial position. Colour words are presented in a conflicting coloured ink, the latter to be named; the word interferes with this task, indicating that it is processed at least as quickly as the colour, even though it is irrelevant to the task. Spatial contiguity is probably not essential to the Stroop effect since interference can occur from acoustically presented words (Morton 1969). Two other differences between the Stroop task and Garner's situation could explain the discrepancy. Words are very familiar and automatically processed and the relevant and irrelevant information are closely related in the Stroop experiments. Since irrelevant words have little effect in Stroop tasks, relatedness is important. Possibly both the spatially separate colour patches are processed in Garner's experiment, but the two 'channels' remain functionally independent, or perhaps the irrelevant patch is not processed because processing of coloured patches is less automatic than processing of words.

Other evidence on parallel processing comes from situations where the second input is outside awareness. Such input can interfere with a main task, show independent effects or bias responses on the main task (Lewis 1970; Corteen and Wood 1972; Mackay 1973). Somekh and Wilding (1973) used a visual analogue of Mackay's task, presenting a bright neutral face to one eye and a dim biasing word outside awareness to the other eye, which affected judgements of the facial expression. These results all show that two inputs can both have effects but do not necessarily demonstrate strictly parallel processing. Philpott and Wilding (1979) used the same technique to present a word or shape to be named to one eye and a dim word or shape outside awareness to the other. Time to name the first word or shape was affected by the presence of the second, increasing as the item outside awareness got closer in meaning, being greatest when the two were identical. The authors suggest that this reflects competition for the same analysing mechanisms, which occurs because gating out of subliminal information outside awareness does not occur, as it may with competing supraliminal cues. Underwood (1976) and Treisman, Squire and Green (1974) obtained similar results using supraliminal competing items, except that there was some facilitation from identical items.

In conclusion, the selection (and closely related) tasks suggest that when some objects or features of objects are to be selected and others excluded, exclusion is difficult when the material to be excluded is highly familiar (though it is not clear whether this is essential). The evidence also suggests that interference occurs when the two inputs require use of related processing systems, even when they evoke the same response, since subliminal stimuli identical to the supraliminal ones caused more delay than conflicting stimuli in Philpott and Wilding's experiment. These results support Allport's views. Interference also occurs when responses compete, as in the Stroop situation.

Evidence from dual task experiments

Difficulty with dual tasks

Turning now to the data from dual task experiments, Moray (1969, p. 47) studied reaction times to tones which might occur in either ear and found reactions were slower when the tones in the two ears coincided, implying absence of parallel processing, but parallel emission of responses could be the source of the difficulty rather than parallel perceptual processing. The experiment is similar to a long tradition of experiments studying the so-called psychological refractory period, which found that when two stimuli were delivered in close temporal proximity the response to the second was delayed more as the delay between the two got less. The results have been attributed both to delays at the perceptual processing and the response selection stages (Bertelson 1966; Kantowitz 1974).

Posner and Boies (1971), using a different type of task, also obtained evidence for interference between inputs. The main task was to carry out same–different judgements on a pair of sequentially presented letters, responding by pressing keys with two fingers of one hand. At any point in the sequence a tone would occur, requiring a detection response with the other hand. Responses to the tone were not affected if it occurred during presentation of the first letter, but were slowed if it occurred after the presentation of the second letter. Posner concluded that letter identification did not require use of limited capacity which had to be shared with tone detection, but letter comparison did. However, MacLeod (1978) subsequently repeated the experiment using a vocal detection response to the tone instead of a manual one and found no slowing of tone detection. This suggests that the original effect depended on similarity of the comparison and tone detection *responses* rather than the actual stimulus processing.

Dual processing tasks have been used quite widely to study micro-attention. In an experiment by Taylor (1976) examining letter matching, same–different judgements were made of letters formed out of straight line segments (like those in digital watches and calculators). Same judgements were made equally quickly, regardless of how many segments had to be matched, but 'different' judgements were slower as the number of segments by which two letters differed decreased. Taylor concluded that same judgements were holistic and different judgements were carried out segment by segment. However, it does not follow that the segment analyses were necessarily carried out serially, since clearly if segments are analysed in parallel, completion of one difference signal is adequate to trigger a response. If the time to complete each comparison varies on different trials, then, the more such comparisons are being made, the more likely it is that one will finish quickly and trigger a response. Hence responses will be slower when letters differ by only one segment than when they differ by several. Obviously same judgements could not be explained in the same way, since time to complete analysis of all dimensions would increase as the number of segments to be handled increased, unless of course extra capacity is deployed for the more difficult task. Most experiments of this type find that same judgements are faster and a number of theories have been produced to try and explain this, the most plausible being that there are two matching processes, a holistic one, which, if positive, produces a same response, and, if negative, just awaits the result of a more systematic analytic process (Bamber 1969). It would take advantage of a straightforward template matching process, while not being misled by the small irrelevant differences which, as we saw above, raise such problems for template matching theories.

Another possible explanation for the faster different responses in Taylor's experiment as the number of differences increased is that holistic processing occurs in both same and different matches but in the latter case more discriminable differences are detected earlier. Consequently, the 'different' judgements are compatible with at least three explanations, though the 'same' judgements imply holistic matching or deployment of extra capacity as difficulty increases.

Parallel processing in initial stages of identification
Sperling (1960) produced more convincing evidence of parallel processing in the early stages of identification. He began by testing memory for a briefly presented matrix of twelve letters (four columns by three rows) and found that although subjects could only report about four items, they claimed that they had seen more. He then tested this by giving a randomly chosen signal after presentation of the letters to tell the subjects which row of the matrix to report. They could report nearly the whole row, implying that almost the whole matrix was present in memory for a short time (about $\frac{1}{4}$ s) in a visual information storage system (VIS). This suggests parallel processing of the letters, though conceivably very fast serial processing could produce the same result. Since the letters could only be reported one by one, the representations decayed before they could all be converted into names (or in Sperling's terms, before they could be passed to AIS, an acoustic information store). This implies that many features can be processed in parallel but a more permanent representation will only be established if together they form some object which is itself identifiable. Presumably if subjects learned to identify each possible row combination as a whole, they could report the whole matrix, just as in reading words. Hence we might say the difficulty is not in stimulus processing but in assigning a label to be reproduced.

Later experiments showed that physical selection cues, such as shape and colour as well as position (Clark 1969; Turvey and Kravetz 1970), enabled selection from VIS, but Sperling had shown that meaningful differences, such as digits or letters, did not. This conflicts with evidence discussed already for the influence of meaning on selection in shadowing and search, but Sperling's method presumably overloaded the system by the brevity and complexity and unfamiliar layout of the input, and induced a strategy which precluded such influences.

Parallel processing aided by labelling and experience

There is a good deal of evidence, some of it fairly informal, and therefore not unequivocal, that having an accessible label for a complex pattern is important. International chess grandmasters were able to reproduce the positions of pieces on a board after a brief exposure, provided the positions came from a real game and were not random placings. Less skilled chess players could not do this (Chase and Simon 1973). The abilities to read X-rays or identify faulty products after practice have already been mentioned, though it is less clear in these cases whether these are examples of holistic matching or parallel but separate feature processing, since this distinction is rarely made clearly and no satisfactory tests are available between the two possibilities.

An experiment by Marcel (1970) suggests more directly that experience does enable parallel processing. Dumas (1972), using a memory search task with shape and colour combinations, also found that four stimuli could be handled as quickly as one after practice. Marcel used geometric shapes varying in several ways and subjects had to respond positively if the stimulus matched a previously defined rule, such as all red squares with a left inclined stripe, and negatively otherwise. Rules were conjunctive (as the above example) or disjunctive (either red or square or with a left inclined stripe). Both sets of data showed that 'same' responses (i.e. matching the rule) were fastest and 'different' responses decreased in latency as the number of differences increased. However, this tendency had almost vanished after extended practice so that all the 'different' responses were made at the same speed. The decrease in time as the number of differences increased in unpractised subjects could be due to serial processing of the dimensions or parallel processing with more chance of finishing early when more differences were present, or to overall similarity, just as in Taylor's experiment, or, as Saraga and Shallice (1973) suggest, to time spent retrieving stimulus-response connections (i.e. assigning a label) which had not been well learned. The last explanation would not readily account for the effect of the number of differences and none of the other explanations is able on its own to predict the practice effect. Saraga and Shallice suggest this could be due to improvement on more difficult dimensions when processing in parallel and this, or Marcel's suggestion of a change from serial to parallel processing of dimensions, are the most plausible accounts of what happens. Deployment of extra capacity for more difficult decisions does not seem adequate to explain the practice effect, as the diffi-culty varied from trial to trial.

Parallel processing in easy tasks

Saraga and Shallice (1973) pointed out a number of methodological problems in studies such as Marcel's and argued that a proper test for parallel processing requires comparison between processing of the same dimension singly and with another present, absence of response competition from irrelevant dimensions, absence of a need to process more than one spatial position and absence of problems of stimulus-response mapping. Hence they used an iden-tification task with correlated stimulus dimensions in which an orange square required one response and a red rectangle another. By changing the ease of discrimination on each dimension separ-ately they could produce an easy discrimination on colour and a difficult one on shape (for example, blue square versus red rectangle), or the reverse (orange triangle versus red rectangle). Subjects were told they could use either dimension to reach a decision, so if speed of decision was as fast as that for the easy decision (blue versus red or triangle versus rectangle) on its own, this would imply parallel processing, since serial processing would sometimes begin with the difficult decision if subjects did not know beforehand which combination they would get. The results supported the parallel processing model, showing no increase in latency in the dual feature conditions compared with the easier single feature on its own. The task is of course much simpler than Marcel's and this is presumably why parallel processing was possible without practice. Since the difficulty was not known before each trial, it is difficult to see how the result could be explained by the deployment of extra capacity in serial processing. Saraga and Shallice point out that their correlated conditions produce no redundancy gain in Garner's sense, since they are no faster than decisions based on the easier feature on its own, and comment that, consequently, redundancy gain is not a good criterion for integ-rality, in the sense in which Lockhead (1966) uses the term. Lockhead says integral dimensions are those that can be presented simultaneously and in the same place while maintaining psycho-logical independence, which fits Saraga and Shallice's situation. However, Garner (1970) uses the term differently and gives only a limiting condition: 'if in order for one dimension to be realized there must be a dimensional level specified for the other' the dimensions are integral, and (Garner 1974) devised the experimental criteria already discussed. He stresses that 'If dimensions are integral, they are not really perceived as dimensions at all' (1974, p. 119). For Garner, redundancy gain is *faster* processing with both features varying than with either one alone varying. Equally fast processing in both cases is not evidence for integrality, nor are Saraga and Shallice's stimuli integral in Garner's sense, so the results present no problem. As they themselves point out, and as I have indicated in the previous chapter, integrality in this sense and independent parallel processing of dimensions are distinct.

Evidence from search tasks

Taken with the selection studies, these results further support the view that parallel processing of different features and of objects is possible (and indeed becomes automatic) when the task is easy or well practised. This conclusion is further supported by the final group of studies to be considered, the search experiments. As pointed out earlier, search tasks require processing of more than one input to enable rejection of non-targets, the degree of processing being dependent on the nature of the target definition. A large number of experiments using search tasks has shown that the number of irrelevant items presented does not affect the speed of identifying the target when letters or digits are used. The Shiffrin and Schneider results have already been described. Search tasks using a single target and variable background search set have shown no increase in time to find a target as the size of the search set increases (Egeth, Ionides and Wall 1972; Ionides and Gleitman 1972; Sperling *et al.* 1971, for digits in letters or letters in digits; Estes 1972, using search for a letter in a dot background). Also Egeth *et al.* (1972), Beller (1970) and Connor (1972) found that deciding whether a display contained homogeneous items or one odd one was carried out as quickly for all numbers of items presented.

On the other hand, Atkinson, Holmgren and Juola (1969) and Estes (1972) found that searching for a letter in letters was affected by the number of non-target items. The difference between this and the above results is explicable in terms of the demonstration of Schneider and Shiffrin, who showed that with practice it was possible to learn to search through sets of all sizes equally quickly, provided that the target items were never used as non-target items.

These conditions did not hold in Atkinson's and Estes's experiments.

One other type of experiment which varies the number of possibilities in memory will be discussed in detail in Chapter 7. It is the choice reaction task in which each of a set of stimuli is paired with one of a set of responses. Stimuli are presented one at a time in random order and speed of identification is the main focus of interest. One of the main phenomena studied has been the effect of the number of stimuli and responses on performance. Typically, speed declines as the number of possible stimuli increases, which suggests that comparison with all the possibilities cannot be carried out in parallel. However the interpretation of this finding is much disputed, as will be seen, and in fact if stimulus-response connections are well learned or highly compatible (automatic) then the number of possibilities has no effect, which once more supports the conclusion so often reiterated throughout this chapter that level of practice combined with naturalness of stimulus-response links is the critical factor.

Conclusions

An irrelevant input usually seems to affect performance on the relevant one if the irrelevant input has well-learned responses associated with it, as shown in selective attention, subliminal perception and object identification (including Stroop) experiments. Gating out of irrelevant inputs is aided by spatial separation and the absence of automatic processing, but the precise effects of these two variables require further elucidation. The relation between the two inputs is also important. In the case of interference, both inputs are of similar type (related words or concepts) whereas in Garner's orthogonal combinations the two separable dimensions were arbitrarily paired in a novel combination for the perceiver. The dual word tasks (for example, Philpott and Wilding) directly suggested that the relation between the words is important, implying that the interference occurs at the later stages of processing, at least when early exclusion is not possible because the second stimulus is outside awareness.

Practice seems critical in dual processing. The more spectacular results described in connection with Allport's criticism of limited capacity theory showed that even complex tasks could be performed simultaneously given enough practice. In view of these findings it is not surprising that the same seems to be true in handling less complex combinations such as letters in words or features of objects. There are several experiments suggesting difficulty in simultaneous handling of spatially separated duplicated features (Lappin's use of the same analyser in several different locations, Sperling's transfer of items to acoustic storage, Treisman's shape and colour combinations). Each of these cases involves spatially separate units which would be segregated into separated objects by rapid automatic processes (perhaps for the reasons given by Treisman discussed above) and it does seem difficult to achieve parallel processing in this situation. However, the effects of extensive practice in such cases, especially practice in learning distinct responses to novel combinations, require experimental investigation.

A more detailed examination of the evidence therefore has supported the view of Allport already described, that most difficulties in dual processing tasks can be overcome with practice and that highly familiar irrelevant inputs are difficult to exclude. This conclusion of course was already present in embryo in Treisman's attenuation theory, but the fixed filter and limited post-filter capacity assumptions of that model were clearly too rigid.

Moreover, no clear specification has been produced of the nature of the difficulty faced by inexperienced subjects with dual tasks or the nature of the change which enables practised subjects to perform multiple processes simultaneously, often with contemptuous ease which leaves the non-expert gasping.

Capacity, consciousness and perception without awareness

Finally, we must say something about the distinction between processing capacity and consciousness. Though we can process more than one input at once, it does not follow that we are conscious of everything that is processed. This issue is of course a major philosophical and psychological puzzle, and the ramifications will not be discussed here. I shall however consider the controversial psychological issue of subliminal perception. Several experiments have been cited showing effects of stimuli of which the observer is not aware. A detailed discussion of these issues is provided by Dixon (1971; Dixon and Henley 1980; Dixon 1981), who takes the view that focused attention is at the opposite end of a continuum of operating modes from that which favours perception without awareness. The former is self-initiated, active and involves high arousal, while the latter occurs when the observer is relaxed, passive and not focusing on any particular task. In support of these distinctions he points out that the most reliable effects have been obtained not when subjects try to report the nature of a stimulus which they claim not to have perceived, but when they are carrying out one task and the effect of an auxiliary input of which they are not aware is measured. Second, he points out that the effects of sub-liminal stimuli seem to be more apparent later rather than early in the experiment. A recent unpublished experiment by Abbott (1981) tried to test the effect of arousal level directly. She repeated part of the experiment by Philpott and Wilding (1979) described above and again found that identification of the supraliminal words was delayed by related subliminal words. However this effect vanished when the subjects were given caffeine beforehand to increase their arousal level.

Dixon (1971) proposes a model in which stimulus analysers are prepared for particular tasks according to expectations, but the selective mechanisms do not become operative until the arrival of some input above threshold. Hence selection of expected inputs and exclusion of unwanted ones do not occur until there is aware-ness that something has arrived. This allows him to account for another paradoxical finding in subliminal perception studies, that the effects of subliminal stimuli are greater when they are well below the threshold of awareness than when they are close to it. Stimuli in the latter case are more likely to switch in the selection device. The theory can also account for some intriguing characteristics of responses to subliminal words, namely that they sometimes show strong semantic associations to the word actually presented, implying that aspects of meaning can be extracted without the perceiver being aware of the word. Dixon suggests that without the selective devices operating, the excitation is diffuse and evokes a range of related responses. Even more interesting is that similar meaning-related responses have been observed in response to supraliminal words from clinical patients with certain types of reading difficulty due to brain damage. These are discussed in the next chapter; in terms of the model to be discussed there, these results imply that access to meaning is independent of access to the name (that is the articulatory representation) of a word and the second can be damaged while the former is intact.

Despite these attractive features of Dixon's model, there is one difficulty with it. In dual input situations, such as shadowing, attention is focused and it should be possible to gate out the unwanted input, yet several results already described suggest the contrary.

Many of these experiments offer no major challenge to conventional perceptual theorizing since the 'subliminal' inputs were at least potentially supraliminal by switching attention and certainly affected the sensory system. There are, however, other demonstrations of effects of subliminal stimuli which are less comfortable. Marcel (1976) presented single words at the point where subjects were fixating, and masked them by a random pattern so that subjects could not tell whether a word had preceded or not. They were offered a choice between:

1   whether a word had been present or not;
2   whether it was visually more similar to one or other of two possible words, or
3   whether it was more similar in meaning to one or other of two possible words.

Some subjects were persuaded to continue 'guessing' as the words were presented more and more briefly. Performance fell to a chance level first on 1 then on 2 then on 3, implying again that meaning is extracted at lower energy levels than physical form. Marcel subsequently used a modified task in which the effects of the subliminal word were measured indirectly by the speed of classifying a letter string following it as a word or non-word (a lexical decision task). A related word preceding the target word speeds up the decision when presented supraliminally and Marcel showed the same effect from preceding subliminal words.

As Marcel points out, the results show that awareness comes late in perceptual processing, a view that is not hard to accommodate in the framework of a model of perception as a sequence of processes. The finding that meaning is available at lower levels of stimulation than physical features is, however, somewhat problematical; it is not restricted to words, since similar effects have been found with pictures (Dixon 1971, Chapter 3). As will emerge in the next chapter, sequences of processing are usually envisaged as requiring extraction of form in order to locate information about meaning in memory. Various rather unsatisfactory efforts have been made to solve this dilemma (for example, Erdelyi 1974). Clearly, if form is extracted in the subliminal perception experiments, the necessary processes and results all occur prior to awareness and something else determines what information enters awareness. This problem, in my view, remains unsolved.

6 Processing stages

Anatomical and neurophysiological evidence for processing stages

In addition to logical and psychological considerations, there is of course anatomical and neurophysiological evidence that input passes through a number of stages. The anatomical evidence shows that neurons from the sense organs link with other neurons at a number of points on the way to the higher centres of the brain, where the interconnections become so rich and complex that detailed mapping is very difficult. These interconnections mean that input is combined and separated in complex ways and the neuro-physiological evidence from single cell recordings shows some of the forms of combination which occur.

Taking first input to the eye, light rays pass through the lens of the eye and by adjustment of the lens a focused image is projected on the central part of the retina at the rear of the eye (the fovea). Rods and cones in the retina are sensitive to light and if stimulated will cause the neurons connected to them to fire (note that though it is possible to see the image on the rear of an eyeball, what is received by the brain is a pattern of neuronal activity not a miniature picture of the world). The retina contains a complex set of interconnections formed by different types of nerve cell (horizontal, bipolar and amacrine cells) connecting with the ganglion cells which carry messages onward to the higher brain centres. These cells make a junction in the lateral geniculate nucleus with cells which go directly to the visual cortex at the rear of the brain (Area 17). Images of objects from the left of the point being fixated (looked at directly) are formed on the right half of the retina and excite retinal cells which project to the right lateral geniculate body and the right visual cortex.

The evidence from neurophysiological recordings of single cells, such as those carried out by Hubel and Wiesel, was described in Chapter 4; it showed units responsive to circular visual fields in the

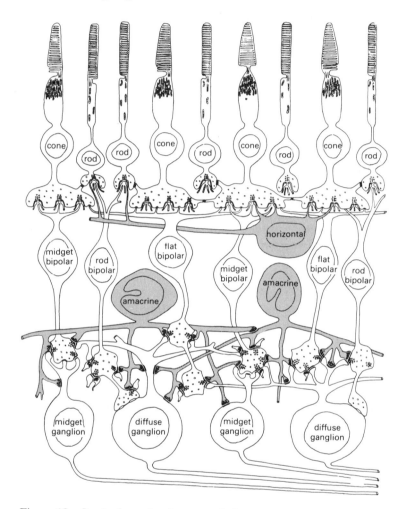

Figure 18 *Semi-schematic diagram of the connections among neural elements in the primate retina (modified from Dowling and Boycott 1966, Figure 23)*

lateral geniculate, to bars and edges in Area 17 of the visual cortex and to corners in Area 18. Penfield (1952), in his famous studies of experiences evoked by direct electrical stimulation of the human cortex, pointed out that stimulation of the sensory areas produces unorganized sensations. For example, stimulation of the visual sensory area produces experiences of form, movement, brightness

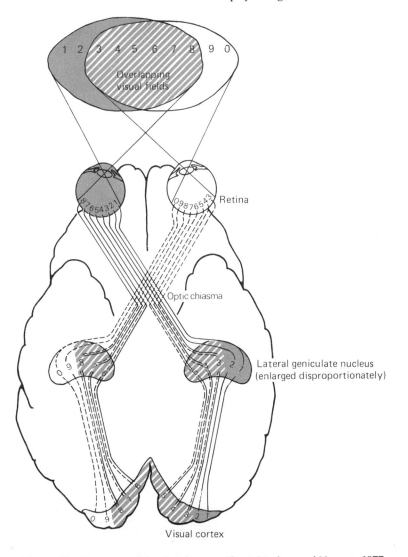

Figure 19 *Structure of the visual system (from Lindsay and Norman 1977, Figure 2.10)*

and colour, such as stars, black forms or moving lights, but no familiar objects, and all subjects tested gave similar reports. The responses could change very suddenly as the point of stimulation was moved forward toward the temporal lobe. Suddenly whole meaningful experiences of scenes with all types of sensory component would be evoked. Of course these were memories, or at least they were assumed to depend on memory (they seemed more vivid than memories, as if the experience was occurring at that time), but Penfield suggests that they reflect a progressive integration of simple sensory information into objects and experiences which occurs in perception. Despite this conclusion, which is similar to that originally drawn by Hubel and Wiesel from their data, there is now evidence that the cells in Areas 17 and 18 do not form a hierarchy but depend on independent inputs. In fact the more complex cells respond more rapidly than the less complex ones.

The ear responds to changes in pressure in the air. At any moment in time the combination of frequencies in a sound is signalled to the brain by a set of receptors, each responding to its own specific frequency. Information from both ears goes to both hemispheres of the brain, passing through a number of junctions on the way; the connections are stronger to the contralateral hemisphere. The auditory cortex is situated just above the ear on each side.

Of course these findings do not go very far toward establishing the full processing sequence which occurs in the identification of complex objects. Our neurophysiological knowledge ceases a long way short of processes involving objects (apart from the occasional intriguing finding such as Penfield's reports or Gross *et al.* (1972) finding of monkey paw detectors). Moreover there is not necessarily any direct relation between the succession of psychological processes and activity in a succession of anatomically different sites. Psychological stages are defined by changes in the way information is represented following transformations, while anatomical stages are defined physically in the brain. If no transformations of the input occur between anatomical stages, but simply one to one connections passing the same message on from one site to another, then no changes of psychological interest occur. Conversely, as in the retina of the eye, a great deal of combining and transforming may occur within a densely packed layer of neuron connections which cannot easily be identified by anatomical methods.

Psychological approaches to the discovery of processing stages

Thus if we wish to map out stages in the central processes of identification we have to devise psychological methods. It is these methods with which we are concerned in this chapter. Unfortunately, as has been indicated earlier in discussing the separation between the classical perception research and the research based on an information processing approach, the investigations into processing stages are based almost entirely on alphanumeric material and conclusions must therefore frequently be limited to two dimensional, already segregated, well-defined patterns. While describing the findings using such material, I shall also try to consider what, if anything, we know from these findings about object segregation, depth perception, scene integration and the constancies.

Obviously the question arises as to how general any model of processing stages can be. Though it is clearly dangerous to draw conclusions from experiments on processing letters about how a scene is processed or how sounds are identified, nevertheless some common principles do seem to emerge. Another question is whether the stages identified are typical only of the task given to the observer and whether brief controlled exposures evoke the same processing strategies as continuous natural perceiving. A similar point was made by Craik and Lockhart (1972) in their attack on 'box' models of memory, in place of which they suggested the more flexible 'levels of processing' framework discussed in Chapter 4. The perceptual processes which psychologists can study most easily must come relatively late in the input processing sequence and therefore are most likely to be varied according to the task, expectations and motives of the observer, which will affect the level of processing and selective strategies employed. These considerations should all induce caution in accepting a stage model based on a particular experimental paradigm as a general model of perception. Nevertheless, they do not present serious difficulties for the basic assumptions on which stage models and the methods of testing them depend, that the input is analysed in a sequence of independent operations which can in principle be studied separately.

One possibility, however, which does raise serious difficulties for these assumptions is that later stages may feed back into earlier stages during a single process of analysis. For example, we sometimes 'hear' an impossible word and recheck our memory of the sound in order to come up with a more plausible one, so part of the sequence is run through again. Of course where we are aware of this (or where it could be detected in some other way) allowance could

be made for it, but what if such reprocessing occurs prior to awareness? When we think we are measuring one cycle of operations we
may be measuring several, and factors which really affect a later
stage may appear to affect an earlier one because the later stage
feeds back to and modifies the earlier one. This presents severe
problems for any theory which tries to separate out stages by
looking at the effects of different variables on different tasks. Some
of these are described below. Rather than give up, the view taken
here is that a straightforward step-by-step processing model, combined with the assumption that errors at a low level can be overriden
by later decisions and excluded from awareness, takes us a long
way, and it is better to test such a model to destruction than to try
and produce another before we are clear about the problems to be
solved.

In addition to the neurophysiological investigations, evidence on
the nature of the successive stages of processing has been derived in
a number of different ways:

1 Studies of attention (which were discussed in Chapter 5) investigating knowledge about inputs which are not attended to.
2 Logical considerations of the necessary sequence of events from
   input to response output, often derived from or supported by
   attempts to program computers to carry out perceptual tasks.
3 Studies attempting to add or delete component stages, or vary
   depth of processing, by varying the task requirements.
4 Studies investigating the effects of different variables on the
   time to carry out a specified task.
5 Premature termination of processing by obliterating the
   input.
6 Premature termination of processing by requiring a speeded
   response.
7 Decomposing distributions of reaction times into components
   which are assumed to reflect different stages of processing.
8 Examination of clinical cases of brain damage showing
   deficiencies in specific aspects of processing which are assumed
   to reflect the activity of specific stages.

Before describing these methods, I must emphasize that they are all
based upon responses to single inputs and the sequences of processes needed to integrate successive samples from a visual scene or
from reading or speech are not considered.

Studies of attention

The previous chapter has described in some detail the evidence from studies of attention that in many tasks there is a broad physical analysis of the input before selection of some part of it for more detailed analysis. Despite the problems raised in the last chapter, majority opinion still accepts that physical features must be analysed before aspects of meaning can be abstracted, because analysis of the former, however complex, is required before matching the input to existing knowledge about the world, from which meaning and further associated information can be derived. There are of course a few exceptions, for example, built-in instinctive reactions to danger, which override selective strategies.

It should, however, be apparent from the last chapter that the evidence in favour of a stage where only physical information is available is inconclusive. I mentioned developments of Sperling's method which showed physical but not meaningful cues to be useful for selection and which therefore supported such a distinction, but also cited a variety of evidence for the effects of meaning on supposedly early processing stages. Sperling used brief presentations, complex inputs and heavy task demands and the results imply that only special techniques will restrict processing to early stages in which meaning is not available. The question then arises as to whether the method is revealing a general operation in visual processing or one specific to a special experimental situation. Neisser (1966) argued that, at the level of the iconic store (his term for Sperling's VIS), objects had been segregated so that figure and ground were separated. Though it is tempting to generalize this conclusion to other perceptual situations, it should be noted that the input consisted of individual patterns (i.e. letters) separated from all the others by white background, without any overlap or distance cues to complicate segregation. It seems likely that rapid automatic processing cannot always produce figure–ground differentiation or construction of three-dimensional representations. More elaborate processes guided by knowledge of the world will be needed (see Figure 12 and the related discussion), so the icon is not always a segregated representation, or, if it is, non-automatic processes must sometimes precede its emergence. Nor need the results of such processes necessarily enter awareness as perception without awareness indicates. In short, there is flexibility in the system, depending on the availability of automatic processes and the task requirements. Consequently we may question Neisser's conclusion. He wrote: 'At this stage, the pattern has already been resolved into one or more segregated figures by the global, holistic process I have called preattentive' (p. 102) and argued that the icon is a necessary stage in all processing and that it enters awareness, so perception without an icon was impossible. The ample evidence for perception without awareness refutes this argument. In conclusion, therefore, the work on attention does not provide any decisive evidence for a fixed sequence of processing from physical to semantic attributes.

Logical analysis of task requirements

When we obtain data on speed or accuracy of identification, the final result necessarily depends on far more than a central process of identification which we are trying to study. Stimuli have to get into the processing system and responses have to get out and variation in the efficacy of these processes will affect the overall time, as well as variation in the central decision process. Hence a proper under-standing of the overall sequence is desirable before the central decision process can be disentangled from the whole. A repre-sentative statement of the possible overall sequence is offered by Theios (1975) who suggests first an Input stage, which includes more than the simple registration of the physical energy in the input, since he refers to a suggestion of Turvey (see p. 154) that input consists of a sequence of transformations or analysis of the stimulation which proceeds from peripheral receptors all the way to the central nervous system. The Input stage is followed by Identi-fication (for example, 'this is a four') then Response Determination ('four is a target letter in this search task'), Response Programme Selection ('select instructions to the motor system to say "Yes" or press Button A') and finally Response Output. Theios goes on to discuss the effect of a number of variables on these presumed stages, but offers no systematic evidence that they do in fact affect the stage he suggests and not some other. Like Theios, our main concern must be to devise a plan of the separate stages then to consider what happens within each one and what variables affect what happens.

Computer identification of patterns

Attempts to program computers to carry out identification of symbols gave some indications of what steps are necessary to match the achievements of natural organisms and provided tests of the feasibility of hypotheses about the nature of such steps. Of course there is no guarantee that the method used by the animal or human matches that of the computer, but nevertheless it is instructive to consider what sequences of processing have been found necessary to carry out identification.

Pandemonium Some early programs attempted a template-matching method in which a visual pattern was converted into a matrix of on and off cells and the overall result was matched to stored images. Provided that the inputs were highly stylized, invariant and carefully positioned, this worked, but performance never reached the level of natural perceivers and of course no natural inputs match the strict requirements needed by these computer programs. Other programs used, in effect, a feature-analysis approach, with separate analysing systems examining the input for specific features such as vertical lines, circles, diagonals. The best known of this type of program was 'Pandemonium' by Selfridge (1959), originally designed to handle identification of Morse code, then adapted to cope with visually presented letters. The system is pictured as having four levels, depicted as demons assigned to different duties. The lowest level are data demons, who simply record the input. Feature demons then simultaneously scan the input for the presence of specific features and shriek with a loudness proportional to their confidence that their particular feature is present. Cognitive demons listen to these shrieks and are responsible for finding particular combinations of features. So the cognitive demon looking for a vertical straight line and the right half of a circle (P) will shriek loudly if both the appropriate feature demons shrieked to him, and the cognitive demon looking for 'R' will shriek somewhat less loudly. At the top is a decision demon who listens to the shrieking cognitive demons and decides which is shrieking the loudest. Notice, however, that the result would be the same in the system as described if the pattern presented had been 'b' or 'ㅂ' or 'P', so clearly the efficacy of the system will depend on careful selection of features to include the spatial relations between the more basic ones. The similarity between Turvey's suggestions from his masking studies (see below) and the order of events in Pandemonium is quite striking.

Uhr and Vossler's learning program Uhr and Vossler (1966)

described a program which could develop its own set of features by recording their usefulness and ditching the ineffective ones. The pattern to be identified was presented in a 20 × 20 matrix and adjusted to a particular position in it. The features were constructed by generating patterns in a 5 × 5 matrix, filling in some squares and leaving others blank. Higher order features could be constructed by combining these. The features were compared with the pattern to be identified at all the possible positions and any matches recorded. On the first encounter the computer was informed of the name of the letter so that it could construct a table of the features associated with each letter. By working out which features were unique to one letter or specified only a few letters, the program could reduce its set to the effective ones.

Programs which segregate objects Later and more elaborate and sophisticated programs have illustrated the complexity of analysis required to separate more complex and 'natural' inputs, such as photographs of objects, into figure and ground, and to segment complex patterns of objects into constituent parts, and thus provide some theories as to how figure–ground separation might be achieved. The program by Guzman (1969), which has already been described in outline (Chapter 3), used a set of intersection features which indicate different combinations of adjacent surfaces (belonging to the same object or to different objects) and by scanning for these it was able to work out which surfaces belonged to a single object. No investigations of how human beings do such tasks appear to have been carried out. A program by Roberts (1965) used half-tone photographs of sclid objects and undertook an immense amount of preprocessing to work out the contours (that is edges) and reduce the photograph to a line-drawing indicating these. The program was supplied with 'templates' of three main shapes, a cube, a wedge and an octagonal cylinder, each of which could be transformed by stretching or compressing on any of the three axes. These were matched to parts of the line-drawing and if the program succeeded the drawing was described in terms of a spatial combination of the three basic components.

Constructing object representations: the work of Marr The most comprehensive and systematic proposals concerning the sequence of operations needed to handle a natural visual input have been provided by Marr (1976, 1980). Marr points out that our ability to identify outline drawings of two-dimensional shapes and stick figures representing (for example) animals implies that these contain the essential information used in identifying the real objects. Hence his analysis of the sequence of processing is designed to extract first contour and then 'object-centred' three-dimensional shape. The sequence begins with a *grey level intensity array* (the retinal image) which records the intensity of stimulation (brightness) of each point. For the purposes of this analysis colour is ignored. The first step is to construct a *raw primal sketch* which records changes in brightness such as those produced by contours of objects, but also edges of highlights, shadows and surface texture. This analysis is achieved by a set of units such as those found in the visual cortex which respond to edges. Marr suggests that if there are units of this type responsive to input from visual fields of different sizes, they are equivalent to sets of filters of different degrees of precision. Units responsive to a very small field will respond to every slight change in brightness including irrelevant ones, while units with large fields will be insensitive to all but major changes (see Figure 20). Changes which evoke responses in units of several different field sizes will be the important ones for coding the input. Changes from bright to dark, or vice versa, which follow a predictable path are then combined to form edges, bars and blobs (presumably by combining the outputs from the filters into single unit detectors). These units are called *place tokens* by Marr and they record size, brightness, position in the image and orientation. This combined record is the *primal sketch.*

The next requirement is to separate out objects from the total pattern. Marr believed that as much information as possible must be extracted from the input before invoking top-down processing involving hypotheses derived from expectations. The next suggested stage, therefore, was to construct a $2\frac{1}{2}$ *dimensional sketch* which provides the orientations of surfaces relative to the observer. This has to use cues about distance from the observer such as texture gradients, stereopsis, motion, colour and shading, in order to obtain the orientations, and requires segmentation of the array into surfaces and groupings of surfaces into objects. Marr found the *Gestalt* criteria for distinguishing figure and ground, such as orientation, similarity, good continuation and so on, were effective methods of achieving segmentation when used in combination; if most of them agreed on a particular grouping, that grouping was selected.

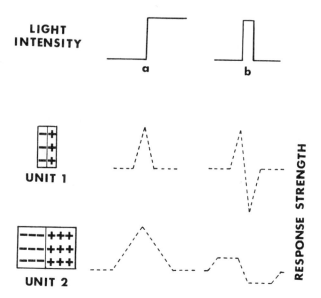

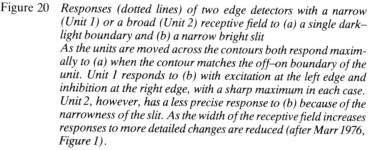

Figure 20   *Responses (dotted lines) of two edge detectors with a narrow (Unit 1) or a broad (Unit 2) receptive field to (a) a single dark–light boundary and (b) a narrow bright slit*
As the units are moved across the contours both respond maximally to (a) when the contour matches the off–on boundary of the unit. Unit 1 responds to (b) with excitation at the left edge and inhibition at the right edge, with a sharp maximum in each case. Unit 2, however, has a less precise response to (b) because of the narrowness of the slit. As the width of the receptive field increases responses to more detailed changes are reduced (after Marr 1976, Figure 1).

To derive objects proper which could be identified the observer-centred descriptions of the $2\frac{1}{2}$ dimensional sketch had to be converted into *object-centred descriptions* which would not vary according to the viewpoint of the observer. To achieve this, basic geometrical properties were calculated such as the centre of gravity, the principal axes and size along these axes. Marr found that many shapes could be adequately described as combinations of basic cylindrical components (Figure 21) in spatial relations to each other.

This gives a very sketchy outline of the sequence of processes envisaged by Marr. The transformations from one level to another were specified in mathematical terms and implemented in a series of

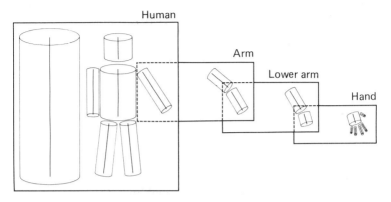

Figure 21   *Analysis of a human figure into a hierarchical organization of cylindrical shapes (from Marr and Nishihara 1978, Figure 3)*

computer simulations which proceeded from a natural and fuzzy two-dimensional input to a three-dimensional description of the shape represented. In the articles cited the successive representations are illustrated as they were obtained from the computing system. Marr's work is important in many ways:

1   he acknowledges the complexity of the necessary series of transformations to get from the input to the identification, and is specific in his suggestions of what these may be;
2   he shows how the transformations can be described mathematically and therefore implemented on a man-made machine;
3   he does where possible relate his theoretical analysis to known neurophysiological findings, such as suggesting that Hubel and Wiesel type cells in Area 17 of the visual cortex are carrying out the transformation to the raw primal sketch.

However, the stages of relating the three-dimensional representation to memory representations are not included in the outline. No doubt, but for his untimely death, Marr would have attempted to elaborate the theory to deal with these later operations.

Adding and deleting stages

The most natural and obvious method of investigating stages in perceptual tasks would seem to be to devise tasks in which different combinations of proposed stages are required. For example, deciding whether two visually presented letters are physically identical does not require that their names be retrieved, while deciding whether they have the same name clearly does in some cases (for example, A and a). One would therefore expect that the second task might take longer if it includes a first stage of analysing the inputs for their physical characteristics followed by a second of deriving the names. This is indeed the case, as has been shown originally by Posner and Mitchell (1967), and subsequently by many others, using two tasks of this kind. Name matches take about 40 ms longer than physical matches. Such measurements of time support the notion of an extra stage or stages but tell us nothing about their nature. Tests can be made about the nature of the assumed extra stages by modifying the task in ways likely to affect the processes believed to be involved. A modification which affects Task A should also affect Task B when the latter includes the operations which make up the former, but a modification which affects the additional components of Task B not contained in Task A should only affect Task B. The problem then is to determine that it is the assumed additional component which is affected and not some other difference between the two, which comes down to the problem of choosing task changes which add one operation only.

Posner attempted to provide supporting evidence of this type by demonstrating that physical matches were affected by how similar the letters were (for example, P and p were judged to be physically different more slowly than A and a). However, if the letters were presented successively instead of simultaneously, the advantage of physical over name matches vanished at longer intervals, suggesting that direct visual matching ceased to be possible if the visual image had to be maintained for too long, and in these cases a name had to be used instead. Name judgements were not affected by the interval. However, name judgements were also unaffected by visual similarity; P and p were judged the same no more quickly than A and a, and this causes problems if it is assumed that name matching includes everything involved in visual matching plus something extra. The reason presumably is that the physical similarity must affect the actual *comparison* of the physical letters rather than the operation of constructing a description of them, and this comparison process does not occur when names have to be matched. In order to carry out name matching the physical descriptions have to be translated into names (a phonemic code) and then these phonemic codes have to be matched (see Figure 22). Of course we do not know whether this translation to names also occurs in the physical matching task, even though it is not needed, nor do we know whether the matching of physical descriptions and name descriptions is carried out in a similar way or at the same speed, so any suggestion that the difference between the times for the two types of match reflects the time to convert the visual code into a phonemic one is clearly dubious.

This method of attempting to add or subtract stages by varying the task was originally devised by a Dutch physiologist, Donders, in 1868. He proposed that different tasks could be devised to include different combinations of the assumed basic processes and the additional time required to carry out the more complex task would indicate the time to carry out the extra processing step. Hence a detailed picture could be devised of the stages of perceptual processing and their durations. He proposed three main tasks to test speed of reaction, differing in the number of possible stimuli and responses, one stimulus appearing at a time:

the *a* reaction: one stimulus related to one response (what we now call a simple reaction task) which he claimed included Stimulus Detection and Response Emission;

the *b* reaction: two stimuli each related to one of two responses (choice reaction task) involving the processes of Stimulus Identification and Response Selection inserted between the two stages of the *a* reaction;

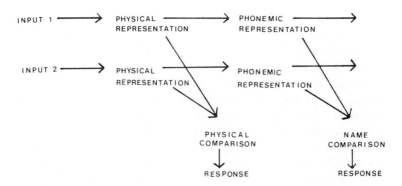

Figure 22 *Hypothesized series of events in Posner's letter comparison task*

the c reaction: two stimuli one requiring a response and the other requiring no response, which Donders claimed involved Stimulus Detection, Stimulus Identification and Response Emission.

If this theoretical analysis were correct then b reactions should exceed c reactions by the time taken to carry out Response Selection and c reactions should exceed a reactions by the time taken to carry out Stimulus Identification. Unfortunately, there are several problems with this proposal, alluring though it is. First, it is not obvious that only the processes proposed by Donders are involved. In the c reaction a form of Response Selection has to occur, namely the decision whether to respond or not, and of course if the c reaction analysis is suspect the whole edifice falls apart. Second, it is by no means certain that adding or deleting a process leaves all else unchanged; putting this another way, do the subjects proceed in exactly the same way having dropped out one step, or do they change to a qualitatively different method. We have already seen this possibility in the Posner matching task, where requiring the naming stage may also alter the nature and duration of the comparison process rather than just inserting an extra operation, and this makes it impossible to measure the duration of the extra stage. Another illustration of this problem occurs in the difference between two choice and multiple choice reaction tasks. One might suppose that, on Donders's principles, increasing the number of stimuli (and responses) which can occur, simply increases the complexity (possibly the number of substages) in the Stimulus Identification and Response Selection stages. In fact, however, there is suggestive evidence that two-choice tasks are often carried out by using sequential rules ('if it is the same as on the last trial then make the same response, otherwise make the other one') which cannot of course be applied in multiple choice tasks. In this case the whole strategy changes.

This assumption of Donders, that complete stages can be taken out or put in like railway carriages, is known as the fallacy of pure insertion. In some cases this assumption is more acceptable than in others. The cases where it seems most plausible are those where extra operations of the same kind as some of the existing ones are added. Examples of this type are the search tasks pioneered by Neisser and Sternberg. Neisser (1963) required subjects to search through a series of rows of letters looking for a target and varied the number of rows to be searched before the target appeared.

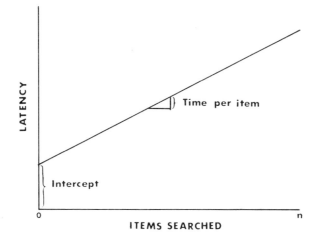

Figure 23   *The type of result obtained from search tasks, illustrating the separation of total latency into two parts, the intercept and the time to scan each item*

Sternberg (1966) presented a set of items to be held in memory, then a target which had to be categorized as present or absent from the memory set (this is a bit like categorizing something as a vegetable, for example, where members of the class have no common perceptual feature). Both paradigms produce a function relating decision time to number of items to be searched and both typically produce a straight line (Figure 23), the slope of which is taken to indicate the time to process each item (though some theorists argue that a logarithmic function provides a better fit than a linear one). Both Neisser and Sternberg argued that this enabled a pure measure of central matching time uncontaminated by input and output time, while the latter processes are assumed to contribute to the intercept of the straight line with the zero point on the horizontal axis. Consequently some manipulations should affect the slope and others the intercept, depending on whether they affect decision time or the input and output processes, respectively. However, this assumption, that the two measures of slope and intercept are completely independent, is questionable. It is equally possible that there is overlap with results of one process being fed to another continuously like water passing through a series of linked containers; each container does not have to fill before the link to the next opens, but all the water has to pass through each one before the operation is complete. If what goes on in the brain is more like this picture then attempting to measure the duration of stages which are distinct in time is a forlorn hope. It does not of course follow that there are no *functionally* distinct stages.

For these reasons, Donders's methods have not been used to any great extent; the Posner experiments described above are an example of the problems of drawing valid conclusions from such data.

Effects of task variation on processing time: the additive factors method

This was proposed by Sternberg (1969) at a symposium to celebrate the 100th anniversary of Donders's original paper. Sternberg offered a method which avoided some of the weaknesses of the original approach, though it still assumed a sequence of discrete stages, each completed before the next began. He argued that if the total time to identify an object (or for that matter to carry out any task) is the sum of the time to carry out a number of component operations one after another, we can proceed as follows. By altering the task in some way (for example, by reducing the illumination) we may increase the time by a certain amount, it may be assumed by increasing the time spent on one stage in the process. What stage this is we cannot be sure, though we can make a reasonable guess; in the above case, for example, it might be the stage of registering the stimulus before more detailed analysis. By altering the task in some other way (for example, by increasing the number of possible stimuli) we may also increase the time, and it seems likely that this would be due to affecting a different stage such as matching the presented stimulus to the possible stimuli. Now if we make both these changes we may find the total increase in time equal to the sum of the two separate increases, which is called being additive; this seems likely if the two changes affect quite separate operations and the effects on earlier operations in the sequence do not carry over to later ones. This last condition is of course debatable since lower illumination may result in a less clear proximal stimulus so that matching to the possibilities may take longer as well as the initial registration. However, if for this reason or because both changes affect one and the same stage, it is likely that their combined effect will be greater than the sum of their separate effects. Such an 'interaction' is taken to indicate therefore that two changes affect a common process. Sternberg also pointed out that if two changes affect separate stages, not only is there additivity in the means but also in the variance and all the higher cumulants (mathematical measures of more complex properties of the distribution of reaction times). Thus, by making a series of changes, singly or in combinations of two or more together, it is possible to work out which of them affect common processes and which do not and then to draw up a sequence of what these processes might be and which of the variables affect them. This is known as the additive factors method.

Though this has proved a very useful methodological framework, most of the assumptions on which it depends can be questioned. As already indicated, there is no proof that stages occur one after another without overlap or any parallel processing or feedback from later to earlier stages. Such feedback would of course complicate any conclusions from the method because a factor might affect Stage 3 which feeds back to and modifies Stage 1, and hence could interact with a factor affecting Stage 1 directly. Also evidence that stages may overlap in time has been provided by Stanovich and Pachella (1977) who found that in some cases an interaction occurs of a different kind to those considered by Sternberg. Degrading visually presented digits with random patterns affected speed of performance *less* when response was by button-pressing than when it was spoken naming, even though the former was slower. They suggest this implies that when one process is slowed down, more overlapping with others can occur so the effect of additional slowing is hidden. Second, if two changes do only produce additive effects, they may still affect a common stage and if they produce interactions it may be because one of them affects an earlier stage and the results carry over to later stages, as in the hypothetical example given above. Also the possibility of changes in caution (or the amount of evidence required before a decision) is not sufficiently considered. This issue is discussed in detail in the next chapter and a method of controlling the degree of caution is described which also involves another approach to separating out stages in the decision process. It will be shown that variables which seem likely to affect the degree of caution may interact with other variables in ways which are difficult to account for by means of a straightforward stages model.

Sternberg did not initially use the additive factors technique in a straightforward identification task, but in the memory search task mentioned earlier. The results were reasonably clear and intelligible. He looked at variation in four factors: stimulus quality (whether or not a checkerboard pattern was used to obscure the target item); size of the memory set; type of response (positive or negative), and the frequency of the positive trials. No interactions were found, and Sternberg suggested therefore that four main stages were involved: stimulus encoding (affected by stimulus quality); serial comparison of target item and memory set (affected by size of memory set); decision (affected by type of response), and translation and response organization (frequency of the positive trials). It should be noted that the nature of the stages is not given automatically by the data, but derived from reasoned intuitions based on the nature of the variables.

Subsequently Sternberg looked at an identification or naming task. Digits were presented and the subject had to identify them, either with their conventional name or the name of the next higher digit (for example, to '1' they had to respond 'two'). By this method the *compatibility* of the stimulus and response was varied. Sternberg varied two other factors – stimulus quality, as in the previously described experiment, and the number of different possible stimuli, which was either two or eight. He found that the number of alternatives interacted both with stimulus quality (weakly) and with compatibility (strongly). Quality and compatibility did not interact. Sternberg concluded that two distinct stages exist; first stimulus encoding and then translation plus response organization, and left undecided what happened in between. The main effect of the number of alternatives, judging from the strength of the interactions, is on the translation plus response organization stages. Further experiments varying other factors would be needed to define and perhaps subdivide these stages more precisely, such as the similarity of the visual forms of the digits to each other, which might be expected to affect the actual matching to representations in memory, that is, the central identification stage which is missing in Sternberg's sequence.

Stimulus encoding is further defined by Sternberg as 'transformation of the visual stimulus into some representation of the numeral or its identity' (presumably this last phrase means its name represented as a phonemic pattern), and in the memory search experiment as the stage which 'prepares a stimulus representation to be used in the serial comparison process'. These definitions are neutral about the nature of the analysis and representation of the stimuli (wholes, feature lists etc.); moreover, the exact method by which the encoded representation is compared with memory is left open, apart from the suggestion that it is compared with each possibility in turn in the memory search task. As already pointed out, no indication is given of the comparable process in the digit identification task and it seems unlikely that 'normal' identification is achieved by this cumbersome process of searching through a set of possibilities until a match is found; face or word recognition would be lengthy processes if this were true.

A further example of the additive factors method is an experiment by Schwartz, Pomerantz and Egeth (1977), who presented two letters to be named, and varied ease of encoding by a masking field or no masking field, the physical similarity of the two letters (which were A and H) and the response compatibility. All these proved additive, once again suggesting a sequence of encoding followed by translation to name codes and then response emission.

Controlled termination of processing

Another approach to the problem of delineating stages is to attempt to halt or tap the process before it is completed. Early experiments simply varied the input duration and asked for reports. There was surprisingly good agreement by observers on what was experienced as the input duration increased. Vernon (1952, Chapter 3) has summarized the evidence, which suggests four stages: a vague awareness of something present or an indefinite object, awareness of a generic object belonging to some general category, awareness of a specific object, and finally understanding of meaning.

Later experiments raised doubts about the adequacy of simply varying exposure time in order to control the length of time the input was available, since Sperling's results discussed above indicated that the effect of brief visual stimulation lasted for up to $\frac{1}{2}$ s, whatever the actual stimulus duration. Consequently, masking fields were used to provide better control, consisting of a bright flash or a random pattern of small squares (known as a visual noise field) or a random pattern of lines similar to the components of the stimuli to be identified (pattern mask). If such an interfering stimulus is presented soon after the stimulus to be identified, it completely obscures the latter; at somewhat longer delays it causes difficulty in identification. This obliteration is known as *masking*. Masking also sometimes occurs when the masking field precedes the stimulus, which is known as forward masking; when the masking field follows the stimulus, the result is naturally called backward masking. Masking can also be used in combination with other variables to restrict the effects of the latter to the stages of processing which remain unimpaired by the mask. The method of operation of the different types of masking is still not fully agreed (see Kahneman 1966) and it is certain that masks can exert a number of effects and different types of mask work in different ways.

The first extensive use of masking in devising a stage model of perception was by Sperling in the partial report experiment described in Chapter 5. Using masking fields to halt the postulated transfer from the visual to the acoustic storage, he showed that one additional item was transferred for every 10 ms delay of the mask. Later work, however, showed that performance on the second item reported started to improve before that on the first item reported reached perfection, and performance on the third item similarly improved before that on the second was perfect and so on, so that it was not a case of strict sequential processing of the letters one at a time.

Turvey (1973) has studied in detail two types of backward masking and derived a more detailed outline of pre-iconic processes using letter identification tasks. One of the types of masking he studied, which he believed to be of peripheral origin, depended on the energy in the masked stimulus (energy being defined as luminance $\times$ duration). The interval (I) required to evade masking was directly related to stimulus energy (E) such that $I \times E$ equalled a constant value. Thus doubling E, by doubling luminance or duration, would enable the stimulus to be seen at half the original delay before mask onset (that is, more easily). Masks had to have a greater energy value than the stimulus for these effects to occur, but above this value changes of luminance or duration in the mask had no further effect. A contourless flash was less effective than random visual noise or a pattern mask. Random noise was even more effective when preceding the stimulus and the same relations between stimulus energy and interval held. However, with forward masking, the effect increased as the mask luminance increased, unlike backward masking, so the energy of the first input in each case was important. No masking occurred in either direction if the stimulus and mask were presented to different eyes (dichoptic presentation). In summary, when two stimuli compete in this system the one with greater energy wins, but the effect occurs before inputs to the two eyes are combined.

The second type of masking, which Turvey believed to occur more centrally, was obtained with a pattern mask. This type of masking did occur with dichoptic presentation and was completely dependent on the interval between stimulus onset and mask onset (stimulus onset asynchrony or SOA). The energy in the stimulus was not important and the mask energy did not need to exceed the stimulus energy. Virtually no masking occurred if the mask preceded the stimulus. This type of masking occurred at longer SOA than the first and it was possible to plot out the decline in the first type followed by the rise in the second type as SOA increased, giving a U-shaped function with the least masking at an SOA of about 48 ms (mask energy being greater than stimulus energy). Thus with this second type of masking, when two stimuli compete, the one arriving second usually wins.

Turvey's conclusions from these results were as follows. Peripheral feature analysers signal properties of the input such as colour, brightness, contour, orientation and size to a more central decision system. The rate at which these analysers work depends on the energy of the input and different features will be passed on at different rates, but all these analysers function in parallel. This is the set of processing operations which is affected by peripheral masking. Two inputs occurring too closely together in time will be combined and the feature analysers will extract properties of the composite input and pass them on.

The central decision system constructs a representation of the input by picking up the messages from the feature analysers one after another and passing them through a decision tree which yields a final output which specifies the whole input. Originally Turvey suggested that the two stages occurred one after the other, but his experiments showed that target duration affected peripheral processing time (that is the interval at which peripheral masking occurred) but not central processing time. Hence the latter could not include the former. Consequently, Turvey suggested that the peripheral and central processes overlap and central decision occurs as the input from the peripheral systems continues to arrive (we shall see in Chapter 7 ways in which this might happen). The times taken to carry out this sequence he assumed to be constant and therefore unaffected by the times taken by the peripheral system to forward information (of course it has also to be assumed that the central process cannot occur more rapidly than the slowest peripheral input). If another set of inputs from the peripheral processes arrives too soon the central decision never gets completed and this is the second type of masking.

Turvey discussed the relation between these systems and Sperling's iconic store. He began by considering the notion of features and pointed out, as we have already noted, that high-order features indicating relations between parts of a pattern are needed for full identification. These he calls context-dependent features, while the simpler features which combine to form them he calls context-independent. The feature-detecting systems assumed to exist in his peripheral system can be taken to be of the latter type. In this case the central decision process can be seen as synthesizing a holistic representation out of these context-independent features; from this holistic representation context-dependent features could be derived. Alternatively, if the features abstracted by the peripheral system include context-dependent features, the central decision process can be seen as leading directly to identification of the input. Taking an imaginary example, in the first case the peripheral systems would signal | and ⊃ and spatial co-ordinates of each, the central process derives from this the relational feature, that ⊃ is on the right and top of |, and the still higher process compares the total information with memory and identifies the input as P. In the second case all the relational information as well as the features would be forwarded by the peripheral systems to the central process which would itself identify the input as P.

Turvey argued that the decisions made by the central process following the peripheral inputs and not the inputs to the central process from the peripheral systems are the material of Sperling's iconic store. These decisions form a global representation of the input (with figures separated from ground and from each other) but the extraction of relational features and identification have not yet occurred. His argument is mainly based on verbal reports from subjects, who claimed a shift 'with increasing interstimulus interval from reporting little or no evidence of the target letter to an intermediate state of noting its presence, and finally reporting not only that it was present but that its form was clear and that the problem was to identify it before it was replaced by pattern mask' (p. 45). These reports parallel closely those obtained from the early studies summarized by Vernon and from partial report experiments of the type used by Sperling. Turvey also added that informal observations suggest that different types of mask are differentially effective and that Mayzner and Tresselt (1969) found that five random letters would mask five random letters but not a five letter word. This implies that similarity of stimulus and mask on physical and semantic dimensions can affect the severity of masking and Turvey suggests that it is competition for the same post-iconic analysing systems that may be the effective factor.

This account is compatible with the view that in Sperling's iconic store the letters have been segregated into separate items; features from the same location would be signalled together and combined. However, in more complex fields such segregation requires additional processing using relational features, as has been pointed out earlier, and may often require sampling over time as when using the results of movement to separate objects from background. It seems unlikely that these more complex operations could be carried out in the brief time which enables information to be entered into iconic memory and this form of memory may therefore be specific to the task and materials used to demonstrate it. However, Treisman *et al.* (1975) did find that information about movement was available at the iconic level, which goes against this view.

Speeded responding

If observers are forced to made decisions under differing degrees of time pressure, for example, on which of several possible patterns has occurred, the rate and order of acquiring different types of information can be discovered. Though this method has been employed with reaction tasks involving relatively simple stimuli to try and uncover the course of identification processes (see Chapter 7) it does not appear to have been employed with more complex stimuli and tasks to discover the order in which different aspects of the input are processed.

Analysis of reaction time distributions

Hohle (1965, 1967) has suggested that the overall reaction time is the sum of several components, an identification process which is distributed exponentially and a number of other processes which are each and in combination distributed normally. That is, he suggests, that the time to carry out the identification process varies from occasion to occasion in such a way that if we could measure it on its own many times we would get a distribution of times like the coarsely shaded one in Figure 24. He advances no reasons for

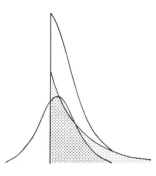

Figure 24   *Hypothetical combination of an exponential latency distribution (coarse dots) and a normal latency distribution (fine dots) to give an overall latency distribution (overall outline) such as would be obtained in an experiment*

making these particular assumptions but such a distribution would result if (for example) one test is made of the input which has a probability *p* of giving the answer and if that fails a second test is made which also has the same probability *p* of giving the answer and so on (whether this actually happens we simply do not know). Similarly he suggests that if we could measure response selection and some other processes on their own we would find each varied randomly from occasion to occasion in such a way that when they are combined we would get the finely shaded distribution shown in Figure 24. The overall outline in Figure 24 shows the distribution which results from adding together Hohle's two hypothetical distributions. Hohle attempted to test these assumptions by varying his tasks in ways which would plausibly affect one of the components and by mathematical methods he separated out the obtained distribution of reaction times into the two suggested components to see if the appropriate one had been affected in each case. Varying the foreperiod between a warning signal and a stimulus in a detection task increased the duration of the normally distributed component, as did the duration of the foreperiod. Stimulus intensity affected both components. The number of words which might appear in a word reading task increased the duration of the exponentially distributed component. Reactions by toe instead of finger affected both. Most of these results, apart from the affect of number of possible words, fail to make much sense in terms of Hohle's assumptions and as the normally distributed component is the sum of several processes, any change in it can usually be explained somehow.

Of course if we had some good reason for assuming what are the components of reaction time and what form the distribution of times for these components take, this would be a very powerful technique, but in the absence of such information its usefulness is rather slight. In consequence, we have little idea why Hohle's data fail to match the predictions.

Clinical evidence

In the light of the picture which is emerging we might expect to find clinical cases in which particular parts of the system had ceased to function. Clearly, wide damage in early stages would prevent all later ones from operating adequately. However, more specific types of damage could occur, such as loss of the ability to segment the field into figures and ground or words and gaps, or loss of particular feature analysers, or loss of the ability to integrate features into objects. At a higher level, connections which enable the results of one sensory input to locate the appropriate information in memory might be damaged, so that naming of visually or tactually presented objects or of sounds, or pronunciation of words would become impossible. Or writing words and drawing pictures in response to spoken names could be impaired. The level at which an object can be named may also be affected. It may be in such cases that meaning (knowledge about use or associations) can still be retrieved from memory so that it is possible to describe what to do with an object but not to produce its name. The reverse pattern is also possible with naming of objects or words retained but access to meaning impaired.

Clinical cases which match some of these expectations have been observed at one time or another, but often multiple injuries are present, since damage due to strokes or impact is not neatly restricted to a particular subsystem, and in any case there is no necessity that these functionally separate subsystems should be anatomically separate. Moreover, there is the usual problem of locating any effects observed in a particular stage of the whole process. Hence it is difficult to draw conclusions from such evidence about sharp distinctions between different stages and functions. Nevertheless, some suggestive results have been observed. A recent survey is provided by Pirozzolo (1978).

Damage to Area 17 or 18 can produce some rather puzzling phenomena. Parts of the visual field may be lost so that no vision is reported but objects which project partly to the missing area will be reported as complete (Poppel, Held and Frost 1973; Weiskrantz *et al.* 1974). Patients may catch a ball thrown to them which they report they cannot see (cortical blindness). These results indicate that appropriate behaviour can occur in the absence of awareness. Either information from earlier in the processing sequence is used or the higher centres receive inputs by another route, or, in the case of completion of missing parts the incomplete input is used to predict the rest, as in constructing a complete object from incomplete data in much of normal perception. Certainly the evidence weakens the assumption of a strict linear sequence of operations in which each stage depends on input from the preceding one.

Inability to segment input does not seem to have been described, but it would be difficult to identify unequivocally. However, disorders of perception of direction and topography have been observed and loss of ability to name or identify from a given name specific features such as colour, and to handle specific material such as faces. Inability to read letters has been reported while numerals could be read (Ettlinger 1967). Kinsbourne and Warrington (1964) showed a difficulty with colour sorting, so it was not just a naming problem, but often colour matching is possible while naming is not (Benson 1981). Some have claimed to observe a specific inability to handle music, but Pirozzolo says that other defects have always been present as well. However, reading of words can be lost and reading of music retained (Benson 1981), which suggests an independent function.

Inability to integrate has been described quite frequently. Patients with right brain hemisphere damage produce disorganized drawings when copying, which contain the essential parts but in no organized relations to each other. Eye movement disorders have also been reported which can affect integration of information from successive samples.

Impairment of naming of visually presented objects and words have both been reported. The former (object agnosia) is rather rare (see Rubens and Benson 1971, for an example) and often occurs with impaired ability to describe or use or give associations, so in these cases it involves impaired access to meaning too. However, ability to use objects without naming them can also occur, though the reverse pattern seems not to have been observed. Naming requires the left hemisphere in most right-handed people. When the two brain hemispheres are separated and words are shown only to the right hemisphere, reading is impossible but the left hand may select the correct object (Gazzaniga and Sperry 1967). Another type of patient can copy drawings but not draw named objects from memory, suggesting that the name cannot evoke the visual pattern. Warrington and Taylor (1973, 1978) found patients with right hemisphere lesions, especially posterior ones, were worse than those with left hemisphere lesions in making same–different judgements of pairs of pictures of objects taken from different angles, but could name and describe the use of the objects. Thus connections from visual representation to name or the reverse can be lost separately and the first sometimes involves the loss of associations from visual representation to use.

Problems in repeating heard words occur in cases of so-called word deafness. Inability to recognize non-verbal sounds has also been reported (Spreen, Benton and Fincham 1965) and also to recognize objects by touch, suggesting separate analyses occur for different senses as well as different types of input. Rubens and Benson's patient could recognize by touch but not by vision and could copy drawings but not name the objects. He could also write but not read. Intact hearing and ability to repeat speech without comprehension can also occur (Geschwind *et al.* 1968).

Returning to word naming, there are several different problems which may be observed (Patterson 1981). The most straightforward is when visual confusions occur between words. It is now widely believed that there are two ways of reading words, one via the sound and the other directly from visual patterns to meaning. Impairment of the first produces patients who can read familiar words, especially concrete ones, but not new words, non-words or function words which have no object they represent. This is called deep dyslexia. Japanese patients of this kind cannot read the syllabic script Kana, but can read the ideographs which form the Kanji script (Sasanuma and Fujimura 1971; Yamadori 1975). The patients tend to produce meaningfully related or associated words instead of the one presented.

Phonological dyslexics read single morpheme content words perfectly, but non-words hardly at all, and have some difficulty with function words and word endings like -ed and -tion. They do not show the meaning-related responses of the deep dyslexics. Letter-by-letter reading is characteristic of another type of dyslexia, suggesting an impairment in processing words as wholes. Finally, surface dyslexics show features which suggest impairment of direct visual pattern recognition. They perform badly on words with irregular spelling, which good readers know how to pronounce by direct recall, not by using spelling-to-sound rules, but they handle unknown words of regular spelling quite adequately. Mispronounced words can be assigned a meaning appropriate to the mispronunciation (for example, 'listen' read as 'liston' with the comment 'that is the boxer'). Japanese patients show loss of Kanji with Kana reading unimpaired.

Thus a large variety of fairly specific clinical deficits has been observed, supporting the general idea that perceptual performance includes many specific skills which can be lost independently or disconnected from other component skills of a task. The data, however, are not sufficiently tidy to permit derivation of particular temporal *sequences* of operations. Rather they provide evidence that different tasks and different types of input are handled by independent subsystems in the brain, as Seymour's model described below assumes. In particular, right hemisphere lesions are associated with difficulty in tasks requiring visual analysis and left hemisphere lesions with difficulties in semantic analysis (Warrington and Taylor 1978).

An integrated model of visual processing

This completes the account of methods of uncovering stages and has illustrated applications of these methods to specific tasks. The psychological methods (attention experiments, stage deletion, additive factors, premature termination) all find that the earliest stage they can detect is some form of already processed physical representation. This may be because of the restricted inputs they have employed or because these methods are inappropriate for detecting the initial processing which is needed to produce such a representation. The demands of artificial intelligence have forced theorists such as Marr to consider these preceding processes more carefully in relation to the analysis of three-dimensional scenes.

In introducing these methods it was pointed out that theorists aim to produce more general models from their analysis of particular tasks, though it was suggested that flexibility was one of the main features of perceptual processing. A detailed attempt to sketch out a stage analysis of the basic achievements and operations in visual processing of alphanumeric and lexical material and objects or pictures of objects is contained in a recent book by Seymour (1979), drawing on data which primarily used the method described in the 'Adding and deleting stages' section above, and sometimes additive factors experiments, clinical cases and termination of processing by masking.

Seymour derives his structure mainly by considering the types of material humans can handle and the possible achievements with these, rather than by a painstaking analysis of the patterns of interaction between different variables. He suggests an outline for the components of the processing systems involved in such tasks as identifying letters, words and pictures, comparing pairs of such items and categorizing patterns as words or non-words, or categorizing pictures as animals, together with the operations these systems perform. Then he looks for tasks which are likely to require the use of these operations, in order to investigate which variables affect the operations. It is only at this stage that interactions between variables or premature termination are sometimes considered as evidence for the distinctiveness of the proposed stages. Hence there is a general weakness of relying on data from different tasks for different components of the system rather than analysing the components of a single task.

Seymour assumes that different types of data are stored in separate long term *data stores* – graphemic (information about visually presented letters), phonemic (acoustically presented letters), pictorial, semantic and so on. This information can be retrieved from any of these stores and placed in a temporary *register*, one of which is associated with each data store. Symbols in one register can be converted into the appropriate symbols in another or two such sets of symbols from a register can be compared with each other. Naming visually presented letters requires conversion from items in the graphemic register to items in the phonemic register then output or *expression* (in Seymour's terminology), while naming pictures requires conversion from pictorial to phonological (that is, word) symbols and so on. Identification is therefore an operation of relating an input of one type to the contents of a data store containing a different type of data and outputting new symbols which may involve uttering a sound, pressing a key and so on. Exactly how one set of symbols must be represented in order to make contact with the equivalent symbols in another form and how this contact could be made is not dealt with in any detail by Seymour, nor is it his major concern, which is to outline the processes at a more general level.

Let us consider only visual input of alphanumeric characters in order to simplify matters. Seymour proposes that following elementary feature analysis a shortlived *iconic* representation is established of the whole input from which part is selected and transferred to the *graphemic* register, which contains specifications of visual features and locations. The contents of the graphemic register can then be converted to other types of representation by means of *interfaces* between it and semantic, phonemic, pictorial and other registers. These interfaces consist of a *pattern recognizer* which reads the symbols from the graphemic register, *address registers* which use the result of this reading operation to find the semantic, phonemic or pictorial equivalent in the semantic, phonemic or pictorial *data store*, and place the result in the equivalent register. This process is called retrieval by Seymour and can also result in rehearsal if the graphemic pattern is used to find itself in a graphemic data store and then this information is passed back into the graphemic register (a process called *representation* by Seymour). The contents of the graphemic, phonemic, semantic registers and others can also be passed to a comparison process for matching to other patterns. An outline of these structures, simplified from several of Seymour's own figures, is shown in Figure 25. Output devices are not considered in any detail by Seymour and sometimes this leads to unjustified conclusions because effects he discussed could be in the output stage. Of course input can also be in the form of phonemic symbols (such as spoken letters), pictorial symbols and so on as well as visual symbols, and Figure 25 can readily be modified to depict these other possibilities. Note that the different boxes are not intended to represent different anatomical areas in the brain, but different functions.

Different tasks can be devised which involve different operations and hence different combinations of these components. For example, an identification task requiring naming of a picture would involve the iconic and pictorial registers followed by retrieval of a semantic representation then a phonemic one via the appropriate interfaces. Much of the evidence cited by Seymour for his distinctions consists of demonstrations that a particular variable affects a task he assumes to include a particular stage. In many cases there is only a high probability that the effect is not due to earlier stages, either because the problem of removing the critical stage to test the

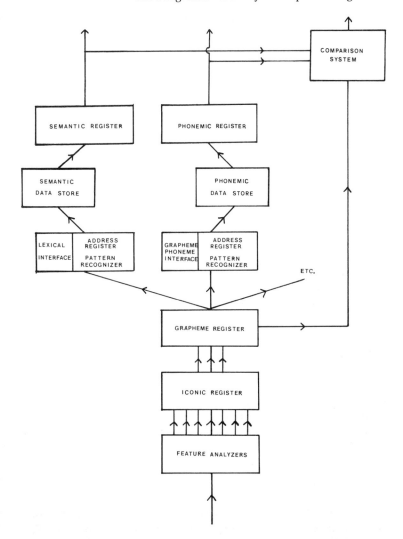

Figure 25   *Outline of Seymour's system, derived from several figures in Seymour (1979)*

effect of the variable on preceding stages only has not been solved, or because, even where the possibility of doing this exists, the relevant experiment has not been carried out. Furthermore, when Seymour does compare two tasks they often differ in several ways, and if a variable affects the more complex one only there is no certainty about which of the additional operations it is affecting; Seymour often makes unjustified conclusions in this respect, without citing any critical evidence such as a demonstration that the variable in question has effects which are additive with those of another variable which is known to affect the other stages in the sequence and therefore the two affect different stages. Hence, while Seymour provides an impressive array of data in support of his proposed structure, there are many uncertainties which require resolution. I will now sketch out the most convincing examples of evidence for the distinctions he wishes to draw.

Iconic versus graphemic registers

Display size has no effects when detection of a specified element is required (assumed to require iconic register only), but does affect deciding whether an element specified after the presentation was present or absent (Eriksen and Collins 1969). The latter task is assumed to require identifying the items as they appear, which requires the graphemic register, according to Seymour, but it could of course require more than just the use of this register and the difference could be due to a later stage, such as transforming the items to a phonemic mode for retention. Less equivocal evidence for the distinction comes from an experiment investigating masking by a bright field. Spencer (1969) presented a circular array of items with one to be named indicated by an arrow. When the arrow was simultaneously present with the display, a bright flash masked the display up to a delay of 75 ms. If however the arrow marker was delayed for 100 ms and followed by the mask, the mask was ineffective, implying that a more permanent representation had been established. At this interval a pattern mask was effective (compare Turvey's results).

Seymour appears, like Neisser, to assume that all input passes through the iconic store, but the evidence for this is weak. Spencer presented his two conditions in separate blocks, so different processing could easily have occurred. No experiment is cited using a task requiring processing beyond the icon but terminating processing prematurely on some trials, or illustrating additivity of variables affecting the iconic and graphemic stages. Moreover, Seymour believes that the contents of the icon can be fed into a comparison process, which hardly tallies with the fleeting relic defined in Sperling's experiments. All this suggests a flexible rather than a fixed processing sequence; the type of preliminary processing outlined by Marr could deliver any one of a number of possible sets of information to the decision-making systems, giving an 'icon' with different properties in different tasks.

Phonemic and graphemic registers

As we have already seen, matching visually presented letters presented successively for physical identity is sensitive to visual but not phonemic similarity (graphemic register) while matching them for nominal identity (same name) is (somewhat) sensitive to phonemic similarity. The effect of visual similarity declines with delay between the items, disappearing for delays over 2 s, suggesting that items are converted into a phonemic code, an interpretation which is supported by an experiment which interfered with this process by making subjects repeat digits while carrying out the task. Visual similarity continued to be effective over much longer intervals in this situation – this also shows that the graphemic code can be maintained if required.

Retrieving a phonemic (name) code for a graphemic code

In a task such as reading letters, Seymour suggests that factors such as the number of possibilities and their probability of occurrence, which affect certainty about the symbol which may appear, affect this operation. This evidence is discussed in more detail in the next chapter, where the complexities of deciding which part of the process is affected by this variable are considered and this suggestion is found to be unjustified. Pachella and Miller (1976) found that under name-matching instructions physical matches were affected by stimulus quality but not by stimulus probability, and name matches were affected by both, with the two effects being additive. This suggests that different stages are involved. Hence probability must affect a later stage than quality and Seymour suggests it is phonemic retrieval, but it could also of course be affecting the phonemic comparisons which follow.

The situation is more complex when the input is a word. Many English written forms cannot be correctly pronounced (named) without use of existing lexical knowledge, since the rules for regular forms are not applicable. Hence two routes to reading would need to be involved, a route from sight to sound (grapheme to phoneme) and a route from sight to meaning to sound (the so-called direct reading route). If reading aloud is required the second route goes from the graphemic register to the semantic register to the phonemic register. With these more complex situations the evidence for the proposed stage breakdown becomes more ambiguous. Seymour discusses a number of tasks which he suggests will involve different combinations of the suggested stages, but is able to offer very little direct comparison between different tasks, or systematic additive factors data to support the suggested combinations. Such data are badly needed.

Seymour discusses recognition of tachistoscopically presented words, decisions as to whether letter strings are words (lexical decisions) and vocalization of presented letter strings, his main purpose being to demonstrate the two-channel access theory described above. Regularly spelled words are recognized more easily than irregularly spelled ones (effects on the graphemic register), regularly spelled non-words or non-words sounding like real ones (brane, for example) are rejected more slowly than irregularly spelled strings, and judgements of whether pairs of words are words or non-words are slowed if they are visually similar but pronounced differently (lemon and demon), all indicating involvement of the phonemic register (but the last effect vanishes if *visual* matching of the ends of the words is required). Evidence for direct access from the graphemic to the semantic system comes from clinical data (discussed above) and from an experiment in which judgements were required on whether pairs of words had a similar meaning or rhymed. Shadowing affected the latter task but not the former, indicating that recovering the sound was not necessary for the semantic judgement.

Processing of non-verbal inputs

Seymour puts forward a similar structure to handle non-verbal visual inputs, whether from three-dimensional objects or pictures. He suggests a preliminary iconic stage followed by a pictorial register which has access via a pictorial interface to pictorial, semantic and structural data stores and can place the retrieved data in the pictorial, semantic or structural register. He argues for differences between these levels by demonstrating that some tasks are sensitive to some variables and other tasks to other variables.

Iconic versus pictorial register
Matching matrix patterns separated by intervals under 20 ms was accurate and not affected by pattern complexity, while at ISIs of 1 to 9 s complexity had a deleterious effect. On the other hand, visual masking and spatial displacement impaired performance at short ISI but not at longer ISI. No evidence involving three-dimensional forms is presented.

Pictorial versus graphemic register
Letter recognition was unaffected by having to retain the position of filled cells in a matrix at the same time.

Pictorial versus semantic register
This distinction is most conclusively established by experiments which demonstrate that same–different comparisons of the colour of the inks in which pairs of conflicting colour words are printed (Stroop effect patterns) are no slower than when the words are replaced by rows of Xs. However, when *naming* of the colour is forced by asking for 'same' responses when a colour name matches the ink colour of a row of Xs of a conflicting colour word, then the word condition is slower than the X condition. The first task is therefore assumed to involve the pictorial register only and the second to involve the semantic register as well.

So far, so good. Seymour also argues that the integral/separable distinction discussed in Chapter 4 is ascribable to processing at the pictorial and semantic levels, respectively, the pictorial level treating the object as a whole and the semantic level deriving a logical or propositional or feature-by-feature description. This distinction simply does not agree with his own earlier specifications. The pictorial code involves (p. 221) 'a two-dimensional interpretation (a statement about points, lines, bounded regions and properties of brightness, size, colour, orientation and two-dimensional shape) and a three-dimensional interpretation which is descriptive of relations among surfaces, edges, and elementary forms'. In other words, it is a feature description, like the graphemic register which it parallels and not an integral or holistic description or a blob. Moreover, the semantic register contains 'attributes and categorical assignments . . . descriptive of the colours of objects, their sizes, spatial attributes, and functional and affective properties' (only the last two of these seem to be truly semantic, while the others are merely copies of information from the pictorial register). Seymour gives no reason why the semantic store requires separated dimensions and in fact one might argue the reverse case, nor is his distinction compatible with the basis for Garner's. The latter is based upon different effects of different combinations of features on the same task and not on differences in what happens in different tasks. Seymour's view requires that changing the task from one requiring pictorial coding to one requiring semantic coding should produce integrality or separability, respectively, and changing the features involved should not have any effect, but he provides no evidence supporting this requirement. Hence, while the distinction between types of coding and hence types of register is acceptable, the tying of these to the integral/separable distinction seems wholly unjustified. That distinction must occur at the pictorial level and involves questions of the nature of the feature analysis; this analysis is of course merely assumed but never discussed in detail by Seymour.

Retrieving a phonemic code for a picture
The sequence is like that for reading words by the direct route to meaning.

Seymour argues that the additive factors method does not provide any access to processes at a more minute level than the broad stages he has outlined. In consequence, he provides no discussion of the details of such operations as figure–ground separation or the nature of feature analysis. He does consider in some detail the comparison process and suggests in relation to this and a number of other decision processes a cumulative count of matches is made until a criterion is reached. This approach to the microprocesses underlying basic operations is discussed in more detail in the next chapter. Seymour believes the main advance in understanding microprocesses must come through artificial intelligence research and he would probably be quite willing to accept Marr's account of the detailed processes involved in constructing the code which enters the pictorial register.

An integrated model of acoustic processing

What then of acoustic inputs? There appear to be no models of the stages of early processing of the level of sophistication offered by Marr. Seymour himself does suggest a similar stage analysis for speech inputs to those he offers for written words and pictures, namely an 'echoic' register and a phonemic register, but he does not consider the details of these as his concern is with visual perception. He does not discuss whether there is a separate input register handling sounds like car brakes and honking geese, analogous to the pictorial register, and in fact this type of auditory perception has been almost totally ignored by all researchers. No experiment has tested whether sounds and words interfere with each other, but there are some indications from clinical cases that perception of one can be lost while the other is retained.

Quite complex outlines have been suggested for the processes involved in the perception of continuous speech, involving analysis at several different levels (acoustic, syntactic and semantic), which will be discussed in Chapter 10. For the early processes investigation has concentrated on the existence of, in Seymour's terms, the echoic register and the phonemic register. Massaro (1975) and his colleagues have presented a plausible stage model which is in essence identical to that of Seymour, with a *preperceptual auditory store* containing lists of unconnected features and a *synthesized auditory memory* containing clusters of such features combined into elementary speech units, which Massaro believes to be syllables. The third stage in Massaro's model is called *Generated Abstract Memory* and corresponds to Seymour's Semantic Data Store and Register.

Massaro claims he has demonstrated the existence of a store with the characteristics of his preperceptual auditory store by demonstrating that a brief tone (20 ms) presented for identification is masked by another tone occurring within $\frac{1}{4}$ s. Holding (1979), however, quotes evidence that tones mask but noises do not, and that the masking effect vanishes with practice, casting doubt on the notion of an early uncategorized trace. Eriksen and Johnson (1964) have shown that if tones are presented randomly when subjects are reading, asking shortly after each tone has occurred whether there had recently been one, greatly increased accuracy of response compared with leaving subjects to respond whenever they heard one (50 per cent versus 11 per cent correct). This implies that the trace of the tone survives and can be checked in the cued condition. However it survived after 10.5 s, since performance was still higher than the uncued condition, so was not like Massaro's $\frac{1}{4}$ s trace. Hence the latter seems weakly supported by the evidence.

A great deal of energy has been devoted to examining a phenomenon known as the auditory suffix effect, which also concerns the existence of a short-term store for verbal items. If a list of syllables or words is presented acoustically the final items are usually better remembered than the rest of the list and also better than when the list is presented visually. However, if a single item is added within 2 s which does not have to be reported, the advantage is removed. This effect occurs at longer intervals than Massaro's effect described above and depends on the physical similarity of the items to be recalled and the interfering items (resemblance to speech, voice of speaker, pitch and so on). Massaro places this effect in his proposed synthesized auditory memory. In doing so he has to account for the effect of acoustic similarity by arguing that the synthesized auditory memory preserves acoustic characteristics such as speaker's voice. In this respect Massaro's model must differ from Seymour's, since for Seymour the items in the phonemic register can be entered from input or retrieved from the phonemic data store (as when converting visual letters to phonemic equivalents) and hence would have to be abstract descriptions without actual voice characteristics. Either we must assume that the voice characteristics can be included but need not be, or that Seymour has oversimplified in assuming one store which can hold both phonemic inputs and self-generated phonemes.

Massaro quotes an experiment by Cole, Coltheart and Allard (1974) in support of his case, who found that same–different judgements for letters presented sequentially were faster if both were spoken in the same voice and this occurred at delays of 8 s, and Craik and Kirsner (1974) found voice information survived for 2 mins. Clearly this effect could not be ascribed to the preperceptual store, but it also raises difficulties for Massaro's assignment of it to synthesized auditory memory, since one may ask why suffix effects do not operate at such intervals. In criticizing theories of a fixed sequence, including short-lived sensory stores, Holding (1979) quotes data from Erwin (1976) who demonstrated that the length of time that visually presented items 'survived' depended on the amount of information which had to be extracted from them. He argues that evidence such of this supports the view that the duration and nature of processing varies with the task, as suggested in the levels of processing framework, even at the supposedly early stages (I have of course suggested above that these stages are not in fact very early). We may note also that, as with the visual data, there is no good evidence that preperceptual storage precedes synthesized auditory memory where the latter occurs, rather than being an alternative for certain forms of input in certain situations.

Conclusions

Drawing together the results of these differing lines of investigation, there is clearly a considerable difference in the level and type of processing which can be investigated by neurophysiological and psychological techniques. A broad separation into Input Stage – Decision Processes – Response Selection – Response Output is generally accepted but not enormously informative, because the important central processes remain unspecified. Although it is important to be able to identify and isolate the additional processes, it is the central decision processes which contain the secret of how identification is achieved. Marr has provided an explicit model of a large part of the visual input stage for fairly complex scenes. These stages are lumped into one by Theios, Sternberg and Seymour because the inputs they consider are of the kind where the problems considered by Marr do not arise and because they were not forced by the precise demands of computer stimulation.

The psychologically-based models are also derived from a relatively narrow range of data. The stimuli used in experiments considered by these authors are two-dimensional, readily isolated, drawn from well-defined sets, evoke highly overlearned identifications and require precisely specified operations on them. Seymour does offer a discussion of picture perception but this is restricted to simple pictures depicting one object. The perceiver has no problems over deriving a three-dimensional representation, including scaling for size and shape constancy, object segregation, the appropriate domain, the possible stimuli, the required level of identification (which is usually specified by instruction), or integration of information from a succession of samples, all of which are necessary in a great deal of our processing. Admittedly, because most perception occurs in familiar environments and observers bring habitual strategies to perceiving, many of these operations may normally cause no great problems. Nevertheless, they could fruitfully be investigated using Sternberg's additive factors technique or controlled stimulus duration. For example, in searching for the presence of a given object, such as a sparrow, in a three-dimensional scene, the adequacy of distance cues, the ease of isolating the object and the ambiguity of the object could be varied independently to discover whether separate stages of three-dimensional scene construction, object segregation and object identification are involved, and by using masking to terminate processing, the time needed to extract different types of information could be investigated. Thus the methods of the information processing approach could be applied to the problems of classical perception.

7 Deciding

The previous chapter has outlined ways of deducing the stages involved in extracting perceptual information from the input and the main conclusions which have emerged from the use of these methods. However, the key processes of matching input, however it is coded, to the information in memory has been glossed over in the stage models. We have already seen that this could not be achieved by a direct matching of the input to stored representations because of the variation in the information, loss of some information or inability to cope with all the information, and would have to be done by making a best bet among the possibilities. Furthermore, the expectations and motivations of the perceiver will obviously play an important part in such decisions; whether they also affect other aspects of perception is a question reserved for the next chapter. This chapter then is concerned with decision processes in perception. First I shall consider an influential theoretical approach developed in the 1950s to cope with problems of separating perceptual sensitivity from response biases in measuring success in detecting simple events. I shall point out some of the inadequacies of this approach from the point of view of a process theory and then describe methods of coping with similar issues in the analysis of reaction time data. This will involve theories about decision processes involved in matching inputs to information in memory.

Effects of discriminability and bias on perception

Suppose you are lying in bed and become aware that there may have been a sound downstairs. Whether you decide there really was such a sound will depend on two things – how loud it was and your assessment of the consequences of coming to a positive decision. The colder the night and the lower your current feelings of heroism, the louder the noise will have to be to convince you of its reality. Again, suppose you are watching a radar screen for enemy rockets;

the possibility of surprise attack has to be weighed against the mockery you might suffer for a false alarm. In such cases the *discriminability* of the possible stimuli or signals and the *bias* of the observer toward one conclusion or other act together to determine the actual response. Such biases are likely to operate in all perceptual decisions – identifying sloppy handwriting, birds, deciding the meaning of ambiguous sentences and identifying squirrels or sounds of cars or of geese.

Broadbent (1971) has made the distinction between perception and bias more strikingly by describing the latter as pigeon-holing. He distinguishes states of the environment, states of evidence (the selected and filtered information arriving at a decision mechanism) and the category states which are the groupings into which the evidence is separated. Pigeon-holing determines which and how many evidence states are mapped into which category states when there is no information about a certain feature in an evidence state. There is, however, some lack of clarity about the distinction between number of categories and number of pigeon-holes. The number of features considered determines the number of category states distinguished (for example, in speech the features of voicing and position of articulation give six possible states – voiced or unvoiced and front, middle or back articulation). Pigeon-holing is said to occur when a feature of the input is uncertain and is assumed to take a preferred value arbitrarily, and is thus not the same as the mapping of feature combinations into categories, which can follow different rules in different situations. For example, the category of 'big men' might include tall and thin men, tall and fat men and short and fat men, and small men would include only short and thin men, or 'big' might be restricted to tall, fat men, or the two features might be used to form four categories, but pigeon-holing would occur if, when it was uncertain whether a man was tall, he was assumed to fall on the short side of the dividing line. Broadbent does not properly consider the first type of information reduction (the category definitions) when discussing the different possible effects of variables such as probability on how the observer behaves.

The Theory of Signal Detection

A decision-making problem faces an observer in a psychology experiment in which the experimenter is trying to discover the minimum energy in a light or a sound which can be detected. Such experiments used to be regarded as measuring the *absolute threshold*, or, if it was the minimum detectable difference between two stimuli, as measuring the *differential threshold*. The *Theory of Signal Detection* was developed to handle situations where stimulus information or discriminability is impoverished and biases are therefore more influential, and in fact in its original form it applies only to situations where a weak signal has to be detected in a background of random 'noise' which is assumed to be due to random variation in the physical signal and random activity in the nervous system which will occur even in the absence of any input. It has, however, been applied more widely by many psychologists to situations where decisions have to be made about which of two or more possible stimuli has occurred.

Let us consider the visual threshold measurement situation. Of course there is little point in presenting a stimulus on every trial; even if you trust your observers' honesty, they will be sensible to say 'yes' when in doubt, thus performing better than strictly they should. So we throw in some trials where no light occurs and ask whether anything was detected. If the task is sufficiently difficult, mistakes will occur. Some lights will be missed and some non-lights will be reported as lights. What are we to make of such cases, especially the latter? There are two traditions of handling these *false alarms* as they are called. One assumes they are simply bad guesses when nothing was seen and the other assumes that information is rarely unambiguous and errors result from processes designed to do the best possible in the face of uncertainty.

Guessing theories make one very straightforward prediction which has been shown many times to be wrong. This is that the number of times the subject achieves a *hit* (reports a stimulus when one was present) will increase at the same rate as the number of false alarms. Putting this more precisely, suppose on 100 trials, half with a stimulus (or *signal* to use the theory's technical term), the observer sees the stimulus on 34 trials, sees there is no stimulus on 34 and on the remaining 16 trials of each kind guesses 'yes' and 'no' equally often. The result will look like Table 1. Suppose, however, that the observer guesses 'yes' on only 2 out of the 16 trials of each kind; the result will then look like Table 2.

Clearly, for every rise in the number of false alarms, there is an equal rise in the number of hits and we could plot out a graph to show this, like Figure 26, which has converted into probabilities the numbers from Tables 1 and 2, by dividing by the fifty trials of each

Table 1

Response

	Yes	No
Signal	42 (hits)	8 (misses)
No signal	8 (false alarms)	42 (correct rejections)

Table 2

Response

	Yes	No
Signal	36 (hits)	14 (misses)
No signal	2 (false alarms)	48 (correct rejections)

type (indicated by the points marked 1 and 2 on the graph). However, when we look at some results obtained by encouraging observers to vary their tendency to 'guess' we get a result like Figure 27, which looks nothing like the prediction offered in Figure 26. The probability of a hit at first rises much faster than the probability of a false alarm, then more slowly, showing that hits cannot depend on guesses in the way the guessing theory suggests. The Theory of Signal Detection offers an alternative account of what is happening inside the observer. Remember that this applies not just to psychologists' experiments and early warning systems but that the basic

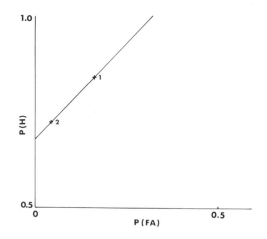

Figure 26   *The relation between the probability of a hit (P(H)) and the probability of a false alarm (P(FA)), as predicted from guessing theory*
The two points marked 1 and 2 represent the combinations of values derived from Tables 1 and 2, respectively.

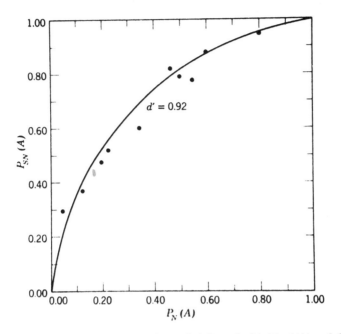

Figure 27   *The relation between the probability of a hit ($P_{SN}(A)$)) and the probability of a false alarm ($P_N(A)$)), obtained by Tanner, Swets and Green in an auditory detection task (from Green 1956, Chapter 2, Figure 2)*

ideas are applicable to any situation where a decision has to be made about whether the input justifies Decision A rather than Decision B, including such everyday events as deciding whether or not you have seen this person before.

The main principles of the theory are as follows:

1   The sensory system varies in the amount of activity it generates.
2   In the absence of input the level of this activity varies normally about a mean; this random activity is called *noise* in the system. If we could sample the level many times and plot the results we would get a distribution like the left-hand one in Figure 28 (the Noise or N distribution).
3   Addition of an input will shift the current level of activity by some amount, the amount depending on the strength of the signal. Thus the level of activity produced by a series of inputs, all the same strength, will also vary normally about a mean

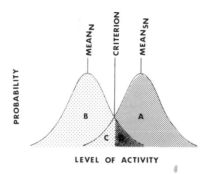

Figure 28   *The probability of each activity level given noise (left hand distribution) and signal plus noise (right hand distribution) assumed by the Theory of Signal Detection, indicating the mean of each distribution and a criterion point. The shaded areas represent the probabilities of hits (A), correct rejections (B), misses (C) and false alarms (D).*

which is separated from the mean of the noise distribution by an amount depending on the strength of the signal. Again, if we could sample the level many times we would get a distribution like the right-hand one in Figure 28 (the Signal + Noise or SN distribution).

4   Observers do their best, but if there is overlap of the two distributions they will of necessity make some errors.

5   Performance depends on a sensory factor (the separation between the two distributions measured in terms of the standard deviations and known as d' or d prime) and the observer's criterion or decision on the level of activity above which a signal will be reported which is known as β (the Greek letter beta). Clearly d' depends on the intensity of the signal, low intensity signals producing small differences between the distributions, and also on the sensitivity of the nervous system to inputs. β depends on rewards for correct responses, costs of the different types of error, and expectations about the probability that signals will occur.

Now if we return to the imaginary results in Table 1 we can match up the proportions of each kind of event with the different shaded areas on Figure 28 as follows.

Area A (hits)   0.84 of the SN distribution
Area B (correct rejections)   0.84 of the N distribution

Area C (misses)   0.16 of the SN distribution
Area D (false alarms)   0.16 of the N distribution.

The criterion must be at a point which produces symmetrical results, that is the point where the two distributions cross. Now how can we calculate d' and β? First d'. We need the distance between the means of the two distributions. The distance from the mean of the N distribution to the criterion in terms of the standard deviation of the distribution can be found in tables of the normal distribution by seeing at what point (or z score) 0.84 of the area will be cut off; the answer is that if we move out one standard deviation from the mean this result will occur. Clearly the distance from the mean of the SN distribution to the criterion is exactly the same, so the total distance between the two means is two standard deviations and $d' = 2$. If we take the data from Table 2 the values of A, B, C, D are 0.72, 0.96, 0.28, 0.04, respectively. The distance from the N mean to the criterion will be the z score which cuts off 0.96 of the N distribution and the tables tell us that this is about 1.75 standard deviations. And the distance from the mean of the SN distribution to the criterion is the z score which cuts off 0.72 of the SN distribution, namely about 0.6 of a standard deviation, so d' is the sum of these values, namely 2.35. Notice the oddity of this result; the probability of a hit has gone down but our measure of sensitivity has gone up. How can this make any sense? Remember that the difference between the two sets of results lay in assuming a greater reluctance to guess in favour of a signal in the second case. This should show up in our estimates of β.

How then can we measure β? To do so we need some scale to represent position along the horizontal axis of Figure 28 and without a method of measuring neural activity in some hypothetical nerve centre, that looks difficult. Fortunately, a single neat assumption solves the problem. As we move from left to right along the horizontal axis of Figure 28 the relative probability that the activity level is due to a signal increases in a lawful way (for any given separation of the two distributions of course) from 0 to infinity. This relative probability or *likelihood ratio* can be calculated at any point from the height of the SN distribution divided by the height of the N distribution. These heights in turn can be obtained by calculating the area of the distribution in a very narrow column, taking the area of the distribution up to just before the required point and up to just after it and finding the difference. Fortunately tables are available giving both d' and β for different combinations of probabilities of hits and false alarms, so I shall not go through this labour here. If we consult Appendices 1 and 2 we can confirm our calculations for d' in the two cases (as the exact values for hits and false alarms are not given we have to estimate) and discover that the values of β in the two cases are 1 (which should be obvious already) and about 3.3, respectively. This second value means that the criterion has moved considerably to the right, making 'yes' responses rarer.

From the assumptions of the theory, we can make predictions about the effects of several different variables on performance. Making the difference between the two situations to be discriminated larger will increase d' but need have no effect on β. Encouraging the observer to say 'yes' by presenting more signals or suggesting there will be more or by giving a reward for each signal which is correctly reported should not change d' but should affect β, moving it to the left. Encouraging the observer to say 'no' should have the reverse effect. Results of this kind have been obtained in many experiments.

One way in which these types of change are often displayed is by working out for a given value of d' the combinations of hits and false alarms which will occur as β is moved from the left to the right in Figure 28. This gives the type of curve which was shown in Figure 27 with a different curve for each value of d', getting closer to the top left hand corner as d' increases. These curves are known as *Receiver Operating Characteristics* (ROCs) and they can be turned into straight lines by converting each of the axes into z scores instead of probabilities. Changes in perceptual sensitivity are represented by moving from one curve to another and changes in bias by moving along a single curve.

Since it is rather tedious to get such data by persuading observers to use a different criterion on different occasions, another method of achieving the same result which is often employed is to ask observers to rate their confidence in each response they make. It is assumed that high confidence responses can be treated as if a strict criterion is being used (so that only signals falling well to the right are included), high plus fairly high confidence responses can be treated as if the criterion is somewhat less strict and so on. The ROC is plotted out using hits and false alarms at each criterion level just as before.

Using this method it should be possible to discover whether expectations, motives, mood and similar variables which I shall be discussing in the next chapter are really affecting perception or only the bias in reporting what is perceived, and to separate effects on perception from effects on response. Note, however, that this method uses the probability of correct responses as its basic data and requires two-choice tasks, so its applications are fairly limited. Another difficulty is that the theory as I have described it requires that the N and SN distributions should be normal and have the same variance, but this problem can be avoided by adopting measures similar to d' and which do not make this assumption (see MacNicol 1972, for a detailed description). Also a variety of effects may be concealed within the perceptual changes, which may be due to attention, some stimuli or aspects of stimuli being selected for more detailed analysis under certain motivation, or to more precise classification of some sort or to observing for longer before making a decision. The next chapter will give an example of how an early criterion variation in respect of colour information could emerge as an apparent perceptual change. The Theory of Signal Detection (TSD) only incorporates the notion of caution or response criterion in the sense of bias toward one response or other rather than in the sense of willingness or reluctance to come to a decision at all. Because it was designed to handle detection tasks with brief stimuli a bias toward saying that no stimulus has occurred superficially looks like general caution about reaching a decision, but clearly the two are different. The second sense of criterion (the amount of evidence required before any decision is reached) is important in cases where the stimulus does not vanish after a brief exposure so that increased caution enables more evidence to be gathered. In these cases such increased caution will increase d' and not affect β because more evidence allows more accurate decisions to be reached. Hence in conclusion, while TSD was an important advance in the analysis of perceptual performance it is not an adequate model for perceptual processes nor an adequate method of distinguishing the different possible effects on perception of expectations, motives and so forth.

Investigation of decision processes through choice reaction time measurement:

I turn now, therefore, to the development of models of decision processes, which aim to specify the processes by which it is decided that the input is the left rather than the right of two lights, or the longer rather than the shorter of two lines, or A rather than H and so on. Use of simple stimuli bypasses questions of whether the input is treated holistically or feature by feature and whether features are handled in parallel or serially, and leaves only (it is hoped) the question of how a single feature is compared with the possibilities, whether serially to one possibility after another, simultaneously to all at once, or by a series of steps, narrowing the possibilities progressively. And is the matching carried out in a single step or by a more prolonged process?

Hick's Law: an information theory approach

The first attempt to produce any kind of model of the process seems to have been that of Hick (1952), who confirmed earlier observations of Merkel (1885) that the relation between the number of possible stimuli and the choice reaction time to press a key identifying a light by its spatial position could be described by the formula

$$L = a + b \log n$$

where L is the latency of the response, a and b are constants and n is the number of possible and equiprobable stimuli (see Figure 29). At the time information theory (see Chapter 3) was beginning to be regarded as a suitable mathematical model for the analysis of psychological processes and Hick therefore wrote his formula specifically in terms of log to the base 2 ($\log_2$), rather than the more usual $\log_{10}$ or $\log_e$. He then attempted to describe possible processes which would produce such a relation, of which two examples will suffice. One suggestion was that replicas of the input are produced

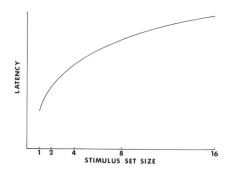

Figure 29   *Example of a relation between latency and stimulus set size which can be described by the function* a + b *log* n

for matching to the set of possibilities which exists in memory; if replication occurred by recurrent duplication so that the input was first used to produce two copies and each of these to produce two more and so on until sufficient were available to match simultaneously to all the possibilities, the obtained result would occur, assuming that each duplication stage takes the same time and the simultaneous matching takes the same time, however many replicas are involved. The other suggestion made by Hick was that the input is first judged to belong in one half of the possible stimuli, then in half of that half and so on until only one possibility is left. Hyman (1953) subsequently varied the probabilities of the stimuli, thus varying the information, and found that the relation found by Hick still held overall for the mean time, but the separate times for the more and less frequent stimuli were not exactly what they should have been if only information in the information theory sense was important. Responses to frequent stimuli were too fast and those to rare stimuli too slow. Furthermore, Hick's theories do not easily adapt to cope with imbalance in frequency or numbers of stimuli which are not powers of two, and though his suggestions are interesting and the attempt to relate an overall result to internal processes is commendable, there are serious inadequacies in the theoretical approach, experimental procedure and the data, not all of which have been satisfactorily resolved in later more sophisticated experiments. Moreover, the second suggestion seems an inefficient process since errors early on would be disastrous and correction slow and difficult, while the first suggestion requires a more precise specification of what is replicated and how matching to memory occurs.

Problems with information theory

Inadequacies in the applicability of information theory to psychological processes soon become apparent in several areas. In the one which is of concern to us, experiments showed that Hick's result did not occur in naming numerals (a well-practised task) nor after long practice in pressing keys to lights. In these cases the size of the stimulus set had at most a very small effect on identification latency. This finding is of course reminiscent of those discussed in Chapter 4, showing that parallel analysis of several stimulus features is possible in well-practised subjects. Recently Teichner and Krebs (1974) showed that the increase in latency as set size increases gets less as the subjects used became more practised and finally drops to zero. Furthermore, Fitts and Switzer (1962) showed that the familiarity of the set as a set was important; responding to either 1 or 2 was faster than responding to any one of the numerals 1 to 8, but responding to 2 or 7 produced results just like those to the set of eight (again we are reminded of Garner's stress on the subjective subset from which a stimulus is assumed to come). To handle this change in the effect of set size the notion of *stimulus-response compatibility* was devised, with compatible situations reducing or eliminating the set size effect. No satisfactory independent definition of compatibility was ever offered or any suggestion of how it affected the processes but the implication of this idea is that the stimulus analysis process is closely tied to the response selection process and it is primarily the characteristics of the stimulus-response relation which affect latency. Of course it might be possible to modify Hick's ideas to account for these effects, but before this could be done two other problems had to be solved, of isolating the critical variable and controlling the subject's caution in responding in different situations. I will consider these two problems in turn.

The effect of the number of possible stimuli on choice reaction time

Work in the classical reaction time tradition has examined the effect of a large number of variables, especially the effect of set size, but has in the process thrown very little light on the internal processes involved in these tasks. Smith (1968) provides a review of the main areas of investigation. The research has tended to be driven by attempts to assign the effects of some variable to stimulus or response processes, but has been bedevilled by inadequate models, inadequate methods of delimiting the site of effects and inability to isolate the variables adequately.

As an example we may consider further the attempts to grapple with the effect of set size on response latencies and to separate out the effect of this variable from probability, sequential effects and discriminability. One might well ask why this single variable attracted so much attention, particularly once it was obvious that its effect depended on the nature of the stimulus-response relationship. It was presumably hoped that an adequate explanation would provide insight into how the formidable task of dealing with the immense variety of possible natural objects could be handled so rapidly and efficiently. Furthermore, the necessity of disentangling stimulus set size, stimulus probability (both absolute and sequential), discriminability of the items in the set and stimulus effects from response effects also involved considerations of how expectancies affected the perceptual process, which clearly were relevant also to the efficiency of decision making in the natural environment.

Unfortunately, the enterprise of disentangling these variables and establishing consistent findings never achieved much success and finally died away under the weight of its contradictions. In the straightforward choice–reaction task, stimulus and response set sizes covary. Attempts to separate the two, by mapping several stimuli on to one response, suggested that whether or not the number of stimuli per response affected reaction time depended on the ease of grouping them together by common perceptual or conceptual features (compare Schneider and Schiffrin's results). Broadbent and Gregory (1962) and Brebner and Gordon (1962) obtained set size effects when probability of a particular stimulus was held constant while set size changed, and Kornblum (1975) obtained set size effects while holding constant the probability of repetitions and alternations, the effect occurring mainly on the alternations. However, Bernstein and Reese (1965) showed that set size effects occurred only when a prediction about the next stimulus was falsified. The last two findings suggest that a match may first be attempted to a predicted stimulus or the previous stimulus, followed by a search through the remainder. Crossman (1955) has argued that the set size effect is due to decreased discriminability as the set size increases and showed that the effect vanished when discriminability was equated, while Gholson and Hohle (1969) showed it was greater for less discriminable sets. Chase and Posner (1965) and Wilcox and Wilding (1970) found a similar result in memory search tasks. Thus part of the effect at least seems to be due to discriminability and a precise model is needed which could handle these findings.

The effect of stimulus and response probability on choice reaction time

In attempts to isolate effects of stimulus probability, experimenters have varied the probability of stimuli assigned to a single response. For example, Bertelson and Tisseyre (1966) used four stimuli, two assigned to one response with probabilities of 0.55 and 0.15 and the other two assigned to the other response with probabilities of 0.15 each. Most such experiments have demonstrated that more probable stimuli elicit faster responses and a few have shown effects of response probability too when the differences in such probability were large.

The effect of stimulus and response sequence on choice reaction time

The effects of sequence are complex and poorly understood. Responses to repetitions are generally faster than those to changes of stimulus, but only when the interval between presentations is less than 2 s. Above that figure the reverse occurs, due mainly to an increase in time to respond to the repetitions. Whether this is the result of combinations of effects of stimulus repetitions, response repetitions and expectancies is unclear.

Other factors affecting choice reaction time

Clearly, apart from the difficulties of achieving consistency of results, these findings do not enable a model to be devised or the effects to be assigned to any particular stage in stimulus processing, so little progress was achieved toward understanding the nature of the central decision processes. This very brief sketch illustrates some of the difficulties and uncertainty in isolating critical variables. Surprisingly very few experiments in this tradition examined the effects of variables such as brightness, contrast, stimulus duration or discriminability, presumably because the investigators were concentrating on error-free performance. A few errors do however usually occur even with highly discriminable stimuli and the tendency to regard these as aberrations to be ignored was an unfortunate one. Common experience suggests that the number of errors in such tasks will depend heavily on how quickly the subject attempts to respond and ignoring errors involves ignoring the dependencies of reaction time on the subject's degree of caution in responding, which was the second problem identified above.

Trading speed for accuracy: caution and choice reaction time

We can pursue this theme by examining performance at different average speeds of responding. We can either divide the naturally varying response times into groups varying from fast to slow and look at the probability of a correct response in each group, or we can force the subject to respond at different speeds in different blocks of trials or from trial to trial. We can also look at differences between subjects in speed and efficiency, and Vickers, Caudrey and Willson (1971) did this and found that the slower responders made fewer errors. Though the different methods of looking at this speed–accuracy trade-off do not produce exactly the same result, they all show a consistent relation between mean response time and the probability of a correct response, an example of which is shown in Figure 30, which was derived by the method of asking subjects to respond at different speeds in different blocks of trials. Discussions of the adequacy of the different methods are given by Pachella (1974), Wickelgren (1977) and Wood and Jennings (1976). As Figure 30 shows, the probability of a correct response is at a chance level at very fast latencies, then rises rapidly as latency increases with the rise slowing down at longer latencies. This type of curve has been called the Latency Operating Characteristic by Pew (1969), by analogy with the ROC of the Signal Detection Theory.

This type of result has implications for a standard choice–reaction time task in which subjects are allowed to choose their own preferred speed. Performance is rarely error-free, but will include anything up to 5 per cent errors. It can be seen from the figure that

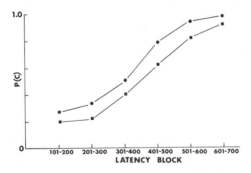

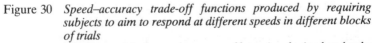

Figure 30   *Speed–accuracy trade-off functions produced by requiring*
subjects to aim to respond at different speeds in different blocks
of trials
The latency blocks are the ranges of latencies obtained under the
different requirements, and the probability of a correct response
(P(C)) is given for each latency block in a four-choice (circles)
and a six-choice (squares) task (unpublished data from the
author).

to increase the probability of a correct response from 0.25 to 0.30 requires only a small increase in latency, but to increase it from 0.90 to 0.95 requires a larger one and from 0.94 to 0.99 an even larger one. Consequently, a small difference in error rate between two conditions in an experiment where the error rates are already low may involve a large latency difference. Suppose in Condition A the mean latency is 500 ms and the error rate 5 per cent, and in Condition B the figures are 600 ms and 3 per cent. The temptation is to ignore the difference in error rate as too small to worry about and to conclude that the change has increased latency. However, all the increase in latency may be associated with the small decrease in error rate so that all that has really happened is that the subject has behaved more cautiously in Condition B, rather than having to carry out some extra operation. One can only conclude that the latter has occurred if both latency and error rate increase or if one increases without the other decreasing. What is more, it is unjustified to derive equations relating the experimental variable such as set size to the latency unless the latencies are obtained without error rate changing.

Putting this another way, subjects can trade speed for accuracy and if we wish to derive conclusions about component processes, we must control this trade-off. Alternatively, we can let it vary, plot the relation between speed and accuracy and determine how this relation is affected by our experimental variables. Returning to Figure 30, we can see that the functions plotted there could change in several ways:

1   the chance level of performance;
2   the latency at which performance begins to rise above chance (intercept);
3   the speed at which performance improves as latency increases (slope).

Changes in caution (criterion) are reflected in changes in the point on the curve (the combination of speed and error rate) at which a subject performs in different conditions, while changes in the nature of the processes carried out will be reflected in changes in the intercept or slope. Moreover, it is plausible to relate the slope to the difficulty of the central decision process itself (but see below for a qualification), with faster improvement indicating an easier task, so that high performance levels are achieved at fast times. If this outline is correct, therefore, we have not only solved the problem of controlling the subject's caution or criterion, since we can compare LOCs from two different conditions with error rates matched, but as a bonus we have also found a way of measuring several different aspects of the decision process separately. The method does of course require the collection of rather large amounts of data, and does not in itself give any indication of the nature of the micro-processes involved in a single decision, but it does give the opportunity to fit predictions to the data from hypotheses about these processes. I shall return to this on pages 196–7.

Two types of error

Before discussing some experiments looking at the effects of different variables on the Latency Operating Characteristic (LOC), it is important to clarify a possible confusion about errors. The errors discussed so far are due to inadequate time to gain information from the input. However, errors can also of course be due to problems of the similarity of the possible stimuli and errors owing to difficulty of discrimination have consistently been found to be slower than correct responses (see Wilding 1971a for a discussion of this). The explanation for this will emerge later.

Factors affecting speed–accuracy trade-off

Only a few experimenters have looked at variables affecting the LOC. In an unpublished experiment I compared a four-choice and a six-choice task, the results of which are shown in Figure 30. The stimuli were lights varying in spatial position and the differences between positions remained the same in the two tasks. The only aspect of the LOC affected by set size was the chance level of performance. Neither slope nor intercept was affected, implying that no extra processes were involved to handle six possible stimuli, though it is of course possible that in an unconstrained task subjects also adopt a more cautious criterion for larger set sizes. The result is somewhat surprising, particularly as one might have expected the stimuli in the six-choice task to be less discriminable than those in the four-choice task. Swensson (1972) showed that lower discriminability produced a flatter slope as one would expect, but did not affect the intercept. Lappin and Disch (1972a, b, 1973) have looked at the effect of several variables on the LOC and found stimulus probability had no effects (implying the previously observed results are due to criterion changes), higher intensity reduced the intercept and produced a steeper slope, stimulus duration had no effects, and a shorter foreperiod between a warning signal and the stimulus produced a steeper slope. Thus set size has no effect on speed of processing (assuming that slope reflects this) while reduced discriminability, lower intensity and longer warning all slow it down (Lappin and Disch suggest that the last result is due to starting processing too soon). Harm and Lappin (1973) also examined the effect of compatibility by asking for left hand responses to right hand stimuli and vice versa and found that this affected the slope. This is puzzling if the slope reflects only stimulus processing and Harm and Lappin suggest that it must reflect 'a stage of information processing where perception is translated into action' and when there is high stimulus-response incompatibility the correct response may be properly selected but incorrectly executed. Suppose the probability of a correct decision at short and long latency points is 0.6 and 0.8 and in a compatible situation the responses directly reflect the probabilities, while in an incompatible situation one out of eight trials produces mistranslation to the response, yielding correct response probabilities of 0.525 and 0.7, respectively, so that there is a smaller increase in the probability of a correct response as latency increases. Whatever the exact explanation of Harm and Lappin's finding, it does mean that we should only compare slopes in different conditions when the stimulus-response compatibility is constant and only use slopes as measures of processing speed when the translation to the response can be assumed to be virtually error-free, that is, in well-practised tasks.

From the LOC the effects of different combinations of effects on the mean time to reach a given level of correct responding can also be worked out (for example, change in slope combined with change in chance level of performance) and hence the effects of combinations of variables assumed to affect the different parameters can be predicted. Without going into details, the main interest of such an exercise is that it shows that changes in criterion (required level of correct performance) will cause different amounts of change depending on the slope and chance level, and changes in slope will cause different amounts of change depending on the chance level. Hence we would expect to find interactions between discriminability and set size. According to Sternberg's argument, presented in Chapter 6, we would then conclude that both affect the same stage, but though this is true in the sense that both involve the decision-making stage, it certainly is not true that both affect it in the same way. More precise models of what is happening in each stage are needed than Sternberg's method can provide.

Explanations of speed–accuracy trade-off: fast guesses

Having shown how the construction of LOCs can enable the locus of some effects to be investigated more precisely, we need to ask about the nature of the processes suggested by the LOC. As with detection data, two opposed positions have been adopted, one being the fast guess view that errors are guesses made when time does not permit a decision to be reached based on the input. Decisions are on this view either stimulus-based with a high probability of being correct, or random guesses, and the trade-off between speed and accuracy occurs because the number of guesses declines as the time to respond increases. Nothing is known about the stimulus until the decision occurs. The opposed view sees the observer as collecting information over time and responding when one of the possibilities accumulates enough information in its favour to justify a decision. A process of this type is implied by the finding that when the decision varies in difficulty randomly from trial to trial (for example, by asking subjects to decide whether a stimulus was on the left or right of centre and varying the distance from the centre), so that the subject does not know beforehand whether a longer wait is desirable before guessing, nevertheless subjects take longer to respond to the more difficult stimuli, and also do less well on them. This is impossible if either nothing or everything is known about the stimulus. Clearly they are not responding after a fixed time nor keeping the probability of an error constant but seem to be waiting until a reasonable amount of evidence favours one of the possibilities. Seymour, in the book discussed earlier, incorporates a process such as this at a number of points in his model of perceptual processes (retrieval, p. 76; comparison, p.89; word recognition, p. 127 and lexical decisions, p. 156) but he does not spell out the details of how it might work. Most of the rest of this chapter will be concerned with describing the possibilities in some detail and the evidence supporting such theories.

First, it is necessary to consider objections to the fast-guess model. One has been given above, that randomly occurring variation in difficulty affects time and accuracy. Second, Pachella (1974) has shown that fast guesses cannot explain the LOC though they could form a proportion of the errors. In an experiment requiring decisions on whether pairs of letters were both vowels or both consonants the number of errors increased as faster responding was required and did so more rapidly for those which were the same only in their class (for example, P and Q) than for those that were the same in class and name (for example, Q and q) which in turn showed a faster increase than those matching in physical form also (Q and Q). Clearly, if guesses occur before any information has accrued from the input, such errors should be equally likely whatever the nature of the pair; the results again imply gradual accumulation of information. Third, Swensson (1972) has found that, when stimuli were quite hard to discriminate and fast responding was enforced, it was possible to distinguish fast guesses from responses made on the basis of some stimulus information. The former were characterized by fixed strategies (repetition, alternation or making the response appropriate to the previous stimulus) and by latencies of under 250 ms. There was a clear separation between the times for these responses and the remainder, since almost no responses were made with a latency between 250 and 280 ms. The remaining responses still showed a clear speed–accuracy trade-off which could not be accounted for by fast guesses.

Sequential sampling explanations of speed–accuracy trade-off and choice reaction time

Turning back then to the gradual accumulation theories, a number of these have been proposed, differing primarily in two respects – the nature of the information assumed to be delivered to the decision mechanism and the type of criterion adopted for making a decision. The information has been seen as either a series of all-or-none 'votes' or as a variable quantity of evidence in favour of one possibility rather than another. The criterion could be a total in favour of one possibility, or a difference or a run of information (Audley and Pike 1965).

I will take first as an illustration a model known as the *recruitment model* originally proposed by Audley (1960). In a two-choice task, two counters are assumed and samples of the input are taken one after another, one unit being accumulated in favour of one possibility or other on each sample; a fixed total (k, for criterion) of such votes is required in one counter before the decision is made. One other variable is required to generate predictions, the probability that each sample will favour the correct decision (p_c). Bias to one response can be included by setting a lower value of k for that response, and of course the probability of a sample favouring the incorrect response is $1 - p_c$. The model can easily be generalized to multiple-choice tasks by specifying such probabilities for all the possible responses ($p_1 \ldots p_n$).

With these assumptions we can work out the mean number of samples required before the criterion k is reached for the correct and the incorrect response for given values of p_c. Suppose $k = 3$. The possible sequences leading to a correct response, where C is a sample favouring the correct response and I is one favouring the incorrect response are:

CCC	ICCC	IICCC
	CICC	ICICC
	CCIC	ICCIC
		CIICC
		CICIC
		CCIIC

The probability of each of these sequences, and of the mirror-image sequences leading to an incorrect response, can be calculated from the values of p_c. For example, the probability of ICCC is $(1-p_c \ p_c^3)$ and the mean latency will be the mean length of sequence with each sequence weighted for its probability.

Table 3 *Values of response probability and latency calculated from the accumulator theory*

	$k = 3$		$k = 6$	
$p_c = $	0.6	0.9	0.6	0.9
Probability of correct response	0.68	0.99	0.75	0.9997
Mean latency of correct response (samples)	3.99	3.31	8.82	6.67
Probability of incorrect response	0.32	0.01	0.25	0.0003
Mean latency of incorrect response (samples)	4.23	4.45	9.63	10.18

Table 3 gives some sample values; one point to notice is that errors take on average more samples than correct responses and this matches the obtained results which were mentioned briefly above.

In fact response speed is directly related to response probability, and errors are one example of relatively rare responses, and so are slow. A second point to note is that a higher value of k or of p_c increases the probability of a correct response and reduces that of errors (in Signal Detection Theory terms it increases d'). A third point is that the calculations do not give exact predictions of latencies unless we know the time to take a sample, but only the changes that occur as the parameters change. Vickers *et al.* (1972) have attempted to calculate sample time and derived a figure of around 100 ms.

It is of course also possible to work out the probability of a correct response after $1, 2 \ldots n$ samples by calculating the probability that a majority of samples favours the correct response, and thus to plot an LOC curve. Variation from sample to sample in the amount of information obtained on each sample or in the time required to take a single sample can also be incorporated in the model with some additional mathematical expertise. What is more, it is not only the mean latency that can be calculated but the whole distribution of latencies for correct and incorrect responses, so that other measurements of the type of distribution can be described in statistical terms. Hence these models can make very precise predictions about a variety of aspects of the data.

Vickers, Caudrey and Willson (1971) compared predictions from several models of this type with results from a task in which sequences of red and green lights occurred in random order and the observers had to decide whether the sequence was predominantly red or green as soon as they could. In this way the probability of red or green samples on each flash (p_c) was under the experimenters' control and did not have to be estimated and the rule for response which was being used could be investigated. They found that their *accumulator model* provided the best, and quite a close, fit to the results. This was a modification of the recruitment model described above, in which a variable amount of evidence was assumed to be gained from each sample and the criterion consisted of a given amount of evidence in favour of one possibility. The present author (Wilding 1974) also compared the various models to data from a simpler task in which subjects had to decide whether a point of light had occurred on the left or right of the centre of a screen. By varying the distance from the centre it was assumed that p_c was varied. The results were very similar to those of Vickers *et al.* and again the accumulator predicted the general effect of the change in p_c, though with some inadequacies. In a further paper Wilding (1978a) pointed out that the obtained latencies in such a task in fact include input and output processes, so do not provide pure measures of discrimination time to match to the theoretical predictions.

An alternative approach is to attempt to fit LOC curves with predictions from the theory. To do this the assumption has to be made that the criterion becomes a time deadline (see Swensson 1972) or a fixed number of samples, after which the possibility with most evidence favouring it is selected. Unpublished work by the present author, which was summarized in Figure 30, showed that a very good fit could be obtained to the data with a variation of Vickers's accumulator model, in which each observation yielded one unit of information but the time to make an observation varied.

The great strength of these sequential sampling models is their flexibility and ability to predict several features of performance. The differences between tasks stressing speed and tasks stressing accuracy can be accounted for by a change in the type of criterion adopted and variation in the criterion to achieve a required level of performance. Given explicit speed instructions or a discrimination so easy that speed is the salient aspect of performance, a time criterion or criterion number of samples can be set, and varied in accordance with feedback from the experimenter or self-assessment; the lower the criterion, the more errors will occur, giving the typical LOC curve and on average errors will be faster than correct responses. Given accuracy instructions or a difficult discrimination without speed being stressed, a criterion can be set for the amount of evidence required in favour of one possibility and this can also be varied in accordance with feedback. This type of criterion produces errors which are relatively rare and slower than correct responses. Swensson (1972) and Wilding (1971a) have pointed out that the two types of error typically occur mainly under the two different types of explicit or implicit instruction.

In conclusion, therefore, some version of a statistical decision process, which envisages the central decision processes as sequences of samples of the input until a decision is reached, seems most likely to handle the facts. Such models are flexible in a number of ways. Changes in caution, discriminability and bias can be included. The absence of set size effects with highly over-learned stimuli can be explained by the very high value of p_c, so that only a single sample is required to achieve the correct response and set size effects which do occur can be explained by changes in discriminability and the chance probability of a correct response. It is also fairly easy to envisage a neural embodiment of these processes.

Vickers's extension of sequential sampling models

In his recent book Vickers (1979) has developed a more elaborate version of the accumulator theory to handle a variety of perceptual tasks. The theory as outlined above incorporated a matching of input to stored representations and incrementing of a counter associated with each representation when a match occurred. Vickers had already considered a version of the model to cope with the task of comparing two lines and responding according to which was the longer, in which differences rather than matches were accumulated. He combines these two ideas into a single model, initially designed to cope with a three-choice discrimination task in which subjects have to say whether a comparison stimulus is less than, greater than, or equal to a standard. Vickers suggests that equal judgements could eventuate when the other two judgements are tied, and the total number of observations has reached a criterion (the higher the number of observations producing a tie, the higher the certainty). The actual criterion he suggests is the sum of the observations in the two counters (for greater and less) minus the difference between them (Figure 31). A multi-choice identification task can be handled by a bank of modules of the same type and multi-dimensional stimuli by separate banks handling the separate features. Vickers also suggested that detection can be handled by the basic module, treating the background as the standard and comparing it with the focal stimulus, and Wilding (1971b) has suggested that in some cases when the stimuli are hard to discriminate subjects compare each with its predecessor and adjust the response accordingly, to circumvent the problem of maintaining representations of all the similar possibilities in memory.

In addition to predicting relations between discriminability, caution, probability of response and latency, the model can also be adapted to incorporate judgements of confidence. Vickers suggests the difference between totals in the counters would be a plausible basis for such judgements and that these judgements could be a means of adjusting the criterion values to meet the task demands.

Thus Vickers argues that a relatively simple general-purpose mechanism or decision module such as this provides an economic account of many aspects of perception and that an evolutionary

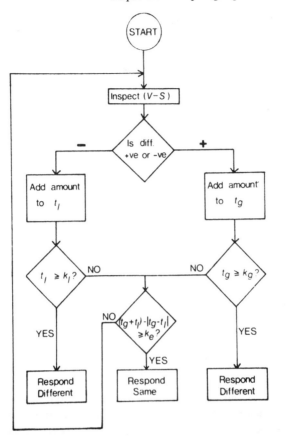

Figure 31   *Vickers's model of an accumulator process for matching an input to a stored representation (from Vickers 1979, Figure 53)*

account of its development and a neurophysiological embodiment are not hard to envisage. These theories are parallel processing theories in the sense that all the possibilities are evaluated simultaneously, but make no claims about whether different features are processed simultaneously or about how responses are initiated, especially responses which are not well-practised and are not therefore closely related to the output from a particular counter in the decision system. In fact the theory suggests possible ways of explaining the changes induced by practice as being due precisely to developing such direct links between decision modules and response processes without any further intervening decision processes.

Deciding between complex possibilities

The decision-making situations which we have been considering have all been relatively simple ones with the stimuli varying in only one way and the problem being to decide whether the evidence favours one or another of the possibilities on that dimension. Most decisions in real life, however, require a complex object to be assigned to one category rather than any of several other possibilities which vary in different ways from this category. Was that a human footstep downstairs, or a book falling off the bed in the next room or a bird flying against the window or the doorpost creaking as it cooled? Some features will point one way and some another. How do we, consciously or unconsciously, put the evidence together and reach a decision? There have been a few interesting studies of human ability to cope with the set of problems involved in attempting to categorize on the basis of varied, variable and unreliable evidence, which we shall consider in closing this chapter.

Bruner, Goodnow and Austin (1956) presented observers with pictures of aeroplanes which could differ in three features (tail fin, wings and air scoop), each of which had two possible values. In different pictures, different combinations of evidence were available, one feature, two or all three. The reliability of different features was also varied so that one value might always indicate a friendly plane and the other an enemy one (100 per cent validity) or in another condition one value would indicate a friendly plane two times out of three and an enemy one on the other time (67 per cent validity). The questions were, how would people react to unreliable cues on their own and in combination with other cues which might be reliable or also unreliable. The results were hardly a triumph for human rationality. Partially valid cues were over-valued, producing the same response 80 per cent of the time and once the partially valid cues had been experienced the valid ones were often under-valued, producing the same response only 90 per cent of the time. Thus subjects did not use the optimum strategy of going for the more probable option every time, nor did they match the actual probabilities. Even more interesting were the results of the combinations. With 100 per cent + 67 per cent obviously the second cue should be ignored. Not so. Subjects made the correct response about 80–90 per cent of the time, apparently treating the object as a whole and allowing the uncertainty of one feature to infect the other, rather as if information on both was accumulated in a single counter irrespective of its source.

Unfortunately this interesting and important work seems to have received little further attention. The other studies to be described did not look at grouping into categories, such as friendly versus enemy, nor at the handling of unreliable cues, but at how combinations of features are handled in rating objects on a single scale of similarity or value. Shepard (1964) showed that, given objects defined by a pair of quite disparate features (size of a circle and angle of a radius in it) no integration could be achieved in judging similarity and ratings were made in terms of one or other feature (see the earlier discussion of separable dimensions and city block measures of similarity). Yntema and Torgerson (1967) were interested in the ability to learn certain sorts of rule relating physical feature combinations to (arbitrarily assigned) value. The stimuli varied in thinness, brownness and saturation and the value increased as any of these characteristics increased. However the increases were not straightforward in that value might increase more rapidly with increasing brownness in thinner than in thicker figures, or it might increase more rapidly with thinness as brownness increased; in statistical terms, the effects of the features interacted. Subjects had to learn the values of 120 of these shapes and while they soon picked up the general rules about what was associated with an increase in value, they virtually disregarded the interactions, thereby simplifying the situation for themselves. Both these studies suggest that straightforward rules for classifying objects are preferred and complexities will tend to be ignored (no doubt one of the facts that makes science hard). Whether this is a learned technique owing to most of the rules we learn being of this type or whether it is a strategy to make the world easier to cope with, and if so, whether this is learned or something the baby arrives with, cannot be decided on the available data.

8 Expectancies and motives

This chapter is concerned with a number of variables which can affect the efficiency and speed of perceptual performance and the decision made. They fall into two main groups – factors affecting the expectations of the observer, and factors affecting motivation, though it is not certain in many cases whether these are the only operative factors or which of them is operative in a given situation. Expectations and motives can obviously be due to very recent events such as instructions, the number of recent occurrences of an event or sequence of recent events and the current state of various drives, or they may depend on experience over a longer period and stable personality characteristics. The effects of early learning, language and culture are examples of ways in which such extended experience may affect current perception. A consideration of these latter effects clearly involves wider questions of the importance of learning in perception which will be discussed in the next chapter. However, some issues have been somewhat arbitrarily included in the present chapter or are mentioned here to be dealt with in more detail later. The main focus of the present chapter is on the effects of current expectations and motives on perceptual performance and as usual we need first to establish what effects occur and then to try and decide where in the process and how they occur.

Ways in which expectancies and motives might affect perception

Most of the experiments investigating effects of these variables were carried out in the 1940s and 1950s and were concerned simply to demonstrate that a given variable exerted an effect on perceptual performance without attempting to outline possible mechanisms. The independent variable was rarely defined adequately (are the different variables we shall look at really different or are they examples of a single underlying variable?) and no adequate specification of the component processes was available in terms of which the observed effects might be explained. There are of course many possibilities and no certainty that the different independent variables exert their effects in the same way. At least the following can be suggested as possible effects:

1 the nature and number of features selected for testing;
2 the combinations of values which are sought;
3 the speed of operating;
4 the amplitude of the neural signal;
5 the amount of evidence required in favour of each feature and combination.

Some of these distinctions are not very easy to grasp when expressed in these abstract terms and a more concrete example may help. Let us consider my identifying a squirrel from my window. Past experience has provided me with a set of features useful in distinguishing different types of small animal, such as colour, size, shape, tail length, movement pattern. Combinations of values of these will single out different animals, with greyness, a length of about twelve in., lowness on the ground, a long tail and an undulating running movement being characteristic of squirrels. When I expect a squirrel I can:

1 restrict testing to these features of colour, length, height, tail length and movement;
2 test only for the combinations of values listed;
3 speed up testing of these;
4 boost the neural signals;
5 require only a little evidence to conclude that the shape is correct or if only some of the features are correct decide that this is a squirrel.

The first four possibilities should all produce rapid and accurate recognition of squirrels and rapid and accurate classification of anything else as a non-squirrel, thereby improving the discrimination between the two groupings (though discrimination of variations within them will be poor), while the last type of change will produce a readiness to classify non-squirrels as squirrels (to make false alarms) as well as rapid identification of squirrels.

Effects of probability on choice reaction time

I pointed out in the previous chapter that increased stimulus probability reduced response latency in choice reaction tasks, but that probability had no effect on the LOC, suggesting that the effect is only on the response criterion. One would expect this would also produce more false alarms to less probable stimuli and this has been shown in an experiment by Audley, Caudrey, Howell and Powell (1975), who used the simplifying device of instructing the subjects before each trial of the probability with which a given stimulus would appear in a two-choice task. This experiment, however, raised a major difficulty for the accumulator theory outlined in Chapter 7. Telling subjects that one stimulus would be more probable in a two-choice task not only decreased the time to respond when that stimulus occurred but also increased the time to respond by about the same amount when the other stimulus was the one which actually appeared. In other words, the reduction for the one stimulus was almost exactly matched by an increase for the other (a linear exchange). This suggests that response bias is the effective variable and that there is a close link between the processes which eventuate in each response, whereas in the accumulator these processes were completely independent and parallel so that the criterion for Response A could be adjusted without affecting that for Response B.

Audley (1973) had considered similar data produced by sequential effects and suggested that the random walk sequential sampling model could explain the results. In this the observer is pictured as starting midway between two goals and taking steps toward one or other as samples arrive until one goal is reached. Bias in favour of one goal is represented by starting off nearer to it and hence further from the other. Another way of looking at this is that a *difference* is required in favour of one possibility and a counter keeps a running total of negative or positive differences (a picture not readily translated into neurophysiological terms, unlike the accumulator model). Bias is assumed to preset this counter with a negative or positive reading.

However, Vickers *et al.* (1971) and Wilding (1974) showed that predictions from such a model failed to describe their results while the accumulator model did. Vickers's model can, however, be adapted to account for the linear exchange phenomenon by assuming that in a two-choice task the subjects compare the incoming stimulus to the previous stimulus rather than to stored standards of each stimulus. Thus a 'difference' judgement leads to a change in response and a 'same' judgement to a repeated response. The model shown in Figure 31 includes mechanisms for both these results in that equal numbers of 'greater' and 'lesser' judgements, either of which on its own can evoke a 'different' decision, lead to a decision of 'same'. If the 'greater' (or the 'lesser') counter is preset according to the bias in favour of differences or against them, this will affect the signals fed into the 'different' and the 'same' counter by an equal amount in opposite directions, producing a roughly linear exchange in latency.

One issue that arises here is the relation between these variations in probability and expectation, as it was suggested at the beginning of the chapter that expectation is a useful concept for organizing these and other effects we are about to consider. If the probability effects and the related changes in criterion are reflected in sub-jective expectations, relations should be found between probabilities, expectations and latencies. Unfortunately there are no data on the direct relation of criterion and expectancy such as could be derived from a experiment like that of Vickers *et al.* (1971) using sequences of red and green lights. Correct prediction does indeed speed response (Hinrichs and Krainz 1970; Hinrichs 1970; Craft and Hinrichs 1975; Whitman and Geller 1971; Williams 1966; Hale 1967) and probability effects disappear when a prediction is correct, suggesting that the same process is involved in both. As indicated above, telling subjects that a stimulus is likely reduces latency. Hinrichs and Krainz mapped two stimuli on to one response and found stimulus prediction (like stimulus probability) rather than response prediction was the important factor. A problem for any integration of probability, expectation and latency, however, is Hale's (1967) result which showed that as the number of repetitions in a run of the same stimulus increased, prediction of the same stimulus decreased but so did latency; this is possibly explained by some automatic priming effect of repetitions overriding the opposed expectancy effect. As indicated in Chapter 7, sequence effects are complex and difficult to understand.

Word frequency and perception

The factor which has been most widely investigated in connection with long-term stable probability effects on perception has been the frequency of a word in the language, mainly because this can be measured with some degree of objectivity, unlike frequency of occurrence of other types of stimulus. Solomon and Howes (1951) pointed out that more frequently occurring words are perceived at lower exposures than less frequent ones. Subsequent research has concentrated on whether the result can be explained by truly perceptual factors or by a bias toward reporting more frequent words. Goldiamond and Hawkins (1958) showed that the latter could explain at least some of the effect. They showed subjects different nonsense words for different numbers of times then asked them to report which word had been flashed briefly, increasing the exposure until the 'correct' word was reported. The correct word was in fact chosen arbitrarily and no word at all was actually flashed. Subjects more often reported the words which they had seen more often in the first part of the experiment, so they 'saw' these at a shorter exposure.

However, Broadbent (1971) discusses in detail the effects of word frequency on probability of correct report, and also the number of possible words which may be presented and the context of the presentation and argues that in no case will such guessing on its own explain the improvement due to increased probability. Either it must be assumed that increased probability also improves the quality of the evidence (see Chapter 7 for his use of this term) or that the relation between errors and correct response is more complex than the guessing theory implies, because the probability of correct reports rises faster than that of false alarms. Broadbent regards the first possibility as unlikely, since the word frequency effect vanishes when the set of possible words is specified, and he outlines a number of approaches to the second possibility, including the Signal Detection Theory with which we are already familiar. All these possibilities incorporate the notion that evidence is variable due to unreliability in the sensory systems and more of the possible states of evidence are attached to some responses than to others (pigeon-holing or response bias). As Broadbent puts it, 'we have found no evidence that people tend to select by filtering those channels from which information is likely to come. All we have found is that they are biassed in favour of responses they are likely to have to make'. This conclusion of course agrees with that drawn from the effects of probability on response latency discussed earlier. In neither case, it should be noted, is it suggested that these adjustments are necessarily consciously adopted changes.

Combined effects of frequency, priming and stimulus quality

This tidy picture, however, is not supported by the pattern of interactions between frequency and other variables. Stanners, Jastrzembski and Westbrook (1975) found no interaction between word frequency and quality of the stimulus (varied by super-imposing a random dot pattern on some trials) in a lexical decision task ('decide whether this is a word or not') and Becker and Killion (1977) obtained the same result when varying stimulus quality by intensity variation. These results are quite explicable if quality only affects the initial stages of forming a stimulus representation, but Lappin and Disch (1972b) found it also affected the slope of the LOC curve, so an interaction with changes in criterion would be expected. The main problem arises, however, because other variables which might be assumed to act on criterion in a similar way to word frequency and which themselves interact with word frequency (Becker 1979) *have*, unlike word frequency, been shown to interact with stimulus quality. Becker and Killion presented a priming word before a target word in a lexical decision task and an identification task, the priming word sometimes being relevant and sometimes irrelevant to the target word. The intensity of the target word had an effect only when the preceding priming word was irrelevant. Meyer, Schaneveldt and Ruddy (1975) found a similar interaction between priming and stimulus degradation, degradation affecting unprimed words more, and Miller and Pachella (1973) found that stimulus contrast had a greater effect for less probable stimuli when they varied the probability of items in memory scanning and digit naming.

These last three results all fit the prediction from the LOC curve that a higher criterion (unexpected words) will increase the difference in latency of responses between discriminable stimuli (with a steep slope) and less discriminable stimuli (with a shallower slope). Why then should the same result not hold when criterion is varied by word frequency? There is a difference between trial-to-trial fluctuation in expectations created by priming, context or within-experiment probabilities and pre-existing stable expectations depending on word frequency. Possibly the latter affects the chance level of response as well as the criterion or has more consistent or greater effects. In terms of the type of process represented in the LOC curve and discussed in the last chapter, changes in discriminability have only very small effects when guessing probability is high and criterion low, so if either of the last two conditions holds we can expect little effect of discriminability. Only additional data can clarify these issues.

Past experience and perception

Colour perception

Let us now consider some other cases of effects of past experience on perception. An experiment by Bruner and Postman (1949) used playing cards with the colour and shape combinations reversed. Not surprisingly the observers took longer to see the true nature of these than to report the nature of normal cards. The question is 'Why exactly?' At very short exposures they tended to report that the cards were normal, thus basing their reports on one feature and assuming the other matched it. At longer exposures they sometimes reported that the colour looked brown or purple which suggests a perceptual distortion and other experimenters have also claimed a similar effect in experiments which required matching the colour of a typical object, such as a banana or a lobster, to that of a meaningless patch, or setting the background to a colour which makes the figure invisible. These experiments have shown that bananas did look yellower and lobsters redder than meaningless patches of the same physical colour. However the results have proved somewhat unreliable (see Epstein 1967, for a review). Setting the colour of an object from memory does seem to be affected by its nature but not matching the colour of an object, and even the former only occurs when the apparatus does not allow an exact match to be made so that subjects are forced to produce a best bet. Setting the background to match the colour of a figure showed only a small effect unless the instructions emphasized the normal colour of the objects.

If these effects do occur they cannot be explained simply in terms of a relaxed response criterion. Recall that in a Signal Detection experiment subjects can, by giving confidence judgements, show that they are able to distinguish the distance away from the criterion that a particular signal was, yet in these colour-matching experiments subjects are matching a red patch some distance away from the point at which they would normally start to call the colour 'orange' to the redness of a lobster which is actually much nearer to the orange boundary. This shows that the red information from the lobster is given a bigger weighting than it deserves. This could happen if at an early perceptual stage, given a lobster shape, the amount of evidence needed to pass on the red signal to the next stage is reduced and the signal passed on is the same irrespective of how high or low this criterion was set. In other words, the criterion change is at a very early stage and the evidence on which it is based is not available as a basis for confidence judgements.

Distance perception

Before we leave past experience let us consider two quite different examples provided by a school of theorists known as the Transactionalists. They believed that what we perceive depends on past experience because the input is always ambiguous and the interpretation selected is the most likely one in the light of what has been perceived previously. They concentrated particularly on perception of distance and size, since they believed there were no cues in the proximal stimulus for distance (mistakenly, as was shown in Chapter 3). Ames produced many demonstrations to support this claim, of which the best known is the Ames room (see Figure 5). When the observer looks through a hole into the room with one eye, thus eliminating binocular and motion parallax, the image projected is identical with that projected by a normally shaped room from the same position, but in fact the room is made with trapezoid shaped walls, ceiling and floor to match the retinal shapes which would be projected by a normal room. When two people stand behind the windows, the one on the right looks large and the one on the left small because of their relation to the supposedly normal windows which are both assumed to be the same size. A single person walking from right to left in such a room appears to shrink, unless, intriguingly, he or she is the spouse of the observer, in which case the person looks normal and the room odd.

Another Ames demonstration presented playing cards, apparently with a nearer one overlapping the corner of a further one. The real situation was that the apparently further card was really nearer to the observer but had a piece cut out of the corner which allowed the other one to be seen in its entirety. In both these cases the viewers were presented with an abnormal situation where the disambiguating cues which head movements and binocular vision would provide were not available, so that the input was indiscriminable from that available for a normal scene. In the absence of any suggestion that anything was abnormal they interpreted it as they would interpret a normal scene. However, there is no proof that this was because of experience, because there is no group with different experience to offer a comparison. It could be that this is how the perceptual system automatically interprets this particular pattern of input. Moreover, in the room experiment, observers also interpret the input in *conflict* with past experience, since human figures are seen to be of unusual size. In the case of conflict some past experience is more powerful than others, and which it is must depend on exactly what is the total situation, as shown by the case of seeing a spouse in the room.

The account just given is basically one in terms of response bias – the expected is accepted. However, even observers who know the true situation have difficulty in seeing the room or the cut-out cards as they really are, so there is more involved. It is possible to learn to see the room aright by poking the walls with a stick. Presumably this information can be correlated with cues which were ignored before, like the presence of the texture changes which would signal a receding wall, so that the visual information on its own becomes more adequate when different aspects receive attention. If this interpretation is correct then the misperceptions are cases of experience restricting the features used to usually reliable ones (linear perspective or relative size) and thereby failing to discriminate the abnormality of the room by making use of a less obvious feature which would indicate the difference from other normal rooms.

Effects of language on perception

Turning to the effects of language on perception, a much quoted experiment is that of Carmichael, Hogan and Walter (1932), who showed pictures of objects with labels and later asked for drawings of the pictures. The drawings were influenced by the labels so that for example O—O when labelled as glasses came out as O⌒O and when labelled as dumb-bells came out as O═O . However there is no proof that these were perceptual effects rather than distortions during the delay before recall. It has also been claimed that labels function to reduce perceived differences within the class of objects which is given a single label and to exaggerate differences between such classes. One example is that of prejudice where differences within a despised group are ignored (Seeleman 1940; Secord *et al.* 1956; Pettigrew *et al.* 1958) and their inferiority to the prejudiced person's own group is exaggerated, but of course prejudice involves a complex mixture of motivational, labelling and expectancy effects which are hard to separate from each other. Tajfel and Wilkes (1963) have shown similar effects with a line judging task where lines were given labels, which led to reduced sensitivity to differences in length within the set given the same label, and exaggerated differences between the lengths of lines in the two groups. These effects are either cases of pigeon-holing in Broadbent's sense (missing information is assumed to fit the label) or of ignoring some features systematically because they are regarded as irrelevant, thus reducing the number of categories considered. Difficulties of discrimination within the class when this is required would suggest the latter.

A similar function of labels was suggested in Chapter 5, when discussing the problem of tying the right features together where several objects are presented simultaneously. It was suggested that having a single label for a complex object permits several features to be 'bundled' together and thus facilitates parallel processing. Obviously this might also involve ignoring some features.

The issue of labelling effects in perception has frequently been referred to as involving the acquired discriminability of cues. Miller and Dollard (1941) argued that 'learning to respond with highly distinctive names to similar stimulus situations should tend to lessen the generalization of other responses from one of these situations to another since the stimuli produced by responding with the distinctive name will tend to increase the difference in the stimulus pattern of the two situations' (p. 174). There is an inconclusive literature aimed at testing this hypothesis (see Epstein 1967, for a review), but the view in any case seems to suffer from a basic circularity, in that discrimination must precede the evocation of the correct response which is supposed to facilitate it (of course storing the label rather than the perceptual features in memory would facilitate subsequent discrimination). What labelling effects do occur seem to occur also with unrewarded observation and are most readily explained as reflecting the learning of relevant features and discriminations, that is, as effects on attention.

The Sapir–Whorf hypothesis

The strongest advocates for the effects of language on perception were Sapir (1929) and Whorf (1956). To quote Sapir 'we see and hear and otherwise experience very largely as we do because the language habits of our community predispose us to do so'. Whorf cited examples from Indian languages in which ideas are expressed very differently from 'Standard Average English'. Navaho, for example, used different verb forms in connection with different shapes and Whorf suggested that shape would therefore be a more important feature of objects for Navaho-speaking children than for English-speaking Navaho children. A study comparing the two groups did show the former preferring to discriminate objects by shape and the latter by colour (Carroll and Casagrande 1958). Whorf also argued that the Hopi perception of time is different because the language does not encode time as a continuum but as a series of repeated events. However, no experimental evidence has been produced on this issue. Another type of evidence cited as support for Whorf's position is cases such as the many words of Eskimos for different types of snow, of Arabs for camels (Thomas 1937) and of the Hanunoo people in the Philippines for varieties of rice (Brown 1965). It is implied that the distinctions enshrined in the words will guarantee distinctions in perception which are not available to those whose language is less precise. However, obviously knowing the words would not guarantee that the perceptual distinctions could be made and people make distinctions for which they have no names. Clearly, where the language does not make certain distinctions it will be because they are not found necessary in the culture so features on which they depend are ignored. Experimental evidence is fairly slight on whether such features can be used if required by those whose language does not enshrine them, and if not, how difficult it is to learn them.

Naming and colour perception

The one case where a quite thorough investigation has been attempted of the Sapir–Whorf hypothesis seems, in fact, to have been a rather special one – that of colour perception. The results initially seemed to support the Sapir–Whorf view, but later and more extensive studies have produced quite a different picture. Brown and Lenneberg (1956) looked first of all at the effect of *codeability* (ease of naming) on memory for colours. Codeability of a colour was assessed by agreement between subjects on the name, the shortness of the name and the speed of naming; high agreement, shorter names and faster naming tended to go together and indicated an easily coded colour. Recognition was better for more codeable colours when sets of four colours were shown and the one previously seen had to be selected, with differences in wavelength between members of this test set matched for all the colours tested. However, more recent research (see Brown 1976, for a review) has studied cultural differences in the colour vocabulary. The Dani, a New Guinean tribe, have only two colour names ('mili' meaning dark, cold colours and 'mola' meaning bright, warm colours) but showed the same superior recognition for codeable colours (codeable for English speakers of course, but not for the Dani). The typical colour for each colour name when a language possesses it, falls at the same point in the spectrum for all the different language speakers. Berlin and Kay (1969) have shown that there is a systematic progression as the number of colour words in languages increases. The two words in languages with only two words distinguish white and black, then in languages with three words the third word is for red. Green and yellow are added next, then blue, then brown, then purple, pink, orange and grey. When a pair of colours are separated by name, they are no more discriminable perceptually than for those whose language only has one word to cover them both. Hence it seems that colour distinctions are based on something common to all cultures, presumably the structure of the visual system, and show only marginal cultural differences. The cultural effects are on the range over which a colour name is used, but this has little effect on ability to discriminate.

In conclusion, therefore, language distinctions are in many cases associated with fineness of discrimination in identifying, but it is likely that this is not so much that the language constrains perception, but that the language distinctions depend on the distinctive features which the culture emphasizes as important. Hence subtle differences in snow or camels or tracks or wines will not be detected by the uninitiated because they have never been picked out as worth detecting. In other words it is a matter of the need to discriminate, skill and attention rather than the language one speaks.

Effects of motivation on perception

Turning to the effects of motivation, Allport (1955) has distinguished six types of effect which have been claimed, due to bodily needs, reward and punishment, individual values, values of objects, personality, emotional connotation. It is, however, possible to consider all these more simply as examples of the rewarding or punishing character of stimuli.

Basic drives

The most straightforward test is to vary a basic biological drive, such as hunger, and several experiments have done this. Levine, Chein and Murphy (1942) showed observers blurred pictures, and, up to 6 hours after eating, the number of food related objects which were reported increased but thereafter declined. No such trend occurred with the non-food objects. Lazarus, Yousem and Arenberg (1953) found a similar trend up to 3 to 4 hours after eating, measuring threshold by increasing the brightness until observers identified objects. Wispe and Drambarean (1953) tested subjects under 0, 10 and 24 hours of food deprivation and found hunger-related words had a higher threshold at 0 and a lower one at 10 and 24 hours of deprivation than neutral words matched for frequency, though the effect seemed to be reversing at 24 hours. They also found a rise in responses naming food objects and food-related acts at 10 hours and a decline at 24 hours. Gilchrist and Nesberg (1952) found that the perceived brightness of food objects but not other objects increased in up to 8 hours of deprivation. All these studies therefore suggest increased sensitivity to food-related stimuli or increased readiness to make such responses up to a certain hunger level then a reversal, partly due at least to unwillingness to respond at all. None of the studies separated perceptual effects from response bias, by measuring false alarms or testing the ability to discriminate food-related from non-food-related objects, but Wispe and Drambarean (1953) found no change in perception of neutral words which suggests subjects were not producing food responses as false alarms, since this would have reduced performance on the neutral words at 10 and 24 hours deprivation.

Association of reward with a stimulus

A second approach is to look at the effect of arbitrary association of reward or punishment with a stimulus; studies have been carried out using three main paradigms:

1   Association of one aspect of an ambiguous pattern with reward or punishment, followed by a test to see whether this aspect is

seen more readily than the other in the full ambiguous figure.

2 Estimates of size after variation on the dimension being judged has been related systematically to reward or punishment.

3 Association of nonsense syllables or words with reward or punishment followed by a test of the ease of identifying them.

Perception in ambiguous situations

Studies using punishment are described later. Studies of the first type using reward have been carried out by Schafer and Murphy (1943) and several others, using visual stimuli and monetary reward. Also Snyder and Snyder (1956) tested listening to two simultaneous voices, one of which had been associated with reward and the other with loss of money, and found that more was reported from the rewarded voice. Rock and Fleck (1950) did not obtain the effects described by Schafer and Murphy, but Jackson (1954) showed that this was because their stimuli were harder to learn and perceive. Positive results have also been obtained by Solley and Sommer (1957) with five to nine year old children, who also reported that the rewarded profile was happier, nearer, brighter and had stronger contours, and by Solley and Engel (1960), who got similar reports from five year olds. In these studies with ambiguous faces, in the training session the experimenter named the face, then showed it, subjects repeated the name and the reward was then given. This could induce an increased tendency to emit the response (or guess) irrespective of the display, but Solley and Engel used a pointing response and presented the profiles facing left or right, so no single response was reinforced, so this type of response effect could not explain their result. Sommer (1956a, b) made reward dependent on the response made to ambiguous faces, and, not surprisingly, obtained more rewarded than unrewarded identifications. The problem with these experiments is that the nature of the effect is unclear. Even if guesses can be eliminated, lower criteria for the rewarded aspect of the stimulus would produce the result, but since the design permits no such thing as a false alarm, it is impossible to distinguish this possibility from others such as attention to particular features.

Reward also arises from the agreement, approval or support of one's fellows and a famous example of effects of social pressure on interpretation of ambiguous stimulation comes from a very different situation – the identification of one's own mood. Schachter and Singer (1962) gave subjects an adrenalin injection which caused a variety of internal responses associated with arousal. Some subjects were not told what to expect and were left to wait with a stooge who indulged in either euphoric or aggressive behaviour. These subjects reacted in a similar way to the stooge, apparently interpreting their internal state according to the social situation, while subjects who had been warned what to expect did not. A common case of a similar phenomenon is the behavioural effects of alcohol which often depend on the social context.

Estimates of size
The second paradigm was used by Proshansky and Murphy (1942) who presented lines and weights to subjects who simply observed them and received or lost money according to the length and weight of the stimuli presented. Subsequent judgements shifted in the rewarded direction, either to overestimation or underestimation. McNamara (1959) rewarded or punished (with money or verbal reinforcement) overestimation or underestimation of the distance between horizontal parallel lines and then tested perception of the horizontal–vertical illusion; subjects tended to distort settings of the horizontal line in accordance with their previous experience, toward the rewarded length and away from the punished one. Thus the effect generalized from the training situation to a different one and did not depend on further expectation of reward. Both these results suggest a general shift in the criterion on one spatial axis. In the absence of any evidence on tasks such as discrimination we cannot know whether other aspects of perception of length were affected but it seems unlikely. Lambert, Solomon and Watson (1949) obtained overestimation of the size of colour chips which had been associated with reward by making them exchangeable for goods.

Another approach has been to look at the relation between the already established value of objects and perception. Bruner and Goodman (1947) reported that overestimation of coin size increased as the value increased (with a reversal at the highest value tested) and the tendency was more pronounced in poorer children. Carter and Schooler (1949) found this result only when settings were made from memory, not when direct matches were required. Ashley, Harper and Runyon (1951) obtained the original result when they hypnotized subjects and induced the belief that they were rich or poor.

The best known experiment showing effects of social pressures in a choice situation is that of Asch (1955). Subjects were shown a standard line and had to select from two others the one equal in length. Subjects performed in groups though in fact the only true subject was the one making the last judgement in the group, the rest being stooges primed to agree on an obviously false judgement. The genuine subjects showed stress and most conformed to the group judgement as the experiment continued. When debriefed afterwards, some admitted that they did not really believe that the line they had picked as equal really was equal; others rationalized by saying they thought the position they were sitting in had caused the lines to look different to them and some still claimed the lines had looked equal. It is difficult to decide the truth of this claim since it may reflect a need to preserve consistency. Though a recent report (Perrin and Spencer 1980) suggests the result may be difficult to replicate in less conforming cultures, the reality of conformity to social pressures in perception and other fields is well established, though the mechanism is uncertain from the available evidence.

Ease of perceiving
There appear to be no experiments associating nonsense syllables with reward, but Rigby and Rigby (1956) associated gain or loss of money with particular letters and found reward lowered the exposure duration to see the letters; loss of money had a slight effect in the same direction.

Related investigations have been carried out investigating the effects of individual differences in the value and importance of different objects or words. Postman, Bruner and McGinnies (1948) found thresholds for perceiving words were lower for words related to the personal values of the observers and also reported that erroneous guesses tended to be made from the same area of interest, implying a response bias effect. Solomon and Howes (1951) argued that the results could be explained by frequency of exposure to the words differing between subjects, but Postman and Schneider (1951) produced new data showing that value had an effect as well as frequency and had its strongest effect with low frequency words. This interaction of value and frequency implies they exert at least some of their effects through the same processing stage, and since it has been argued that frequency affects criterion setting, this supports the view that value does the same. McClelland and Liberman (1949) found that people with high need for achievement (measured by a questionnaire) saw achievement-related words more rapidly than those low in this motivation, an effect which again could be related to frequency of exposure, though there is no evidence to decide one way or the other. Atkinson and Walker (1956) demonstrated what appears to be a genuine perceptual effect of a personality-related motive, when they showed that people high in need for affiliation, when shown four pictures at high speed and asked to say which stood out, tended to report faces more often than those low in this motive. Objectively both groups should be equally familiar with faces, though possibly the former group pay more attention to them and discriminate more features because faces are more important to them. Unfortunately no evidence is reported on reports of faces when none were present because all the slides contained a face.

Summary of reward effects

Thus the evidence does suggest that association of some aspect of the input with reward will cause that aspect to be reported more readily. It is not necessary that any overt response be made and associated with the reward, or for the reward to be contingent on a response, or for reward to be anticipated when the test responses are made, or for exactly the same response to be made at the test as in the training period. All the evidence which has been considered could be explained in terms of changes in the criterion set for decisions in the type of model discussed in the last chapter and no evidence has been cited which suggests enhanced perceptual sensitivity or discrimination.

Association of punishment with a stimulus

Considering now the other side of the coin, there are several studies of punishment and perception of ambiguous faces, but the results are less consistent than those using reward. Punishment has always been known to be more variable in its effects than reward, and subjective strength of the punishment and attitudes toward it seem to be more important with punishment. In addition the possibility of avoidance or escape and of different expectations in the test situation further complicate the effects.

Ambiguous situations

There are several studies of punishment and ambiguous figure perception. Smith and Hochberg (1954) found weak evidence that the profile associated with electric shock was reported less often. Ayllon and Sommer (1956) used a tactile version and gave the shock three seconds later. They obtained fewer reports of the shocked profile by those who reported the shock as mildly unpleasant and a slight reversal of this effect in those who reported it was moderately or very unpleasant. McNamara *et al.* (1958) found no effect with shock delayed in this way, but if it was administered concurrently when the subjects felt the shape a second time (to allow feeling it without distraction the first time) then there was a strong tendency to report the unpunished profile, increasing as the shock level increased. However, if there was a chance to escape the shock, then the punished profile tended to be reported, the tendency being greater at lower shock levels. Smith and Hochberg had used concurrent and unavoidable shock, so overall the results suggest that unavoidable shocks produce defence (reluctance to see the punished aspect) and avoidable ones produce sensitization. Smith and Hochberg left their subjects in doubt about whether shocks would occur during the test, Ayllon and Sommer made it clear there would be no more and McNamara *et al.* give no indication of their procedure in this respect, so the effect of this variable is uncertain. Solley and Long (1958, Experiment 2) used removal of money as a punishment in the same type of experiment and found a tendency to report the punished aspect (loss of money followed the subjects' repetition of the name uttered by the experimenter, and was not expected in the test, so neither of these factors explains the reversed result). Solley and Engel (1960) got no clear effects of punishment and some indications that the effects changed with the age of the children, and Sommer (1956a, b) got no effect of punishment even when it depended on the responses, so was avoidable.

Size judgements
As already indicated, McNamara (1959) tested length judgements and found punishment of overestimation or underestimation produced a trend in the opposite direction. Bruner and Postman (1946) got their subjects to set a circle of light to match the size of a plastic dish then gave them the task of retrieving the dish from a grid which delivered shocks. There were no differences from a control group, which received no shocks, in the estimations made after the retrieval task, but when the experimenters announced that no further shocks would be given, the previously shocked group showed a marked overestimation. The cessation of shocks seems to

have acted like a strong reward on the size estimates.

Ease of perceiving

There are many studies of the effect of association with electric shock on the perception of nonsense syllables. Also Hochberg and Brooks (1958) found that association with an unpleasant noise reduced the frequency with which a figure was reported. Lazarus and McCleary (1951), in a follow-up study to that of McGinnies described below, demonstrated that a Galvanic Skin Response could occur to syllables which had been associated with shock at exposures too short for subjects to report what the syllables were. However there was no indication of difficulty in seeing the shocked syllables compared with syllables not associated with shock (tested in a ten-choice recognition task) and in fact there was a slight tendency in the opposite direction. Subjects were led to continue expecting shock during the test and Lysak (1954) showed that when this was so, and shocks were still given for the critical stimuli/ responses in the test session, these syllables were seen less easily, but the reverse occurred when subjects knew that no more shocks would occur. However, Chapman and Feather (1972) used shapes and obtained faster perception of shocked shapes even when some shocks were given for making the critical responses in the test session, and Pustell (1957), also using shapes but no shock in the test session, obtained a similar result in male subjects and the reverse in females, so this variable does not seem to be critical. Pustell suggested that the subjective level of shock could be the reason for the sex difference. Reece (1954) showed that when no escape from shock was possible, the shock associated syllables were more difficult to see, but when escape was possible they were seen as quickly as in a neutral condition. Dulany (1957) showed that when shock depended on the response, the shocked response declined in frequency.

Several of the latter group of studies show sensitization, though with exceptions such as when shock was still expected in the test session by Lysak's subjects and Pustell's female subjects and Reece's no-escape condition, even though this was not obviously different from several of the other experiments. The ambiguous face studies are rather less consistent, but more unpleasant shock and the possibility of escape seem to induce faster perception. It should be noted that anticipation of an unavoidable punishment may also be beneficial, for example, in enabling preparation to receive the shock. Certainly the data are far from consistent and not all the relevant variables seem to have been identified. Once again sensitivity and bias changes cannot be distinguished.

Turning to the effects of pre-existing unpleasantness of the stimulus on perception, a slightly clearer picture emerges. The classic experiment of McGinnies (1949) already referred to will serve as a starting point. He presented words, some neutral and others emotive (mainly sexually related and taboo in polite conversation at that time, like penis, whore and raped). These were presented at short exposures increasing on successive trials until the word was correctly reported. Not only were the required exposure times for the emotive words longer, but recordings of Galvanic Skin Responses (an indication of emotion) showed that the emotive words produced greater GSRs than neutral ones before subjects could report them. The result caused major problems for many theorists who asked how aspects of words which seemed to require detailed knowledge could be seen before the words could be seen, but at that time perception was not generally conceived as a sequence of processes where such effects could occur but as an all or none event (see Erdelyi 1974, for a discussion of this issue). This phenomenon, with one measure showing perception while the more usual one of verbal report does not, is known as subception or subliminal perception, and I have discussed in Chapter 5 the considerable body of evidence that the meanings of words can have effects even when the observers are unaware that any word has been presented. The further effect observed by McGinnies, that subliminally perceived words which evoke unpleasant emotions take longer to perceive at a conscious level, was called by him perceptual defence. As we shall see, the contrary result of quicker perception of emotive stimuli (known as perceptual vigilance) has also been observed, and it is not clear what situations will produce which result, though personality and degree of unpleasantness seem to be important factors (Eriksen 1951; Carpenter, Wiener and Carpenter 1956) and a distinction between repressors and sensitizers helps to explain some of the discrepancies (Byrne 1961).

A number of alternative explanations of the effects observed by McGinnies have been advanced. Solomon and Howes (1951), in an early response, suggested that taboo words were rarer than neutral ones so the effect was really a probability effect, and that subjects would be unwilling to name taboo words until certain (a caution effect) and finally that the GSR effects could occur because any one of several possible interpretations might evoke them (it was unclear why this should be restricted to the emotive words). Postman, Bronson and Gropper (1953) did find that warning subjects about the words eliminated the effect, but Cowen and Beier (1954) found such a warning did not eliminate the effect; other tests are equally conflicting. Several experiments described below where this factor could not be operating have found, contrary to McGinnies, that thresholds were *lower* for the emotive words, so it seems possible that this factor may have affected McGinnies's result. Elimination of possible probability effects has also tended to produce vigilance rather than defence. However, in a reply to Solomon and Howes, McGinnies and Sherman (1952) reported an experiment in which clearly presented taboo words raised the threshold for neutral words presented after them, thus demonstrating that the arousal of unpleasant emotion independently of the object to be perceived could have an effect. Dixon (1958) and Hardy and Legge (1968) have later demonstrated a similar effect of taboo or unpleasant emotive words on detection of a light and these results are not of course open to Solomon and Howes's frequency argument. However, Zajonc and Dorfman (1965) conditioned responses in animals to a tone, then added a light which had been associated with shock; the conditioned responses then occurred to tones of lower intensity.

An improvement in design over the straightforward identification experiment, to avoid the complication of response bias, has been to use a forced choice situation in which the subjects must select from a pair of possibilities the word which they believe has just been presented. Dorfman, Grossberg and Kroeker (1965) and Dorfman (1970) found that when the choice was between a neutral and taboo word guessing rates favoured neutral responses when no word had actually been presented, but accuracy for the perception of presented taboo words was actually superior to that for neutral ones once the exposure exceeded 30 ms. However, this could be due to the taboo word raising the threshold for the neutral word rather than a low threshold for the emotive word. Bootzin and Natsoulas (1965) found that when the choice was between a pair of words both of which were neutral or both of which were taboo, perception was more accurate in the former case.

Broadbent and Gregory (1967) controlled pleasantness and probability and found that unpleasant words were harder to hear than neutral ones but pleasant words were also harder to hear than neutral ones if they were common but not if they were uncommon.

Hence the effect of unpleasantness was clear-cut but not that of pleasantness. However, Fulkerson (1957) found a similar complication for taboo words, which had lower thresholds than neutral ones if rare, but higher thresholds than neutral ones if common. Gilchrist, Ludeman and Lysak (1954) found the reverse – common pleasant and unpleasant words being easier to see than neutral ones. Sales and Haber (1968) asked subjects to report all the letters they saw or to guess the word and found even in the former case that performance was worse on taboo words than on rare or frequent non-emotive ones. Subjects who were better on the non-emotive words were also better on the emotive ones, which hardly supports a response–suppression explanation. The effects were also present on the first exposure, also unlikely if they are due to response suppression. There is thus reasonable consistency in the finding that perceptual thresholds are higher for taboo words; there is less evidence for other unpleasant words and it is less consistent. Since perceiving the word makes the unpleasantness unavoidable, this seems to fit the pattern of results suggested earlier where it was concluded that unavoidable unpleasant consequences produce avoidance of the associated stimulus.

There are no studies of the relation between major personal dislikes and perceptual sensitivity to related stimuli.

Conclusions concerning effects of reward and punishment: perceptual effects or response bias?

I have now outlined several different types of investigation of the effects of reward and punishment on subsequent perception. There are many apparent inconsistencies and obscurities in the data but the weight of the evidence suggests that association of some aspect of a stimulus or some stimuli with reward or individual interest facilitates perception, but none of the reward studies excludes the possibility that these effects are other than changes in response biases. Unpleasant associations do not, however, always have the opposite effect. It seems that where the unpleasantness is not too great and rapid perception permits avoidance or escape, sensitization will occur, but if the consequences are too awful and unavoidable, perception of the associated stimulus is avoided. The question that remains concerns the nature of these effects. Few studies have used methods which enable the separation of sensitivity and response bias, still less methods which could narrow the effects down to a particular part of the perceptual process. Enough studies have exercised sufficient control over response suppression to conclude that this can be ruled out as a complete explanation of the emotive word results, but this does not of course rule out the possibility of higher criteria being set for decisions in the case of emotive words, which would produce misidentifications of emotive words as non-emotive words. However, what evidence there is suggests the effects are not response bias effects. In the forced-choice task used by Dorfman, Grossberg and Kroeker (1965) there was a tendency to increased caution in reporting taboo words, but nevertheless there was still an *increased d'* for the taboo words. Chapman and Feather (1972) also obtained increased d' to shock-associated words together with increased caution. Furthermore, McGinnies noted in his experiment that errors to neutral stimuli often preserved some of the letters while errors to emotive stimuli were very unlike the original, and Newbigging (1961) has observed that fewer letters are identified at the same exposure for emotive words, suggesting perceptual blocking. Finally, Broadbent and Gregory (1967), in the experiment already quoted, found no evidence that the difficulty of perceiving unpleasant words (or pleasant ones) was due to a low probability of giving them as errors (that is of low response bias to them). Hence they concluded that the effect is different from the probability effect and must involve some impairment of the intake of perceptual information. Thus there is enough evidence to support the view that the sensitizing and desensitizing effects of unpleasant emotion on perception are not due solely to changes in response criterion, though there is little similar evidence available concerning the effects of pleasant emotion. Exactly where the effect lies requires some more sophisticated experiments, for example, looking at patterns of interaction and effects on reaction time, especially on the LOC, none of which exists at present. Further clarification is needed also concerning the conditions which produce vigilance to unpleasant stimuli and those which produce defence.

Effects of non-specific variation in arousal on perception

The results discussed so far are almost all concerned with specific motivational pressures to perform in a particular way. We may also be concerned with the effect of general differences in the internal state of the subject on perceptual performance, such as differences in personality, anxiety, current mood and level of arousal. Evidence on the relation between these factors and the kind of perceptual performance we have been concerned with is not common, but some relevant findings on more general effects of these variables are suggestive and indicate that further experiments would be worth doing. Some results have been quoted above indicating that a task-irrelevant emotive stimulus may impair sensitivity to a task-relevant stimulus (Gilchrist, Ludeman and Lysak 1954; Dixon 1958; Hardy and Legge 1968).

An attempt is often made to unify these variables under the general heading of arousal but it is very doubtful whether such unification is justified and several different types of arousal probably exist. Some of the distinctions which have been suggested are between trait arousal (fairly permanent personality differences, with extraverts low and introverts high on arousal) and state arousal (sometimes called activation) or between arousal (extraversion as a trait or activation as a state) and anxiety (neuroticism as a trait and state anxiety as a state) or between behavioural, cortical and autonomic arousal and between arousal associated with attention to incoming information and arousal associated with active response making.

Several results have suggested that high arousal either narrows attention to dominant information or causes more superficial processing (which could be a special case of the first suggestion). Hockey (1970) showed that in a dual-task situation in which subjects were required to track a moving point with a pointer and press buttons in response to lights on the periphery of the field, subjects performing in noisy conditions improved on the main tracking task and were impaired on the secondary light detection task. A similar result occurred with heat and incentives, but subjects who had been deprived of sleep showed the reverse effect. If the importance of the tasks was reversed by changing the instruction, the effect also reversed. However, it should be noted that Forster and Grierson (1978) have not managed to replicate this result when a small change was made in the tracking task.

Mueller (1976), using memory tasks, has found that anxious subjects do less well than less anxious ones in recalling faces after they had to judge 'deep' characteristics like honesty, but were no worse after they had to judge superficial ones like length of nose. Consequently anxious subjects seem less able to make use of the deep characteristics of faces. Mueller has also shown that anxious subjects make less use of the meanings of words in recalling them.

Some evidence is beginning to emerge showing that different personality types, such as extraverts and introverts, concentrate on different types of information in prose, either pictorial, temporal or some other type (Riding 1979).

Most of this evidence does not directly involve perceptual identification. Even Mueller's experiment with faces does not enable us to say that the effect occurred at the perceptual stage. However, there is enough evidence of effects of these variables on performance to suggest that a careful investigation is desirable of relations between perceptual performance, especially the type and range of features attended to, and such variables as personality and current level of arousal, environmental stresses and drug effects. As with the more specifically perceptual investigations we have been considering, it would be necessary to try and pinpoint exactly which parts of the perceptual processes were affected in each case.

9 Learning and knowledge

The questions

Quite obviously many of the aspects of perceptual identification which have been described must be affected by or depend upon learning or maturity of the organism. Most perceptual tasks show improvement from birth at least up to the age of six years. The problems are to decide what abilities are present at birth, in which tasks improvement occurs with age, and in the cases where improvement does occur whether this is due to maturation or experience. Where improvement does occur we also want to know which components of the task are affected and how they are affected. A further question concerns the possible existence of sensitive periods, during which some ability has to be developed if it is to develop properly so that experience which comes too late is useless.

The first three questions cover the traditional argument as to how far perception is innate and how far learned, and the experimental work to be considered is mainly concerned with attempting to answer these, rather than the more precise, questions about changes in specific processes. I shall consider the questions in relation to three main aspects of perception which have been identified in previous chapters:

1   The perception of objects in space or on a background, including figure–ground differentiation, perception of distance and the constancies. The evidence will naturally be almost entirely drawn from visual perception.
2   The processes leading to object identification, such as selective attention, holistic or analytic processing, feature analysis, automatic and parallel processing.
3   The derivation and nature of the models of the world possessed by the perceiver, including the learning of conceptual categories, combining information from different senses and use of context to guide top-down processing.

There has been a long and indecisive controversy over whether perception in general is learned or innate, but the question is of course much too imprecise to permit of an answer. The *Gestalt* psychologists argued that no learning was needed and Gibson has implied that little or no learning is necessary to extract the structure on which in his view perception of space depends in normal viewing conditions. The Transactionalists, on the other hand, have argued that past experience determines the interpretation of the ambiguous input and Hebb (1949) has put the argument for learning in its starkest form by suggesting that the baby must learn even to identify a simple shape like a triangle by building up a sequence of activity in the brain, initially dependent on scanning the corners of the shape in order and later triggered by a single element of the sequence.

Evidence on these issues has been derived from studies of the physiological and behavioural effects of early deprivation or special experience, adaptation to distorted inputs and of course direct observation of the abilities of infants and older children. I shall discuss the three areas distinguished above in turn, though the evidence often does not clearly apply to one of them rather than another. Naturally the methods which have been used in developing the theoretical approaches toward perception in the mature organism are not usually readily applicable to infants, so indirect evidence, such as that from learning, often has to be used to infer processes.

Scene perception

Recovery from early blindness

Several reports on recovery from early blindness were collected by von Senden and used by Hebb (1949) in support of his case for the importance of learning in perception. However, most of the evidence was anecdotal and unreliable. A better controlled recent study is that by Gregory and Wallace (1963), who found very rapid acquisition of many perceptual abilities such as visual guidance for movement, and transfer from tactile experience which was shown by the patient's ability to identify upper case letters which he had been taught by touch, but not lower case ones, which he had not been taught. However, Gregory and Wallace found that the early promise was not sustained. More complex perceptual tasks which certainly require learning, such as reading, proved very hard and the patient became very depressed, as happened in many of the cases reported by von Senden. The investigators point out that the successful habits of a lifetime had to be superseded and that evidence from such cases is not directly relevant to the issues of perceptual learning in the normal infant. An experiment by Drever (1955), showing that the earlier blindness occurs, the better performance is on tactile discrimination, neatly complements the visual evidence, and Rauschecher and Harris (1981) have found that kittens deprived of vision had more neurons responsive to auditory stimuli.

Deprivation studies on animals

Controlled studies of early deprivation naturally have to be carried out on animals. Prolonged deprivation of all light produces neural damage and some species are more vulnerable than others. Deprivation of patterned light (by wearing opaque diffusing goggles) is a more satisfactory technique (Gregory and Wallace's patient had very similar pre-operative visual experience to this). E. Gibson (1969), in her invaluable book on perceptual learning and development, concludes that such experiments have not however answered many questions. A departure from the normal environment of the species 'deprives the organism of typical stimulation and thus results in organic degeneration, emotional maladjustment, the supplanting of behaviour controlled by one kind of sensory information with behaviour controlled by another and the failure of the usual differentiations to develop'. Gregory and Wallace might have written that too. Consequently the only easily interpreted evidence from such experiments is when an ability is found to survive the deprivation and when this does happen it is not possible to generalize from one species to another.

Rats appear to be unimpaired in depth and form perception unless the deprivation is for about ten months and even then rapid recovery occurred. Similarly, kittens recovered depth perception after four weeks in darkness and monkeys did the same after two months deprivation of pattern vision, but chicks were grossly impaired in form discrimination after ten weeks in darkness. Moreover, in the cases where recovery occurred after the deprivation ended, general exposure to light was all that was needed, without specific experience of the test situation. These data show that specific learning is not necessary in several species for depth perception and separation of figure from ground, and agree with the conclusions from Gregory and Wallace's patient.

Neurophysiological studies

The neurophysiological evidence is intriguing. Hubel and Wiesel (1963) examined units in the cortex of a kitten as soon as its eyes opened and found the pattern of edge and line detectors virtually identical to that in the adult cat. Keeping both eyes closed for a time had some effects but left at least two-thirds of the neurons still responsive, though somewhat sluggish (Wiesel and Hubel 1965). Keeping one eye closed for a time between the ages of four and sixteen weeks could eliminate responses through that eye (Hubel and Wiesel 1970) and prevent visual guidance of paw placement and pattern vision (Dews and Wiesel 1970). Closing an eye after the kitten was four months old had no effect. However, Smith (1981) showed some recovery in the deprived eye when it had to be used because the previously open eye was then deprived of vision, so the effect is not totally irreversible; he refers to similar evidence from humans with impaired vision. Hubel and Wiesel (1970) allowed only one eye to be open, and found this destroyed responses in the closed eye so there was no binocular perception though all else was normal. Hence binocular disparity cues for depth were no longer extracted. Banks, Aslin and Letson (1975) showed similar results in humans who had strabismus at birth. The earlier a correction was made by surgery (up to at least three years of age) the better was the development of binocular perception.

Blakemore (1973) kept kittens in an environment consisting solely of vertical or solely of horizontal lines from two weeks of age to five and a half months and examined responses in the cortex. Units responded only to orientations around the one experienced and animals behaved as if blind to the non-experienced orientation. This and the monocular deprivation studies suggest that there are initially cells able to respond to all the visual orientations, but if no appropriate input occurs they adapt to another orientation. Since no dead cells were observed, modification rather than elimination was indicated.

To complicate the picture Stryker and Sherk (1975) repeated Blakemore's experiments with better controls for possible experimenter bias, due to knowing how each animal had been reared, and sampled more units; they found units responsive to all orientations. In the same paper they refer briefly to unpublished data from an experiment in which kittens were reared with goggles which presented a different and restricted set of orientations to each eye and which did show the Blakemore effect. Also, Leventhal and Hirsch (1975) have found that exposure to horizontal and vertical lines prevents the appearance of any units responsive to diagonals, but units responsive to horizontal and vertical lines can be found even after exposure to diagonals only; this suggests that the units responsive to horizontals and verticals are more basic or robust.

Effects of specific experience

Studies of other effects of specific variation in the environment of animals have looked at the effect on subsequent discrimination of exposure to cut-out or painted geometric shapes in the home cage (Gibson and Walk 1960). The effects were neither large nor consistent, nor was there any benefit if the test stimuli were very different from those in the cage (horizontal and vertical stripes in the test, triangles and circles in the cage) (Gibson *et al.* 1958). Gibson (1969) interprets the results as indicating a biasing of attention to shape features, cut-out shapes being more effective because depth cues at the edges attracted more attention. More evidence is needed on the effect of the similarity of the cage and the test patterns.

Held and Hein (1963) kept kittens in the dark for eight weeks and then one group walked around in a lighted environment while the others were pulled round. The first (active) group performed better on the visual cliff and the authors argued in consequence that active experience was necessary for adequate perceptual development. However, Miller and Walk (1975) refined the experiment; they tested animals raised for only eighteen days in the dark then trained for three hours a day up until four weeks of age. They found that the active group was superior only on the very first test. A light-reared group was superior to both active and passive dark-reared animals and a dark-reared group was inferior to all others. The authors concluded that depth discrimination is innate but can be improved with experience.

Direct investigations of the effects of training on humans' ability to make distance estimates have been carried out by Gibson and Bergman (1954), Gibson, Bergman and Purdy (1955) and Wohlwill

(1964). Gibson *et al.* trained subjects to estimate distances in yards and found this improved performance in subsequent tests of the same sort but not on setting a target to match the distance of a standard. This suggests that all that was learned was to calibrate a scale in yards with distance on the ground rather than better distance perception. Wohlwill looked at the effect of training on bisection performance and found some, but not a dramatic, effect.

Cultural differences

Another type of evidence of the effects of experience in humans comes from comparing people raised in different cultures or occasional cases of children raised in unusually deprived conditions or brought up by animals. The latter type of evidence is usually fairly unreliable. It has been reported that children reared by wild animals show unusual abilities of smell or night vision (see Zingg 1940, for a review).

The cross-cultural evidence consists mainly of investigations of responses to visual illusions and other two-dimensional patterns or pictures rather than perception in real three-dimensional situations. No differences in the efficiency of the basic sensory systems have been found and it seems likely that all cultures must be fairly adept at getting around in a three-dimensional world and any differences in three-dimensional perception would depend rather closely on the exact relation between experience and the test situation. Turnbull (1961) reports that a pygmy brought up in the forest, and consequently without experience of seeing over long distances, when he was taken to the plains believed a distant herd of cows were ants, thus demonstrating lack of size constancy. Cole and Scribner (1974, Chapter 4) report a similar observation of a Kpelle child who thought that distant oil tankers were small boats. However size constancy does not operate over very long distances in the same way as over shorter ones. In the latter case we do not notice the change in projected size, but objects at greater distances do actually look small when we know they are not. Clearly it was the latter experience which was not familiar to the pygmy and the girl. Controlled measures of size constancy over shorter distances give a different picture. Thouless (1933) and Beveridge (1935) measured regression to the real object, which is the failure to match projected retinal sizes and shapes due to taking real (constant) size and shape into account. They found that Indian and West African students, respectively, showed more such regression (that is, less ability to discount distance and match retinal shape and size) than British ones but Mundy Castle and Nelson (1962) got the reverse result with Knysma forest dwellers (an isolated white group) in South Africa. Winter (1967) showed that size constancy measured by matching shapes at different distances up to 12 m decreased from Kalahari bushmen to South African whites to Bantu to optometry students, and Bantu women showed more constancy than European women and men the reverse. There is therefore no consistent evidence for a relation between type of experience and size constancy, but there were differences in the tasks used, most requiring neglect of real size and shape, while Winter requiring matching of these.

The Transactionalists, it will be recalled, claimed that some ambiguous inputs, such as the Ames room, are interpreted as three-dimensional regular patterns due to experience. Consequently, absence of the appropriate experience should reduce the illusion. Stewart (1973) found that Tonga children were less likely to see the room as normal than Europeans. Allport and Pettigrew (1957) investigated perception of the Ames trapezoidal window illusion by Zulus. This illusion occurs when a trapezoidal surface painted on both sides to look like a window viewed from an angle (Figure 32) is rotated. The observer usually sees a rectangular window oscillating from one side to the other, an interpretation which avoids the conflict which would occur when the larger edge was seen as further away. The illusion is assumed to depend on experience of a 'carpentered environment' with lots of right angles. Zulus have little experience of such an environment and did show reduced susceptibility to the illusion, but only in the most difficult viewing condition where the illusion is strongest for those who experience it (monocular viewing from 6 m).

Some of the geometric illusions too are best explained as due to interpreting two-dimensional patterns as representations of three-dimensional objects, so another popular area of research has been

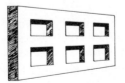

Figure 32 *The Ames trapezoidal window (after Ames 1951)*

to investigate the perception of illusions in different cultures. Stewart, in the study mentioned above, found the Tonga children less susceptible to the Mueller–Lyer illusion as well as to the Ames room and several other studies support the view that lack of experience of a carpentered environment with its parallels and corners will reduce the illusions. However, part of the explanation for these reduced effects could lie in differences in perception of two-dimensional representations in general which have no particular implications for three-dimensional perception. Cole and Scribner (1974) and Deregowski (1980) review these areas of research. Both recognition of objects in pictures and perception of depth in pictures may be reduced in those unfamiliar with two-dimensional representations. European five year olds show similar inadequacies. However, presenting the picture on a more familiar material, such as cloth (Deregowski, Muldrow and Muldrow 1972), will improve performance. The most powerful and earliest developed cues for depth in three-dimensional scenes, binocular disparity and motion parallax gradients, must be ignored in a two-dimensional representation because they prove there is no depth, and it seems possible that the weaker cues of relative size, perspective, overlap, elevation and so on may not be much used when the others are available in a three-dimensional environment and hence observers need to learn to attend to them in two-dimensional representations. Furthermore, Hagen and Jones (1978) have shown that the pictures which have been used in many of the cross-cultural studies did not produce very reliable judgements of depth in sophisticated observers – they were rather crudely drawn outline drawings rather than veridical copies of real scenes.

Two studies have looked at reproduction of three-dimensional objects. Jahoda (1979) showed that constructing shapes from blocks to match a model which had to be remembered was worse in Ghanaian than in Scottish children only when working from a photograph or line drawing and not when working from a three-dimensional model. On another task of assembling pieces to form a two-dimensional shape the Ghanaians were also worse, but whether or not this was owing to experience of such tasks as jigsaw puzzles is not clear. Serpell (1979) presents results strongly favouring an explanation of differences in terms of specific experience. Zambian children were better at reproducing wire models, of which they have plenty of experience (the boys especially), while Scottish children were superior when copying drawings. Obviously these differences could be due to more than perception; what they indicate is that differences between cultures, where they occur, are very likely owing to specific rather than general components of the task set.

Adaptation to distorted vision

Studies of adaptation by a normally reared human to changes in the nature of the perceptual input began with Stratton's (1896, 1897) wearing of inverting spectacles for an extended period. I. Kohler (1964) and his associates at Innsbruck have carried out a large number of studies of this type, and others such as Held, Harris and Rock have carried out a large number of investigations of less drastic distortions, such as lateral displacement, curving of straight vertical lines and size changes. Although a good deal of the interest in these studies is related to how quickly movements can be recalibrated to match the distorted input, reports of perceptual experience are interesting but not always completely enlightening. Motor co-ordination adjusts quite quickly, and Kohler's experiments have shown ability to ski, fence and cycle while wearing the distorting device. The subjects also report that after a while the world begins intermittently to look the right way up, for example, when touching an object or viewing something like a lighted candle where the top is unambiguous. When the distorting device is removed the world may appear inverted again. The studies using less drastic (quantitative rather than qualitative) distortions suggest a number of important facts about perception in general rather than learning in particular:

1   Constant distortions, such as colour fringes at all contours which are produced by distorting prisms, are not seen at all after a short period of experience, and appear in complementary colours when the prisms are removed. Thus stimulation enters awareness only when it is discrepant with expectation and it is perceived in relation to that expectation.

2   The important features are relational, not absolute, and are not extracted from a static image. A line is not seen as straight or vertical because it projects a straight vertical line on the retina, but because it is transformed in a certain way when the eye moves. Thus Held found that subjects wearing spectacles which made all vertical lines into concave to the left curves learned to

see these lines as straight even when they were exposed only to an environment of spots without any straight lines. The only source of such adaptation would be the pattern of flow of the spots as the head moved up and down, which would be along the curve induced by the distortion and not up and down. Clearly such regularities determine what is seen. It is even possible to adapt when the top half of the scene is distorted in one way and the bottom half in another, showing that expectations can be modified according to the direction in which the eye is looking (Kohler 1964).

3   Ability to adapt depends on phylogenetic level. Humans can, monkeys can but less easily (Foley 1940), hens cannot (Pfister, quoted in Rock 1966, p. 52; Hess 1956) and amphibians cannot, as is shown when their eyes are surgically rotated and they never learn to strike for flies in the new direction (Sperry 1951). There is, however, some evidence for an inborn but adjustable prefer-ence for the normal relation between location and position of stimulation on the eye. Bishop (quoted in Rock 1966, p. 53) put inverting spectacles on kittens reared in darkness until they were two months old and they showed little difficulty compared with normals in moving around, though they improved somewhat less rapidly. When both groups had their condition reversed, the controls were somewhat more impaired by the change but not much. Schlodtmann (1902) found phosphenes (light sensations) elicited by pressing the eyeball in children blind from birth were reported as lying in the direction in which corresponding stimu-lation by light would appear to lie. Once more, therefore we have evidence for a preferred innate structure, which can adapt to different situations if required.

4   Active interaction with the environment facilitates adaptation, probably by providing more information on the nature of the distortion.

5   Far from vision depending on touch, as empiricists at one time argued it must for knowledge about distance, vision is dominant and objects are felt where they are seen or felt to be the size they appear to be to vision (Rock 1966).

Perceptual development in infants

In recent years direct studies of basic perceptual abilities in human infants as well as animals have been carried out successfully and provided us with much more straightforward information than the indirect evidence from the types of investigation I have been discussing. These direct studies confirm the conclusions from the indirect evidence that many basic perceptual abilities are present at birth or develop very quickly and that we need to look for the effects of experience to more complex factors, such as attentional strategies, the analysis and synthesis of feature information and the development of schemata or models of the world.

In addition there is now more information available about the development of the human nervous system. Myelinization in the cortex and development of the fovea are not complete until around the fourth month after birth, so efficient transmission of information cannot occur before this age, and the visual cortex is not completely mature until about ten years of age. Electrical activity in the retina is barely present at birth and increases during the first year and regular electrical activity in the brain (the electroencephalograph) develops in the second to fourth month. Accommodation of the lens to focus the image sharply does not reach adult standard until three months after birth and convergence not until seven to eight months. While acuity is much better than was once supposed it is still below adult levels (Fantz and Ordy 1959).

A number of different methods have been employed in investigating the abilities of human infants. One, pioneered by Fantz, is to present a pair of stimuli and examine the time spent looking at each. In a modification, single stimuli can be presented and a variety of behavioural measures taken, such as time spent looking, heart rate, movement and the effect on these measures of changing the stimulus. Interest declines with repeated presentation, as shown by habituation of the measures, but will recover if the new stimulus is perceived as different. Consequently, ability to discriminate the old and new stimuli can be measured. Another method, developed by Bower, used an operant conditioning technique whereby the infant is rewarded in some way, such as a peek-a-booing adult, for a simple head turning or sucking response to a particular stimulus and the generalization of the response to other stimuli is tested to determine which aspects are important. With older children, matching and discrimination tests have been used by investigators such as Eleanor Gibson and Eliane Vurpillot to determine which aspects of patterns are attended to by the child.

Fantz (1961, 1963) has shown that very young babies prefer patterns to plain surfaces, even if the latter are coloured, particularly face-like patterns. However, at under one month of age no distinctions are made between correctly organized faces and scrambled ones, suggesting that relations between the elements are unimportant at this stage. Three-dimensional objects are preferred to two-dimensional representations at one to six months. Held, Birch and Gwiazda (1980) showed use of binocular disparity increased rapidly from four to five months of age. Bower, Broughton and Moore (1970a, b) have shown reaching for a real object at six to eleven days and no reaching toward a photograph of the object, and claimed that discrimination of the object's size is indicated by finger–thumb separation, but other investigators claim that reaching does not appear until much later.

Using the operant conditioning method, Bower (1964, 1965, 1966a, b) has demonstrated that both size and shape constancy are present at one month old. He conditioned a response to a single shape then tested for its occurrence to other shapes. In the size constancy experiment a cube of 30 cm side at a distance of 1 m was used, and for the generalization test the same cube at 2.7 m and a 90 cm cube at 1 or 2.7 m. All these elicited fewer responses than the original stimulus and the 90 cm cube at 2.7 m elicited fewest of all, implying that both size and distance changes were detected. Walters and Walk (in Walk 1976) also showed that at six to seven months babies lowered towards the visual cliff put out a hand to save themselves earlier on the shallow than on the deep side and Mackenzie and Day (1972) showed that infants of six to twenty weeks look more at a nearer object, and Bower *et al.* (1970c) showed that a twenty day old infant will make defensive reactions to an approaching object when it gets close. This occurred even with one eye closed, but did not occur in response to equivalent pictures on a screen, so Bower concluded that motion parallax was the critical cue for distance. A similar conclusion had been drawn from visual cliff experiments with rats by Walk and Gibson (1961), who put larger check patterns under the deeper side to project the same visual angle and found animals still preferred the shallow side. However, more recent work, while confirming that textured patterns produce better discrimination than plain ones, has also shown that some check sizes are treated as indicating a near or a far surface, whatever their true distance, and has thus thrown the earlier conclusions into some disarray (Walk 1976).

In the shape constancy experiment Bower (1966a) used a rectangular board turned at 45° so that the image projected was a trapezium. He tested response generalization to the same board in the fronto-parallel plane, a trapezoid in this plane yielding the same projected shape, and the trapezoid at 45°. The trapezoid elicited far fewer responses than the same board at a different angle.

Thus it is quite clear that no lengthy learning is needed to interpret the retinal image but rather that objects are seen as separate objects in space, and depth and distance perception are quite well developed in very young infants, who presumably use the type of cue suggested by Gibson, such as motion parallax and binocular disparity, though Walk's recent results suggest that size cues can override this. However it does not of course follow either that performance would be as good as that of adults if it could be tested adequately, nor that infants see the more distant parts of the scene as adults do. Experiments examining the ability to estimate distance and size in older children and adults have shown strong age effects. Beyrl (1926) and Zeigler and Leibowitz (1957) found that children made larger and larger underestimates and ones which diverged more from those of adults at distances over 18 m. Harway (1963) got subjects to estimate successive one foot distances across a field and found that children of five to ten years behaved similarly and showed a bigger effect of distance, judgements being closer to visual angle matches, than twelve year olds and adults. Wohlwill (1963) got subjects to bisect a 90 cm distance stretching away from them, and varied the texture of the surface. There was a change from setting the midpoint too near (underconstancy or overuse of the visual angle) to setting it too far away as age increased from five to sixteen. Texture affected all groups alike, with the exception of the texture with maximal density and regularity, suggesting that it is used at all ages. In another experiment, Wohlwill (1965) found underconstancy in all subjects, decreasing with age, especially from thirteen years onward, and found no difference in the effects of texture with age. Hence the results agree in showing improvement in size and distance estimates as age increases, with the improvement accelerating at adolescence, which suggests it may be related to the development of spatial ability, but no change in use of one major cue.

Development of picture perception

The remaining source of evidence for the development of ability to segregate the fields and isolate objects comes from studies of picture perception, already discussed briefly in connection with the cross-cultural studies. Eye movements in scanning pictures have been studied in addition to ability to interpret pictures correctly.

Evidence on the ability to interpret pictures correctly as representations is somewhat mixed. Some of the descriptions suggest piecemeal observation in young children without integration and others suggest misinterpretation of the overall shape without concern for the critical details. These may both be ways of coping with complexity. Potter (1966) says that young children do well when 'only one leap from stimulus to hypothesis is required – and when there is one simple object to be identified' but not when integration of evidence is needed. Judging from the evidence of Hochberg and Brooks (1962), even a young child of nineteen months can recognize pictures of single objects with minimal previous experience of pictures; unfortunately they did not test the effect of making the main object harder to isolate or including more than one object.

Children under five make only limited use of depth cues in pictures. Jahoda and McGurk (1974) found that elevation of objects in the field was the main cue used and adding line perspective and density gradients had only a small additional effect. Leibowitz and Judish (1967) found children of this age did not demonstrate the Ponzo illusion, even when extra cues for depth were added. In the same vein Yonas and Hagen (1973) got children to pick the larger of two triangles presented either in a three-dimensional display or in a two-dimensional one. The children were less influenced by texture cues for distance than adults were and adversely affected by having to carry out the three-dimensional judgements monocularly and through a peep-hole instead of a rectangular hole. Hence binocular disparity and motion parallax seem to have been their main cues and these are, as has been pointed out above, not available in the two-dimensional display.

Studies of eye movements provide more precise indications of what is happening when a picture or pattern such as a geometric shape is presented to an observer. Very young infants show systematic scanning but it is restricted to one local feature such as the corner of a triangle. Older ones start to scan all round the triangle and select key features, suggesting that ability to segregate the whole figure has developed, as opposed to becoming locked on to one informative part (Salapatek and Kessen 1966). Mackworth and Bruner (1970) compared adults and six year old children in scanning more complex pictures and found adults fixated mainly on the parts which contained most information, while children were more likely to become fixed on a small part and to miss the important features. Hence once again we find a lack of controlled strategy which needs prior knowledge about meaning and importance.

Conclusions

Now to attempt to draw some conclusions in relation to the problems raised at the beginning of the chapter:

1 What spatial perception abilities are present at birth?
2 In what ways does improvement occur?
3 What is responsible for such improvement, maturation or learning?
4 When learning is important, what processes does it affect?

The evidence is fairly consistent in suggesting that perception of depth and constancy are present early even in species with a slow development. This also implies ability to separate objects from background. However, deprivation of appropriate conditions can distort or destroy the abilities and conversely a proper environment can develop and extend them. Constancy and distance perception over longer distances still improve up to adolescence in humans. Initially binocular disparity and motion parallax are the main sources of depth perception, but from five years onward there is more use of other cues which are necessary for perception of depth in pictures. It is not clear whether use of these is due to experiencing of pictures or whether it develops without such experience. The cross-cultural evidence on depth perception in pictures, which might answer this question, is unfortunately not clear-cut. Even if it were clear that experience of pictures is necessary before the depth cues are used, it would still be uncertain whether all that is required is a switching of attention to these, or some more fundamental learning process.

Object identification

Some of the evidence already discussed is also relevant to this issue, such as generalization from touch to vision in Gregory and Wallace's study, Bower's work on size and shape constancy which implies that some features of the input are ignored and others selected, and the demonstration of recognition of pictures of simple objects in a nineteen month old child (Hochberg and Brooks 1962). I shall now consider the available evidence concerning development of the component processes of object identification discussed in the preceding chapters, namely:

1 The method of representing objects – wholes or features.
2 Attention – selection, ability to carry out dual or multiple tasks.
3 Stages of processing.
4 Decision-making processes.

Object representation

Piaget (1955) has argued that there is no concept of a permanent object until eight months of age, because a child fails to look for an object covered by a cloth. However, Bower and Wishart (1972) have shown that with a different type of disappearance (turning out the light) infants do reach out for the vanished object. He and others such as Donaldson (1976) have suggested that the experiment with a cloth shows an inability to understand the possibility of two objects in the same place.

Wholes or features?

There is a dispute as to whether young children treat objects as unanalysed wholes or can abstract features. This is really two questions – do young children attend to global or local information, and do they separate different features such as shape, size and colour? On the first issue, it seems that young children have problems in taking into account more than one separate feature at a time (Vurpillot 1976a, b), as already noted in the discussion of picture perception above. Bower (1974) has shown that infants respond to isolated elements of a complex pattern rather than to the whole and will generalize their response to parts and not restrict them to the whole pattern until sixteen weeks of age. Zaporozhets (1965) has shown that children of three and four do not explore objects systematically and even five and six year olds tended to become locked on to a salient feature. As a result of these processes, children may miss differences between objects or concentrate on details ignoring the whole or on the whole ignoring the details. Hidden figures are very difficult for young children to see and ambiguous figures can be seen by them in only one way. Hence a picture of a cyclist made up of pieces of fruit cannot be seen as both (Elkind 1969). Whether the whole or the details is primary depends on the nature of the input. Vurpillot (1976b, p. 212) showed that the size of the elements was important in determining whether the whole or the parts was primary. Infants of four months were shown a cross made up of crosses until their attention habituated and then either a cross made up of squares or a square made up of crosses, to see which would be treated as a new stimulus and reactivate attention. They reacted to the second when the original figure was fairly small (that is a natural whole) and to the first when the original figure was fairly large.

On the second issue, the nature of children's representations of objects, Posner has argued that prototypes are a primitive form of concept and E. Gibson has described perceptual development as primarily a process of differentiation. Werner (1961) has put forward a similar view. Recent results have to some extent supported these views but have suggested some qualifications.

Many experiments on discrimination learning (which is one method of discovering how objects have been coded) have used a procedure known as the reversal shift or intra-dimensional shift (IDS). Subjects learn one response to white objects (for example) and another to black, ignoring whether they are large or small. They are then transferred to a new task in which the opposite response has to be made to the white and black objects, still ignoring size (IDS), or in the extra-dimensional shift they have to learn responses on a basis of size, ignoring brightness. It was originally claimed (Kendler and Kendler 1962) that young children and animals performed better on EDS than IDS, implying that they did not isolate the relevant feature but treated the objects as wholes (half the responses would continue to be correct in EDS and none in IDS). Older children and adults did better on the IDS, implying they used the same dimension of difference and simply reversed responses; the Kendlers suggested that linguistic labelling aided this process. However, later work using different features has shown that children as young as three years can be superior on the IDS (Esposito 1975), so the results depends in part on dimensional salience, which may differ between children and adults. Different dimensions may be salient for children and adults; younger children attend to colour rather than shape, for example, while the reverse is true in older children.

Several investigations of the child's handling of integral and separable combinations of features have suggested that five and six year old children treat as integral some combinations which children of ten and adults treat as separable. Shepp and Swartz (1976) examined children's sorting speed using correlated combinations or orthogonal combinations. As explained in Chapter 4, these respectively facilitate and impede sorting performance in adults compared with that involving a single dimension, but only when the two features are integral; no effects occur when they are separable. The six year old children showed these effects on combinations which are integral for adults, but they also showed them on combinations which are separable for adults (brightness and shape). However, it is possible that the children do separate the features but cannot select one and exclude the other, that is that this is a failure of selective attention. Other studies suggest that young children certainly can distinguish separate features when they have to.

Smith and Kemler (1977) showed that when given four stimuli which could be divided up into two pairs either on the basis of one feature or on overall similarity, the use of the feature as a basis for sorting increased from five to ten years, but even the younger children referred to features when justifying their choice. Kemler and Smith (1979) found that in a different task (two stimuli were presented requiring one of two responses, depending either on overall sameness versus difference in the one condition or on which of two separable dimensions the difference occurred on in the other condition) both five and ten year olds found the second (dimensional) rule easier. Finally Smith and Kemler (1978), using colour and size combinations, which are separable for adults, confirmed the finding of Shepp and Swartz described above, but in addition they showed that five year olds found sorting by dimensions easier than sorting by overall similarity. These results all indicate that the young children could and did use dimensions to some extent and did not simply treat the objects as unanalysed wholes. Smith and Kemler conclude that young children are in process of learning to distinguish separate features when they have to. Other evidence can be cited in support of the view that still younger children than these five year olds can separate dimensions. Bower's results already described indicate that generalization of response depends on similarity of certain features and not others. Carey and Diamond (1977) using faces as stimuli found a tendency in young children to use single features of faces rather than the whole in making comparisons, with a development of holistic perception later. It was suggested in Chapter 5 that two types of development occur – improved ability to isolate dimensions and improved ability to combine them into patterns or higher order features.

Language learning too shows a spontaneous use of features in generalizing the use of a word to objects or situations other than the one for which it was first learned. Bowerman (1977) has shown from recordings of the spontaneous speech of her children in the second year that they used words for a 'family' of objects related to a prototypical instance by one or more features. For example, 'moon' was used for the moon, half a grapefruit, a lemon slice, a shiny round green leaf, a ball of spinach, a green magnetic capital D. A similar conclusion emerges from a study of five year olds' ability to learn an identification carried out by Pick (1965). She presented letter-like shapes with a set of variations transformed in various ways (straight lines to curves, size changes, mirror images, rotations and perspective changes). Children learned to select a copy of the standard from among the transformations and were then transferred to a new task which involved either new transformations and the same standards, new standards and the same transformations, or both new. Performance was superior in the second group, indicating that knowledge of the relevant dimensions to be compared was more important than familiarity with the standards to be matched. The evidence, therefore supports the view that from an early age children can make use of dimensions, but not always consistently, and the demands of the task and the salience of the dimensions will affect how readily they do this. Smith and Kemler (1978) describe how five year olds would suddenly discover during training the rule being used and announce it.

An example given by Gregory (1970) may illustrate in adults something like the situation which faces the young child. Gregory shows how when the planet Saturn was first discovered, astronomers had to make sense of what they saw through their telescopes and drew some very strange shapes indeed. Several of these look like attempts to portray a single undifferentiated shape, where the elements (the sphere and the rings) combining to produce it have not been separated.

Development as differentiation
Gibson and Gibson (1955) have argued that perceptual development consists primarily of progressively finer differentiations. They

appear to be referring both to the separation of features which have previously been ignored or have been combined with others and to finer discrimination along a single dimension. One of the most obvious examples of the first type of development is in speech, where Jakobson *et al.* (1961) have outlined the normal course of phoneme differentiation, beginning with the consonant/vowel distinction, each of which is then further subdivided, consonants into nasal/oral, oral into continuous/discontinuous and so on. Each child learns the distinctions which are important in the language it is exposed to and finds it difficult to hear and produce new distinctions not in that language after a certain age. Whether this is due to a sensitive period for language development or the interference from the first language learned is not entirely clear. Babies who suffer brain damage in the speech hemisphere of the brain can go through the sequence all over again, establishing language in the other hemisphere, provided the injury occurs early in life, and children brought up by animals seem to have difficulties learning language, which supports the idea of a sensitive period. Also the regularity of the order in which the different distinctions develop suggests it may be largely preprogrammed.

Attention

Several conflicting claims have been made about attention in the young child. Some theorists have argued that the infant is 'stimulus bound', attention being attracted by features of the environment without any ability to control what is selected or to maintain attention on a given input, and that control of voluntary directed attention has to develop with age. Others, however, point to the alert attentive scanning of the environment which can be observed in young babies, which certainly does not give the impression of being uncontrolled, and suggest that what has to develop is knowledge of the significance of particular inputs for the current task. Again Vurpillot has argued that what changes is the type of concept or rule used to direct sampling of the environment. Because young children have a different concept of 'sameness' they scan in a different way when comparing two patterns. Finally, it has been argued both that the perceptual process develops from being single channelled to handling several channels in parallel (as was suggested happens with practice in adults) and also, as we have seen in the earlier discussion of integral and separable dimensions in children, that they have to learn to distinguish or select dimensions within the global whole.

I shall look at the evidence on selection and on multiple processing in an effort to resolve some of these conflicts. An additional distinction which is important in considering children's performance on this type of task is that between what they do spontaneously and what they can do if instructions or the task force them. Age changes could be due to changes in strategy or changes in the component processes.

The evidence suggests consistently that ability to select some information and ignore other improves with age. Smith and Kemler's results discussed above have already shown this, but no instruction to select was given, so it could be that the difference is one in strategy rather than ability. Hale (1979) compared a task where no selection instructions were given and a selection task. In the first case children had to learn the positions in a row of five stimuli differing in shape and colour and were then tested with shape and colour only and asked to give the position in the row. Five year olds and eight year olds did not differ on the preferred dimension (shape) but the older children were superior on the non-preferred dimension, suggesting they attended to both to a greater degree than the younger ones. However, when learning of only one dimension was required in the instructions, performance on that dimension improved in both age groups, but the older children also showed a decline on the other dimension, while the younger ones showed no change. This suggests that the older children adopted a strategy in line with the instruction and improved on the required dimension at the cost of the other one, thus showing more efficient selection. Crane and Ross (1967) also showed more selection in eleven than in seven year olds. This is probably due to a better ability to adapt to task requirements in general, rather than a specifically selective ability. Using selective listening tasks, Maccoby and Konrad (1966) and Doyle (1973) have shown rapid improvement from five to eleven years.

Dual tasks

On dual tasks it has already been pointed out that young children have difficulty in seeing both aspects of an ambiguous figure and Hale's result above suggested increased ability to process two dimensions in older children. Siegel and Stevenson (1966) had obtained a similar result in an incidental learning task; incidental learning increased from seven to eleven years, then a decrease occurred at thirteen and a further increase in adults. They suggest that the decrease at thirteen is due to applying a more efficient selection strategy and the increase in adults occurs when the task becomes easy and permits the other aspects of the stimuli to be examined as well as the main one. It thus seems that several factors will combine to determine performance and that increased age will bring both the ability to process more input and to select more efficiently when this is useful.

Search strategies
A third type of research is concerned with search strategies. A careful and clever series of studies by Vurpillot (1976a, b) examined children's attentional strategies when they were required to decide if two complex patterns (pictures of houses with objects in the windows) were 'just the same' or not. Four to five year olds would look at only a few of the windows before deciding that the houses were the same, while six to nine year olds scanned until they found a difference or scanned all the windows before deciding the houses were the same. However, even when made to point at the windows in turn and describe the contents, younger children still responded 'same' to different pairs and Vurpillot suggests that they use a global equivalence, counting the two as the same if they are both houses. Unfortunately no test of this was made by altering the shape of the house. Interestingly Zelniker and Jeffrey (1976) have shown that reflectives, as measured by the speed and accuracy of a matching task, performed better than impulsives when differences were in local detail and worse when they were in overall shape, but they reject an interpretation of the differences in terms of developmental lag. Vurpillot also showed that switches of the location of objects in the windows were not treated as differences by over half the five year olds tested, even though they were perfectly competent at deciding whether two objects were in the same window, suggesting that they still have a different rule for sameness from adults. The importance of Vurpillot's work is in emphasizing the need to consider the concepts and rules being used to direct attentional behaviour. Like the work discussed earlier it suggests that the object which children of different ages are using may be defined very differently from that of an adult experimenter. In the youngest children it may include little or no detail, and in five year olds it may be a list of details with no spatial relations specified (in terms of the

discussion in Chapter 4 these are rather bare templates and straight-forward feature lists without relations between the features, respectively).

Processing strategies

Wickens (1974) reviewed the rather meagre evidence available on the relation between age and performance on a number of reaction time tasks, with the aim of discovering the reasons for the common finding that young children are slower on such tasks. Simple reaction time decreases from the age of three onwards. Increased motivation, ability to maintain attention and practice all contribute to this improvement but some of the difference seems to be due to processing speed. Pew and Rupp (1971) found on a tracking task which maintained attention that time to react to changes in the target position decreased from nine to fifteen years and Miller (1969) found eye movement latency was about 130 ms slower in eight year olds than in adults.

Evidence from studies of reading items from iconic storage has shown that without masking seven to eleven year olds performed alike, but masking impaired the younger children more, implying that their rate of reading the items was reduced. However, familiarity with the letters and digits might well be responsible rather than a general impairment of processing speed in the younger children. Also Haith *et al.* (1973) have found that if only one item is presented, younger children are not slower, suggesting once again that it may be the ability to handle several items presented simultaneously that is the weak link.

Visual search tasks have suggested that familiarity with the type of item is important. Searching for geometric shapes showed little increase in speed with age (Forsman 1967) while searching for letter targets showed rather more of a change (Gibson and Yonas 1966). Children were able to search for two items as quickly as for one, like adults. Younger children were slower overall on these tasks but the increase was a constant one, however many letters were searched; that is the rate of search or speed of comparing the display with the target was not slower in younger children, but some other component of the task in the input or output stages was.

Choice reaction time tasks have found that the effect of set size was somewhat greater in younger children (Alluisi 1965) but the uncertainties of interpreting such data have been discussed in detail in Chapter 6. None of the more refined methods of measuring components of reaction time which were discussed in that chapter seem to have been used with young children, so firm conclusions about the source of any slowing are quite impossible. Hohle (1967) compared eleven year olds and sixteen year olds in one experiment attempting to decompose the latency distribution into components, but found no significant differences. The available evidence suggests that practice rather than maturation is the important variable.

Decision making

No evidence has been found concerning the decision-making processes which were discussed in Chapter 6 in children.

Conclusions

Summarizing this section, younger children have difficulty in adapting their processing strategy according to the task. They have problems with separating or selecting single features, but since they can do this spontaneously the problem is probably that feature dominance, rather than self instruction, controls behaviour. They are unable to carry out parallel processing of several features or parallel comparison of the input to several possibilities, and processing is generally slower than that in the mature organism. Some or all of these abilities continue to improve at least up to the age of ten to eleven years.

Models of the world

The third area in which we need to consider the role of learning concerns the stored information with which the input is compared. I shall consider four sorts of knowledge about the world which contribute to the internal model of reality against which experience is evaluated. The first two, and perhaps the third, appear to be present in their essentials very early, but the last is clearly learned as far as the actual groupings are concerned, though the tendency to group and ways of grouping may be unlearned:

1   The world consists of relatively stable three-dimensional objects.
2   Various qualities or events tend to occur together so that it is

possible to predict from one observed characteristic that another will be present or will shortly occur, or that a given action will produce a particular perceptual change.

3 Information from several senses can be ascribed to one object and equivalent information can sometimes be obtained from two senses.

4 Objects and events can usefully be grouped in certain ways, simplifying perceptual and action decisions.

The stable world

Evidence for early size and shape constancy has already been described. Bower *et al.* (1970a, b) have also shown that infants will reach for an apparent figure, produced by polarizing goggles with stereoscopic pictures, and show bewilderment and distress even at eight days old when the hand encounters nothing. No reaching for photographs of objects occurred. The evidence against Piaget's theory that infants have no conception of permanent objects has already been discussed and the point made that infants seem to identify an object with the space it occupies. Change of an object which remains in the same place (by switching projectors) does not surprise infants up to five months old. Distress is, however, apparent at this age when three simultaneous images of the mother are shown, though not in younger infants (Bower 1974).

Combining of evidence from different events and senses

Wertheimer (1961) showed that immediately after birth an infant would turn its eyes toward the source of a sound. Infants aged five to eight weeks show distress if the mother's voice comes from a different position from that in which she is seen (Aronson and Rosenbloom 1971). In the experiment cited above, extending the hand was clearly expected to produce contact with a solid object. Bryant *et al.* (1972) showed that infants under twelve months of age, after touching an object, would recognize it visually, so information presented through one sense could be used by another. Gregory and Wallace (1963) showed the same in their case study of an adult blind from an early age. Bower, Broughton and Moore (1971) found that by sixteen weeks infants were surprised by objects reappearing at an inappropriate place from behind a screen or reappearing as a different object.

Obviously more complex tasks like processing print and speech depend heavily on ability to predict ahead for efficient performance.

Categorizing

There is an extensive literature on concept learning and on the structure of semantic memory which can only be touched upon here, but which is important for an understanding of the levels and types of identification that are easier and preferred. Studies of adult concept learning began with Bruner, Goodnow and Austin's *A Study of Thinking* (1956). Subjects were shown a set of cards formed of all combinations of three colours × three shapes × three numbers of objects × three numbers of borders. They were told that a particular card represented the concept or rule to be discovered and asked to deduce this by picking cards and asking if they were or were not exemplars of the concept. This was called the selection paradigm. Bruner, Goodnow and Austin worked out possible ideal strategies and attempted to categorize subject behaviour in terms of them, but in fact subjects tended to be somewhat variable and unsystematic. In an alternative experimental situation subjects were shown cards in random order (reception paradigm) and told whether or not each one was an exemplar of the concept to be discovered. The latter is assumed to be closer to the situation of a child attempting to discover the definition of a word or the concept it represents.

However, this situation is different in several ways from the natural one. The rule was exactly specifiable, the relevant features were separable and clearly defined, the values on them discrete (no shades of red or random variation in size occurred). One only has to consider real concepts such as 'dog' and 'vegetable' to realize the artificiality. Natural concepts are frequently ill-defined in the sense that no single feature is essential or reliable and the boundaries between exemplars and non-exemplars are imprecise. In a famous discussion Wittgenstein considered the notion of 'games' and argued that such concepts are related by a 'family resemblance' whereby all have something in common with a central prototype but pairs of exemplars may have nothing in common with each other.

Rosch, whose work was introduced in Chapter 4, has investigated the nature of natural concepts in depth. Her distinction between superordinate, basic and subordinate classifications has been described earlier. The basic level is the most commonly used, and distinctions at this level depend heavily on perceptual features. Rosch *et al.* (1976) argue that the way the world is divided up is not arbitrary but this preference for the basic level gives the most inclusive groupings in which 'all items in the category possess significant numbers of attributes in common and, are used by means of similar sequences of motor movements and are like each other in overall appearance' (Rosch and Mervis 1975, p. 602). Children learn the basic level concepts first. However, even at this level all items do not usually possess any single attribute in common. Some are more typical exemplars than others.

So much for adults' structuring of the world. What do we know about how such systems develop in children? Piaget and Bruner, though their views are not identical, both believe that the infant proceeds through three main stages of representation, termed by Piaget the stages of sensori-motor operations, concrete operations and formal operations and by Bruner stages of enactive, iconic and formal thought. In the first stage, representations and distinctions are made in terms of actions (anything that can be thrown may be regarded as a ball), in the second in terms of images and in the third in terms of abstract rules. Thus in the second stage Bruner and Kenney (1966) have shown that a child shown a matrix of objects systematically organized by height and width can reconstruct the same matrix in the same orientation, but not when a ninety degree rotation is required. The pictorial memory is present but not a rule which survives the transformation. Bruner also suggests that at this stage children have a problem in classifying under one heading (a superordinate category in his terms, though he does not use the term in the same way as Rosch) objects which have no obvious common perceptual attributes. Vygotsky (1962) had made a similar suggestion that early systems of classifying were unsystematic. Bruner and Olver (1963) carried out an experiment in which they presented children of five, eight or eleven years of age first with a pair of words and asked what the objects they named had in common; they then added a third word, asked how it differed from the other two and how all three were similar, and so on for ten words. The classifications produced were separated into several types, distinguished in terms of their simplicity and sophistication. The simplest and most sophisticated rule was a single superordinate one ('they all make a noise'), then there were combinations of two or more groups, a key ring structure (one central item with others related to it by different attributes), a chain (each pair linked by a different attribute such as 'banana and peach are yellow, peach and potato are round' and so on), with a connection in a story being the most complicated and least sophisticated strategy of linking. Use of the superordinate increased with age and was linked to use of functions rather than just perceptual features. The younger children used perceptual features nearly as often as the older ones when giving a superordinate rule, and used function much less often than older children when giving other types of rule. This suggests that as functional features are used more with increasing age, they facilitate use of superordinate rules. Nelson (1977) has shown that even very young children have some appreciation of function. Bruner sees conceptual development as creating simplifying structures for knowledge rather than a process of cumulating un-related information. The ability to achieve such simplification may well be related to the more precise matching rules observed by Vurpillot in her subjects.

Theorists like Bruner, however, and following him Posner, have tended to think of all concept learning as proceeding toward a formal structure, definable by a superordinate or common feature rule, whereas Rosch stresses in the light of her work on real-life concepts in adults that this is not the case. She points out that some of the structures which Bruner observed and assumed to be immature are in fact like the family resemblances which she found in adult concepts. Moreover, the same structures appear in still younger children on the evidence of the way Bowerman's children used new words. Hence, while young children may use such family resemblance structures where adults would discover a formal rule, and Bruner may still be correct in asserting that the latter is not possible before a certain age, it is by no means true that adult conceptual structures are all or even mainly of the formal type. Children certainly, according to extensive work by Piaget, do not have the ability to construct hierarchical structures (a canary is a bird, a bird is an animal, an animal is a living thing) until after the age of seven, so their conceptual structures must remain fairly simple. They cannot understand that an object can be a member of two classes simultaneously, and faced with five red and four blue flowers, they will say there are more red flowers than flowers. This inability to see two aspects of an object has also of course been discussed in more directly perceptual terms above.

In conclusion, the evidence suggests that there is a preferred level for classifying objects which is learned first and used most readily by adults. Children have problems in classifying objects at higher levels and learn superordinate classification rules relatively late. However they show an early tendency to group objects in terms of family resemblances, which is like much adult classification. This suggests a well developed ability to extract several different perceptual features, though they have difficulty in considering more than one at a time. It has been suggested that this is a problem of selective attention rather than a difficulty in distinguishing single features; that is to say, two features may both be picked up but the problem is to ignore one and use the other to guide behaviour.

10   Speech perception and reading

Speech perception

Units and features

Some of the problems of devising an acceptable model of speech perception have already been discussed in Chapter 4, when considering attempts to define critical features. It was pointed out that linguistic considerations suggest that phonemes should be the basic units of speech perception because they are the smallest temporal element, changes in which affect meaning. Vowel sounds can be distinguished by combinations of frequency bands known as formants. These show up clearly when speech sounds are plotted graphically as *sound spectrograms* in which the frequencies present at each moment in time are shown (Figure 33). The dark bars are the formants, bands of frequencies in vowel sounds which derive from relations between different parts of the vocal tract. This method of representing the sounds matches up with the way the ear extracts frequency patterns over time. Another way of representing the sound is by plotting amplitude against time (Figure 34).

Though different speakers show different absolute frequencies of the formants, variation within a speaker is quite small and listeners seem to adjust their perceptions in relation to the characteristic frequencies of each speaker (Broadbent, Ladefoged and Lawrence 1956). Artificial spectrograms can also be made and used to produce artificial speech sounds.

It has, however, proved much less easy to identify invariant frequency patterns for most consonants, because they change according to the following vowel. The frequency of noise which is heard as a particular consonant can vary quite widely. Hence syllables have to be taken as units rather than phonemes. Schatz (1954) cut off the initial consonants from words and spliced them to other words. Table 4 shows that subjects heard different initial consonants depending on which vowel followed. There is really no precise temporal segregation of different phonemes because the

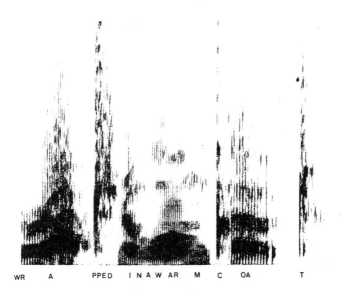

WR   A   PPED   I N A W AR   M   C   OA   T

Figure 33   *Sound spectrograms showing the combinations of frequency bands for different vowel sounds*
Time is shown on the horizontal axis and frequency on the vertical one and the presence of a given frequency at a given time is shown by a dark point. The three formants show clearly as dark bars in the vowels in 'wrapped' and 'coat', while the consonants cover a wide range of frequencies (provided by M. Judd).

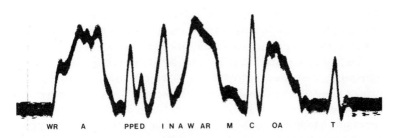

WR   A   PPED   I N A W AR   M   C   OA   T

Figure 34   *A plot of amplitude (vertical axis) against time (horizontal axis). The overall shape is known as the envelope (produced by M. Judd).*

characteristics of adjacent ones overlap and individual phonemes last only about 80 ms, which is too short for separate identification, at least on the evidence of non-speech sounds.

Table 4   *Reported words from different consonant vowel combinations Vowel + final consonant*

		(h)eap	(h)op	(h)oop
Initial consonant	k(eep)	keep	top	poop
	c(op)	peep	cop	poop
	c(oop)	keep	pop	coop
		peep		

In attempts to solve these problems, some theorists have suggested that speech sounds are identified by recourse to the listener's speech production system, since articulation shows less variation on different occurrences of a phoneme than the sound (though it is doubtful in fact if articulation is sufficiently consistent either, according to MacNeilage 1970). Others have looked for different types of feature or pursued consistency in larger units than phonemes or invoked sequential probabilities and listener's expectancies.

Production-based theories of speech perception

The motor theory of speech perception (Liberman *et al.* 1962) and the analysis-by-synthesis theory (Stevens and Halle 1967) both implicate the listener's speech production system in perception. The former claims that 'articulatory movements and their sensory feedback (or more likely, the corresponding neurological processes) become part of the perceiving process mediating between the acoustic stimulus and its ultimate perception'. The latter theory suggests that a preliminary analysis of the input gives rise to a hypothesis, which is used to generate a covert auditory pattern; this is matched to the input and if the match fails the difference is used to generate a new hypothesis. This is, of course, assumed to happen prior to awareness, though we are sometimes aware of this type of process when we fail to hear what someone has said. These theories seem quite inadequate. First, no explanation is offered of how the preliminary analysis occurs; if it is adequate for producing a reasonable hypothesis, why is it inadequate for identifying the input?

Second, no explanation is offered as to how the hypothesis is generated; once again we may ask why it is usually a good hypothesis. If it is derived by predicting ahead, then the theory can be regarded as a way of explaining the effects of expectancies on perception, by guiding the analysis of the input. Finally, the comparison of the pattern generated from the hypothesis and the input requires that the input is analysed in an appropriate way and this is left unexplained. If features can be extracted for matching to the internally generated pattern, what are they, how are they extracted and why were they not extracted in the first place?

A bottom-up theory

A detailed case for the importance of several types of information in speech perception has been provided by Cole and Scott (1974). They discuss three types of information – the frequency characteristics of the specific phonemes, the transitions between consonants and vowel sounds and the overall variation in amplitude of the waveform shown in Figure 34, or envelope as they call it. Each of these, they argue, contributes independent information about the nature of the sounds being uttered.

They provide a detailed breakdown of invariant frequency characteristics of each consonant, which in some cases specify a single sound unambiguously and in others reduce the possibilities to two or three. One example will suffice. /s/ and /z/ are distinguished from /sh/ and /zh/ by noise of specific frequencies and from /f/ and /θ/ (as in thick) by the amplitude of the noise, while /s/ and /z/ are distinguished from each other by energy at 700 Hz in the latter case, together with greater intensity and duration of the noise.

Transitions between consonants and vowels provide information which can enable further distinctions to be made. Figure 33 shows that the formant bands are not horizontal but show swoops or glides linking them to the preceding or succeeding consonant noise. Figure 35 is an example of artificial spectrograms which produce the sounds /b/, /d/ or /g/ before different vowels and shows how the transition to the second (higher) formant seems to originate from a frequency of about 720 Hz for /b/, 1800 for /d/ and 3000 for /g/ in the case of vowels to the left of the picture and from a frequency just above the second formant for vowels to the right of the picture. These transitions can yield perception of a specific consonant preceding the vowel, even if no other consonant noise is actually

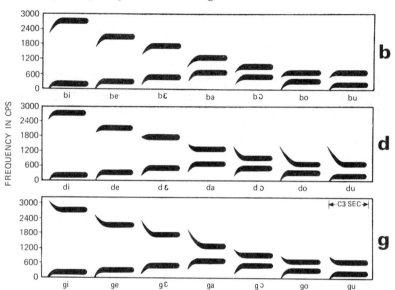

Figure 35   *Artificial sound spectrograms which produce perception of the consonant–vowel combinations indicated when converted to sound (from Delattre, Liberman and Cooper 1955, Figure 1)*

present. Consonant noise on its own, however, is not even heard as speech, but as chirps or hisses or other noises. In a sense consonants have no existence apart from vowels.

Cole and Scott therefore stress that different sounds are characterized by a cluster of cues which can be jointly sufficient. If transitions are removed some distinctions are lost and they give an example of what would be left: 'Motice vat vis steech is mot very diffitult to umderstamd'. If the invariant cues are removed the effect is drastic, sounding like a speaker with a very heavy cold indeed: 'Dotid, dat did dbeed id berry dibbicult to uderdtad'.

Transitions are also important in other ways. They tie the sequence of phonemes into a single ordered sequence. Speech is perceptible even at 50 phonemes a second (that is 20 ms per phoneme), but a sequence of non-speech sounds must last for 700 ms *each* before the order can be judged. When transitions were removed and a consonant-vowel sequence was repeated continually subjects heard two separate 'streams' of sound, one of consonant chirps or hisses and one of vowels. When a series of different consonant–vowel units of this type was played, listeners had problems in judging the order. This evidence encourages the belief that the speech perception system is special and has evolved to deal with a special type of input.

The third type of cue discussed by Cole and Scott is the waveform envelope (see Figure 34) which provides information about amplitude and thus about stress and intonation, but also about some phonemes which are distinguished by amplitude changes or silent pauses. Cole and Scott suggest that these three types of information are handled by different processors, since they operate over different time periods. They point to the segregation of consonant noise and vowel sounds under repeated presentation as one supporting piece of evidence and the fact that only the latter are heard as speech on their own; /sa/ when presented repeatedly may be heard as hissing plus /da/, the /d/ being signalled by the transition and therefore independently of the invariant information which signals /s/. However, more conclusive evidence, such as the loss of one system with retention of the others or a selective effect of a particular manipulation, is needed to support this idea. If there are three independent processes they must be integrated at some point and integration of invariant and transition information requires at least syllabic units. Basically the vowels with transitions are units of this size and invariant information is used to resolve ambiguities about the consonant. Thus the phoneme is not a natural speech unit (at least in the case of consonants which can neither be uttered nor perceived on their own) but a linguistic abstraction. At some pre-conscious automatic level phonemes must be abstracted but they are not separately available to our awareness without sophisticated conscious understanding of what sound changes cause changes in meaning in words.

Nor are vowel sounds exempt from variations which we ignore. Word forms with the same root will often show phonemic differences due to consistent stress changes in the language which are ignored. For example, the first 'e' differs in 'telegraph' and 'telegraphy' and the 'a' differs in 'nation' and 'national'. Conversely, identical phonemes can be ascribed to non-identical base forms; the first vowel in 'telegraphy' and 'Canadian' is the same sound but few of us appreciate that. Knowledge of the rules of stress change in English enables us to recover the underlying form in these cases. Gleitman and Rozin (1977) give a brilliant exposition of these issues and their significance for reading difficulties which I shall discuss below. The written form preserves the meanings rather than the actual sounds. Whether the preliterate child still hears the sound differences is not, however, clear, since no test seems to have been done. Untangling the knot requires the listener to abstract stress patterns and know stress change rules. The envelope information, which was the third component in Cole and Scott's analysis, can help integrate syllables into larger units and derive stress.

Use of context and probability

Thus a detailed analysis of the nature of the speech input does provide a somewhat more optimistic picture with regard to the possibility of identifying speech sounds by 'bottom-up' processing. However, such processing is clearly not adequate, since in natural speech words isolated from context are often impossible to identify (Pollack and Pickett 1964), but present no problem in context. The speaker's individual sound patterns, together with sequential probabilities due to syntax and meaning, are needed to aid the decisions. Likewise probable combinations of features and of phonemes and syllables into words will aid identification of the basic sound by reducing the amount of evidence required in favour of the probable elements. This was the interpretation of the effects of probability and expectation which was favoured in Chapter 7 and it presents no problems for a straightforward stages model such as that discussed in Chapter 6 where the widely accepted view was described that speech perception proceeds from a preperceptual auditory store holding unanalysed sounds through a synthesized auditory memory holding phonemes or syllables to analysis of word meaning and sentence meaning. It was indicated that the evidence for these separate stages was in fact not particularly strong (since information about characteristics of the speaker's voice could survive for much longer than the unanalysed sounds are assumed to survive), though the sequence seems plausible.

However, if there should be feedback from later stages in the process to earlier ones *while analysis of the input is proceeding*, for example because the results arriving at the later stages are obviously in error (which seems a reasonable assumption), then the testing of a stage model becomes very difficult indeed. Fry (1964) has produced one such model with feedback to explain the rarity of errors in speech perception. He suggests a sequence of unit detectors proceeding from simple analysis of component dimensions through phoneme detectors, morpheme detectors, word detectors and units handling sentences. At each level the possible sequences in English are available for predicting the likely next element and guiding the analysis at the next level down. For example, if 'thr' occurs, features of vowels will be tested next. Second, when later input reveals an earlier error a correction is made at the appropriate level. 'Cads chase mice' might be corrected to 'Cats . . .', perhaps erroneously, and the predictions based on the error are recomputed at lower levels where appropriate. The main effect of later stages, that is stages handling larger units, on earlier ones is therefore in guiding *subsequent* processing and in consequence no problems arise for a straightforward stage model. As far as error correction goes, it seems that either lower level errors are simply overriden by higher level corrections, so that the former are preconscious, or that corrections are made after the error has reached awareness, as in the example above. Neither of these possibilities raises difficulties for a stage analysis, provided in the second case that the occurrence of the error prior to the correction can be detected. Fry's model is a hierarchical one. An alternative approach is Reddy and Erman's (1975) 'blackboard model' in which the results of many different types of analysis of the input are 'written' into a store (the blackboard) and made available to all the concurrent analysing systems, enabling choices in one system to be guided by information from another. This is a heterarchical model. A choice between these approaches must await the development of more refined experimentation.

As these models imply, speech perception and reading (to be discussed shortly) involve much more than identifying words. Relations between words have to be worked out, as signalled by syntax and function words, in order to derive the meaning of phrases and sentences. At a still higher level sentences are organized into a sequence of argument or description. To discuss comprehension would involve us in an enormous and currently very active area of research outside the scope of this book. Clark and Clark (1977, Chapter 2) provide an excellent introduction to this work.

Development of speech perception

Development of speech perception proceeds very rapidly and many believe that it is based on an innate system developed specifically for this purpose. Infants as young as one month show ability to discriminate /pa/ and /ba/ in a way identical to adults, who hear all sounds with less than a critical value of voice onset time as /ba/ and all with more than this as /pa/. Eimas *et al.* (1971) showed that infants also did this, by giving them one sound repeatedly then changing it and measuring change in sucking rate as an indication of attention to a new sound. Sucking rate changed only when the change in sound crossed the value of voice onset time which is critical for adult perception. As the child gets older more sounds are distinguished and the order in which the distinctions appear is fairly uniform, but this could of course reflect difficulty rather than an innate sequence of development. Children can distinguish percept- ually before they can produce the distinctions; sip and ship may be pronounced alike as sip but the child knows they are different (Smith 1973).

As already described in Chapter 9, meanings of words are learned gradually by first applying the word to a wide range of objects which show resemblance on some feature to the object first associated with the name. Sometimes this may be one of the relevant charac- teristics and at others the child may pick an irrelevant one. Griffiths and Atkinson (1976) tell of a child who used 'door' for any separ- ating action, such as taking a toy apart or a lid off a box. This shows that learning involves selection and the selected attribute may then be tested by using it and finding out how adults react.

The child's learning of structure in spoken language is a fascin- ating and complex topic. Children of four years old know something about possible sound sequences since they mispronounce sequences which do not exist in English to make them more like English, and presumably such knowledge begins to develop well before this age. Children can supply plurals and regular tense endings by the age of five (Berko 1958). Irregular forms (plural sheep, went) may be produced correctly as early as two years, then comes a stage of regularizing them (sheeps, wented) and finally the correct regular forms reappear, suggesting first direct learning, then overuse of a rule, then acknowledgement of exceptions. The child also uses simplified grammatical forms and cannot repeat correct ones even after many repetitions. As with sounds though, it does not seem that they are unable to hear adult versions correctly, but unfortunately much less work has been done in studying perception than pro- duction of speech so this is not entirely clear.

Reading

I shall consider three main issues: how are words identified; what processes occur in continuous reading of text, and what happens in learning to read.

Word identification

A good deal has already been covered relevant to the first issue in previous chapters. The persistent questions are why meaningful units are perceived more readily than meaningless ones and what is the role of phonological (acoustically based) representations in processing visually presented language.

The word superiority effect

Not only are words perceived more easily than strings of letters which do not form words, but letters in words are perceived more easily than letters in random strings or letters on their own. Reicher (1969) and Wheeler (1970) demonstrated this by briefly presenting a word or string of random letters or a single letter, followed by a masking pattern, then requiring a decision between two possible letters at a particular position, the type of stimulus and the position tested varying from trial to trial. Thus either WORK, OWRD or D might be tested with the alternatives D or K; as both of these would yield a word in the fourth position of the first display, guessing bias was assumed to be minimized. Accuracy was better for the first display than for either of the others and since the observers did not know which position would be tested this implies that all the letters in the word are perceived more easily than a letter on its own. Strings of letters resembling words, such as WURD, also show advantages over random strings but are inferior to real words and some variables influence the gain due to being a real word but not the gain due to using English letter sequences, which suggests that two effects may be involved. Deaf subjects show the effect (Gibson, Shurcliff and Yonas 1970) and it vanishes if subjects can concentrate on a single position or if exposure is not limited by masking (Johnson and McClelland 1973) or if reading aloud is required (Mezrich 1973).

Possible explanations are:

1   parallel independent processing of letters in words, but this

could not explain the *superior* performance on letters in words;

2   processing of words as wholes using emergent features;

3   knowledge or partial knowledge about some letters guides analysis of the others or guesses about them (Rumelhart and Siple 1974). For example, if only part of the D is seen and the observer knows it is in a word, no other possible letter may exist, though another possibility will exist in the case of a single letter or non-word;

4   the trace of words can be converted to a more durable form;

5   results of letter analysis do not enter awareness, while results of word analysis do, so letters require additional processing to recover them (Rozin and Gleitman 1977).

Advantages have also been found for words presented with letters alternately in upper and lower case (McClelland 1976), which rules out (2) and the advantage of word-like letter strings rules out (4), at least as a complete explanation. Rozin and Gleitman offer no explanation as to why processing of single letters should not enter awareness. We are left with (3), which also has some difficulty with the advantage of word-like strings, but can explain this if responses are biased toward English-like combinations, since this would also impair performance on random strings. A bigger problem is presented by the finding of Smith and Haviland (1972) that when words and nonsense strings are matched for predictability by replacing letters in a limited set with a consistent substitute, word perception is still superior, even after lengthy practice to familiarize the subjects with the sequences. However, the non-word sequences were constructed by replacing vowels with consonants so were not even like parts of English words or pronounceable as single units. A combination of processing letters in parallel in words, treating words as wholes and use of predictability is offered below as an explanation of the word superiority effect.

This effect is of course a gain in accuracy. Wheeler measured latencies in choosing the correct letter and found they were longer for word displays than for single letters but this was probably due to time spent locating the position being tested. Since at least some features of each letter in the word become available at the same exposure as that required for a single letter, parallel processing is strongly implied. Moreover, the experiment of Schiffrin and Schneider, in which they demonstrated parallel processing of sets of unrelated letters after extensive practice with them as a set, certainly indicates that parallel processing is possible. Some experimenters have tried to resolve this issue by using search tasks, and comparing search for a letter in words, English-like non-words or random letter strings. Generally, but not invariably, search is faster for letters in words and word-like patterns. However, Juola *et al.* (1979) showed that the difference lay in the intercept and not in the slope of the function plotting time against number of letters (see Figure 23), so the words were registered more quickly but a similar letter-by-letter search occurred with words and random strings to find whether the target was present. Moreover the intercepts for words did not change up to words of about five letters long, implying that parallel encoding of letters occurred up to this length.

The difficulty with this finding is that if the letters can be encoded in parallel a serial search process should be unnecessary since the relevant letter in the word should trigger the 'yes' response. The way to resolve this problem seems to be to assume that the parallel encoding does not produce identification of individual letters when the system is set to identify words, but the results are fed straight into a word identifier, which responds when enough information has arrived to meet a criterion, as in the accumulator process described in Chapter 7. Johnson (1975) found that, when a display consisted of words, a target word was found faster than a target letter and similar results have been found for speech, words being located faster than syllables and these faster than phonemes (Warren 1971). McNeill and Lindig (1973) showed, however, that this was not a case of larger units being processed faster than smaller ones but that searching for one type of unit was slower in a display formed of another type than in a display formed of items of the same type as the target. Hence if the nature of the display and instructions sets the subject to process words, then words will be processed faster than letters. If the depth of processing used is inappropriate for the target type, additional processes will be required to recover the target units from the initial constructs.

This would explain why Smith and Haviland obtained a difference between words and strings matched for sequential dependencies, the latter having no ready-made 'master units' responsive to them. This explanation of the word superiority effect is not just in terms of guessing or using information from one letter to help identify or guess the next, but in terms of extracting enough evidence in favour of one word rather than others to justify a decision. The proposed model is in fact an extension of

Pandemonium (Chapter 4) with word units added above the letter units (in Pandemonium the accumulating evidence is more picturesquely described in terms of demons shouting). A similar but more detailed model is proposed by McClelland and Rumelhart (1981). At first sight the model might seem to imply that false responses might occur quite frequently. Suppose a unit exists looking for the word WELT and each letter can deliver up to four units of evidence to this unit and a criterion of only eight units is set. If PERT is presented and E and T each deliver four units the criterion is met, even though the other letters are incorrect. However there are other independent word units, one of them looking for PERT, which is likely to reach criterion before the WELT unit. Once a word unit has responded, the individual letters can be constructed from it, even if only some evidence in favour of each letter was actually extracted, so a letter in a word can be reported but not a single letter. The advantage of word-like sequences over random ones could be explained as due to units for parts of words or (as some evidence suggests it differs from the word effect) simply to guessing in accordance with sequence probabilities in English.

Phonological coding in reading

Coming to the second question about phonological processing, some complex and speculative models of word identification have been produced (see Gibson and Levin 1975 and Henderson 1977, for examples), some involving a phonological stage and some not. None of these models provides a satisfactory explanation for the word superiority effect and any model which includes an obligatory transformation to a phonological code before access to meaning faces insuperable objections (Rubenstein *et al.* 1971; Gough 1972). Once the visual representation of a word is lost, distinctions between homophones (right, write, rite, wright) are lost. Clearly readers can distinguish these words, even without context. This is not of course to deny that learning to read involves associating visual patterns to already known phonological ones, but it does not follow that the skilled reader does this or only this.

There are some results which suggest phonological coding is important. Rubenstein *et al.* (1971) used a lexical decision task ('decide if this is a word') and found non-words which sounded like words (brane, brite) took longer to reject as words than non-words which did not sound like words. However they may also look more like real words. Meyer *et al.* (1975) found faster decisions that two words looked alike when they rhymed (bribe – tribe) than when they did not (couch – touch), and Baron (1973) got subjects to decide if phrases made sense and got more errors when the sound and sight conflicted (as in 'peace of pie'). Coltheart *et al.* (1977) suggest that both direct visual and indirect phonological access to meaning can occur and may compete, which would explain these results. Other evidence for dual access was quoted earlier, such as activation of meaning when observers are unaware of what word has occurred, absence of interference from shadowing on judgements of synonymy (Kleiman 1975) and clinical evidence for selective loss. Mezrich (1973) found that when subjects had to read aloud, the word superiority effect vanished and in fact performance was better on letters, which suggests this task changed the normal reading process in some way.

Children learning to read and adults faced with difficult reading situations do use overt phonological coding. Liberman and Shankweiler (1979) and others have suggested that phonological coding provides a more durable memory of earlier input which is held for combining with later input into a complete version of the sentence. On this view it is important for comprehension rather than initial word identification Kleiman showed that shadowing lists of digits interfered with decisions about whether lists of words formed an acceptable sentence more than decisions about whether a sentence contained a word that sounded like a target word, looked like a target or belonged to a specified category, which he claims supports this view of the role of phonological coding, but it could of course merely reflect the greater difficulty of the first task. Hardyck and Petrinovich (1970) found that delayed feedback affected comprehension of difficult passages and Levy (1977) found suppression of subvocal speech by counting aloud affected memory for visually presented but not auditorily presented language (i.e. reading but not listening).

Reading continuous text

The processes discussed so far involve stages of processing such as those outlined in Seymour's model described in Chapter 6 (iconic, graphemic and lexical stores). Reading of text obviously requires further processes and in particular use of earlier inputs in memory and their integration with incoming information. This type of operation is assumed by many theorists to require the existence of a working memory or central processor (Baddeley and Hitch 1974). Systematic attempts to separate processing stages in reading sentences by experimental methods are rare but Calfee and Spector (1981) have recently described one such attempt by Juel (1977), using an extension of Sternberg's additive factors method. Calfee (1976) proposed that for complex processes several measures of performance should be taken, each assumed to be affected by several independent variables. Thus Juel looked at three hypothetical stages – decoding from print to sound, identification of word meaning and sentence comprehension – and the effect of six independent variables – number of syllables and spelling regularity (assumed to affect the first), word frequency and concreteness (affecting the second), and sentence length and reversibility (whether the subject and object can have their roles reversed or not which affects ease of comprehension). The measures of efficiency of the three stages were accuracy of pronunciation, word meaning definition and choosing a picture to match a sentence. However Sternberg's analysis was based on processing time and requires a proper measurement scale; the extension to variables of this type is not justified except as a rather crude guide to what may be happening.

The expectation that variables would only affect the measure for the appropriate stage were not all fulfilled. Number of syllables and spelling regularity affected pronunciation as predicted but also affected word definition; frequency and concreteness affected definition as predicted, but also pronunciation, and reversibility as predicted affected choice of the correct picture. Moreover there were interactions between variables supposed to affect separate stages (frequency and spelling regularity, frequency and number of syllables). It is claimed that good readers conformed more closely to the model but the data presented only partially support this claim and in any case it seems quite reasonable that decoding problems would carry over to deciding meaning giving some of the observed effects. Measurement of sentence reading time, the only measure to which the additive factors method can properly be applied, showed effects of all six variables but no interactions even between those assumed to affect the same stage. Though this was an interesting study, the results are not very illuminating and I have described it mainly to illustrate a possible methodology and the traps for the unwary.

The relevance of studies of single word identification to reading continuous prose is often questioned. Naturally the latter is more complex, but while word identification may be modified when a word occurs in context, it is unlikely that there is a complete change in the strategy compared with that used for single words. Not all the information, even in a single word, needs to be processed in order to identify it, as has been shown, because letters differ from each other in many ways. Not all the possible combinations of features exist (on any simple minded view of features). F and H are letters but many other combinations of these straight lines are not. The same is true of words and these restrictions reduce the information in a letter or word and are known as *redundancy*. There are other forms of redundancy in prose, due to restraints of syntax and semantics (grammar and meaning) which allow only some words following a given sequence. A reader who knows the language can predict ahead and need only look for enough evidence to (probably) confirm the predictions. There is also information available other than the component letters; lower case words have overall shapes which may often be enough to confirm a prediction (see Haber and Haber 1981, for a detailed discussion).

Reading is therefore partly a case of confirming predictions by sampling from a continuous input, rather like Hochberg's description of sampling from a scene to confirm an internal model. Much reading research has been devoted to studying the nature of the eye movements which are the overt sign of this sampling process. Quite early it was discovered that the eye moves over the print in a series of fixations lasting around $\frac{1}{4}$ to $\frac{1}{3}$ s, separated by jumps to the next fixation (saccades lasting about 100 ms). At the end of the line a return sweep occurs to the beginning of the next line. Modern technology has permitted more detailed study of these movements and the information available during each fixation. It used to be asserted in textbooks that fixations occurred regularly every few words but more recent studies suggest that nearly every word is fixated and the time spent on each word varies quite widely. Short function words, such as articles and prepositions, are usually the words which are not fixated (Just and Carpenter 1980). Rayner and McConkie (1977), in an intriguing series of studies, investigated what types of information were obtained on each fixation, especially from the areas to the right of the fixation point. The text appeared on a TV-screen controlled by a computer which kept check of the position of the reader's eyes. In some experiments the amount of text (the window) was varied, the rest of the screen being occupied by Xs. As the reader's eye moved, the fixated area was changed to text. In other conditions they presented the complete text on the screen but might provide misleading information in the periphery of the fixation. Take a sentence 'The robbers guarded the palace with their guns'. With the reader fixating on 'guard' the word actually presented instead of 'palace' might preserve word shape (qcluec), first and last letters (pyctce) or both (pcluce). When fixation moved to this word the correct one would be substituted by the computer to discover whether the misleading information slowed reading compared with the unchanged text. By this means they were able to demonstrate that changing the meaning had no effect for words more than six letters away from fixation, while shape and initial letter changes had effects when they were ten places from fixation and word length up to fifteen places away. Rayner and McConkie summarize the findings as indicating that reading involves a number of 'windows' of different widths from which different types of information are available. These windows extend mainly to the right of fixation. Thus the complexity of reading is revealed, depending on a whole set of simultaneous processes using different types of information and all occurring in parallel.

Just and Carpenter (1980) present an outline model of the whole reading process and examine the effects of a large number of variables on time spent fixating on each word. They make the assumptions that the eye remains fixated on each word as long as it is being processed and that each word is encoded, its meaning interpreted and its place in the sentence worked out as it is fixated, even though decisions may have to be changed when later words arrive. Thus reading is a continuous construction and reconstruction process, the time course of which can be studied through fixation times. This processing is described by Just and Carpenter in identical terms to those used for an influential theory of problem solving advanced by Newell and Simon (1972). Units known as *production systems* are the basic building blocks, each consisting of a condition-action rule, which fire one after the other and enter information into a working memory; in addition, Just and Carpenter accept the existence of parallel automatic processes which activate existing knowledge and thus affect the sequence of active production units. Many different production units are postulated and they suggest variables which affect them, but in the end we are left only a global picture of many factors affecting the single measure of reading time, and no suggestion as to how the separate components of the process are to be teased out.

Learning to read

The third topic in reading I propose to discuss is learning to read. It is obvious from the preceding discussion and some of the discussion of clinical defects in reading described in Chapter 6 that efficient reading demands the co-operation of a large number of component processes, and failure or partial failure of any one of these can impede the whole process. Evidence from defects in previously skilled readers is not of course necessarily relevant to an understanding of problems in the learning process, but should certainly induce caution in accepting the claim which is frequently made that there is one specific developmental reading deficit (dyslexia) which is assumed to depend on some specific but undefined neurological impairment and is distinct from a general learning deficit, because it occurs in children who otherwise show normal progress. This is 'identified' when no other explanation is apparent, but no diagnostic criteria are offered and careful studies suggest that there is a variety of problems in children who have reading difficulties (for example, Clark 1970; Mattis 1981; Satz and Morris 1981). This is not of course to say that difficulty in visual pattern perception or auditory pattern perception or sequence memory is never due to a specific neurological impairment, but it is to say that there is no single identifiable dyslexic syndrome and that such a diagnosis arises from the inadequacy of our models of reading and inability to isolate different components by proper tests.

Provided a teacher sets out to instil rules rather than rote visual–auditory pattern associations, learning to read words initially requires segregating single letters from a string, identifying the visual pattern, associating it with a phonemic pattern, and combining a string of such patterns to form words. Learning to read sentences involves storing already identified words in order to combine sequences into sentences, the structure of which can be worked out and the meaning comprehended. Children may have problems with any or all of these operations and some of the evidence in the last chapter showed how many of these different abilities improve with age.

It was argued in Chapter 9 that young children have problems in selectively attending to part of a complex pattern, because salient elements or the whole shape tend to attract attention and switching attention or simultaneous appreciation of other aspects of the input is impossible. However, Smith (1974) found that four to five year olds could easily learn to indicate which letter in pit and pat differed, so the problem is not serious in most children. As already indicated, the problem is likely to be more acute in speech. Phonemes are not natural speech units and children have difficulty in segregating them. Moreover, different physical sounds may be the same phoneme and be written alike to indicate this (telegraph and telegraphy) and identical sounds treated as different phonemes (telegraphy and Canadian). An even more striking example also provided by Gleitman and Rozin (1977) is the difference between nouns, such as writer and rider, which is written as if it were in the central consonant but is in fact physically in the length of the central vowel. The written form indicates the difference in the base forms write and ride, which is in the consonant. English written forms signal meaning relations as much as sound but children have to begin with the latter – small wonder some are confused.

Several theorists have been suggesting that an understanding of basic linguistic notions, such as what a letter, phoneme and word are, is essential for learning to read. Ability to carry out tests which show such knowledge predicts future reading performance. Of course young children have an implicit knowledge of such notions. They play rhyming games and know that cat and bat are different, but they have difficulty in answering explicit questions which demand such knowledge, for instance, what word is left when 'p' is removed from 'pink' (Bruce 1964; Gleitman and Rozin 1977; Rozin and Gleitman 1977)? Much of learning to read is greatly aided by understanding such notions, at least when letters relate (roughly) to separate sounds. Significantly, Rozin *et al.* (1971) found that poor readers of English had no trouble learning to read Chinese ideograms, one for each word. Gleitman and Rozin show how writing systems develop from direct representations requiring lots of distinct symbols to representations of sound requiring few symbols, but complex relating rules. They state 'the lower the level of the language feature that must be attended to and accessed for any language-like activity beyond comprehension . . . the later its accessibility to the language learning child' (p. 90). In terms of earlier discussions, spoken words are integral stimuli which become separable with maturity and/or training.

Development of ability to distinguish features and use more than one feature in classifying objects was discussed in Chapter 9. One difficulty which often appears with letters is in discriminating mirror images, a distinction which is unimportant in 'normal' perception because objects retain their identity when seen from the opposite side.

It has been claimed that poor readers have problems in relating visual spatial ordering to acoustic temporal ordering (Birch and Belmont, 1964), but later studies have shown the difficulty also occurs when matching two orderings within a sensory modality, so is not specific to the type of matching required in reading. Jones (1974) found that poor readers had a specific problem with auditory memory, which would of course create problems in learning phoneme segregation and the relating of written and spoken forms.

Improvement in reading skill requires learning to use the redundancies discussed earlier and to read at least word by word instead of letter by letter. There is a variety of evidence for differences in these abilities between good and poor readers. Samuels *et al.* (1978) found the size of unit used increased with age and Levin and Turner (1968) found good readers' eyes were further ahead of their voices when reading aloud than were poor readers'. If the spaces between words are moved or filled, eleven year old readers are impaired more than eight year olds (Gibson and Levin 1975, p. 357). Speed of reading simple phrases such as 'two red trains' differentiates good and poor readers less well than speed of picking out a matching picture; the latter is done more slowly than reading by poor readers (Rudishill 1956). If the passage to be read is interleaved with an irrelevant one on alternate lines, good readers show more intrusions from the latter when tested for memory of the former. Liberman and Shankweiler have argued that good readers make more use of phonological coding to integrate meaning, and therefore show more impairment from acoustically similar stimuli (but the tests did not involve reading continuous text). Thus poor readers are locked on to small units and so involved in decoding words that meaning is not processed. Yet only by making use of meaning can reading be speeded up. Poor readers are in a 'Catch 22' situation.

11 Epilogue

'How can we know what this thing is?' was the question I suggested as a focusing point for this book. In pursuit of the answer I have considered separation of the input into objects and background, selection of specific parts or objects to guide current behaviour, the stages of analysis required to categorize such objects adequately and to emit appropriate actions and the way in which choices may be made between the competing possibilities at these different stages. I have also looked at the role of expectations, motivation and past experience in varying these processes, and finally I looked briefly at two important human perceptual activities.

Perception, as discussed in this book, is obviously not some distinct activity or achievement which can be separated from memory or problem solving or comprehension. The whole person perceives and interprets the world, working with the information received by the senses and using past experience, particularly in the case of object identification. But in turn perception is fundamental to these other cognitive activities and they cannot be understood without a grasp of how input via the senses activates complex procedures of memory, thought and action.

Though it is obvious that our knowledge of all the component processes in perception is extremely sketchy, it is probably true that our understanding is least of those processes which are specifically perceptual, namely the early processes of segregating figures from ground, calculating depth and the angle of inclination of surfaces. These occur very rapidly in natural perception, are least accessible to psychological methods and are of course carried out efficiently by organisms which are much less complex than humans. A fly must have exquisitely accurate distance perception involving size and shape constancy, yet its object identification mechanisms are very primitive. Extraction of the essential features for achieving such perception has proved generally more challenging for artificial intelligence theorists than has devising methods of solving supposedly more complex 'logical' problems, where humans can describe how they are operating. Such a consideration should ensure that this book ends with an appropriately humble admiration for the sophisticated and highly efficient mechanisms which have evolved to enable living organisms, even relatively humble ones, to cope with their environment, and an appreciation of the enormity of our ignorance about how these mechanisms work.

Appendix 1 Table of d'

Probability of false alarm / Probability of hit	0.05	0.10	0.15	0.20	0.25	0.30	0.35	0.40	0.50	0.60	0.70	0.80
0.05	0.00											
0.10	0.36	0.00										
0.15	0.60	0.24	0.00									
0.20	0.80	0.44	0.19	0.00								
0.25	0.97	0.60	0.36	0.16	0.00							
0.30	1.12	0.75	0.51	0.31	0.15	0.00						
0.35	1.26	0.89	0.65	0.45	0.28	0.13	0.00					
0.40	1.39	1.02	0.78	0.58	0.42	0.27	0.13	0.00				
0.45	1.51	1.15	0.91	0.71	0.54	0.39	0.26	0.12	-0.12			
0.50	1.64	1.28	1.03	0.84	0.67	0.52	0.38	0.25	0.00	-0.25		
0.55	1.77	1.40	1.16	0.96	0.80	0.65	0.51	0.37	0.12	-0.12	-0.39	
0.60	1.89	1.53	1.29	1.09	0.92	0.77	0.63	0.50	0.25	0.00	-0.27	-0.58
0.65	2.03	1.66	1.42	1.22	1.06	0.91	0.77	0.63	0.38	0.13	-0.13	-0.45
0.70	2.16	1.80	1.56	1.36	1.19	1.04	0.91	0.77	0.52	0.27	0.00	-0.31
0.75	2.31	1.95	1.71	1.51	1.34	1.19	1.06	0.92	0.67	0.42	0.15	-0.16
0.80	2.48	2.12	1.87	1.68	1.51	1.36	1.22	1.09	0.84	0.58	0.31	0.00
0.85	2.68	2.31	2.07	1.87	1.71	1.56	1.42	1.29	1.03	0.78	0.51	0.19
0.90	2.92	2.56	2.31	2.12	1.95	1.80	1.66	1.53	1.28	1.02	0.75	0.44
0.95	3.29	2.92	2.68	2.48	2.31	2.27	2.03	1.89	1.64	1.39	1.12	0.80

Appendix 2 Table of beta

Probability of hit	Probability of false alarm											
	0.05	0.10	0.15	0.20	0.25	0.30	0.35	0.40	0.50	0.60	0.70	0.80
0.05	1.00											
0.10	1.70	1.00										
0.15	2.26	1.32	1.00									
0.20	2.71	1.59	1.20	1.00								
0.25	3.08	1.81	1.36	1.13	1.00							
0.30	3.37	1.98	1.49	1.24	1.09	1.00						
0.35	3.59	2.11	1.58	1.32	1.16	1.06	1.00					
0.40	3.74	2.20	1.65	1.38	1.21	1.11	1.04	1.00				
0.45	3.83	2.25	1.69	1.41	1.24	1.13	1.06	1.02	0.99			
0.50	3.86	2.27	1.71	1.42	1.25	1.14	1.07	1.03	1.00	1.03		
0.55	3.83	2.25	1.69	1.41	1.24	1.13	1.06	1.02	0.99	1.02	1.13	
0.60	3.74	2.20	1.65	1.38	1.21	1.11	1.04	1.00	0.96	1.00	1.11	1.38
0.65	3.59	2.11	1.58	1.32	1.16	1.06	1.00	0.95	0.92	0.95	1.06	1.32
0.70	3.37	1.98	1.49	1.24	1.09	1.00	0.93	0.90	0.87	0.90	1.00	1.24
0.75	3.00	1.81	1.36	1.13	1.00	0.91	0.85	0.82	0.79	0.82	0.91	1.13
0.80	2.71	1.59	1.20	1.00	0.88	0.80	0.75	0.72	0.70	0.72	0.80	1.00
0.85	2.26	1.32	1.00	0.83	0.73	0.67	0.62	0.60	0.58	0.60	0.67	0.83
0.90	1.70	1.00	0.75	0.62	0.55	0.50	0.47	0.45	0.44	0.45	0.50	0.62
0.95	1.00	0.58	0.44	0.36	0.32	0.24	0.27	0.26	0.25	0.26	0.29	0.36

References

Abbott, I. (1981), 'Semantic interference from subliminal stimuli in a word-naming task: the effects of manipulating subjects' arousal level', unpublished project, Bedford College, University of London

Abercrombie, M. L. J. (1960), *The Anatomy of Judgment*, London: Hutchinson

Alivisatos, B., and Wilding, J. (1982), *Cortex*, vol. 18, pp. 5–22

Allport, D. A. (1980), in G. Claxton (ed.), *Cognitive Psychology: New Directions*, London: Routledge and Kegan Paul

Allport, D. A., Antonis, B., and Reynolds, P. (1972), *Quarterly Journal of Experimental Psychology*, vol. 24, pp. 225–35

Allport, F. H. (1955), *Theories of Perception and the Concept of Structure*, New York: Wiley

Allport, G. M., and Pettigrew, T. F. (1957), *Journal of Abnormal and Social Psychology*, vol. 55, pp. 104–13

Alluisi, E. (1965), *Perceptual and Motor Skills*, vol. 20, pp. 815–16

Ames, A., Jr (1951), *Psychological Monographs*, vol. 65, whole no. 324, pp. 1–32

Aronson, E., and Rosenbloom, S. (1971), *Science*, vol. 172, pp. 1161–3

Asch, S. E. (1955), *Scientific American*, vol. 192 (5), pp. 31–5

Ashley, W., Harper, R., and Runyon, D. (1951), *American Journal of Psychology*, vol. 64, pp. 564–72

Atkinson, J. W., and Walker, E. L. (1956), *Journal of Abnormal and Social Psychology*, vol. 53, pp. 38–41

Atkinson, R. C., Holmgren, J. E., and Juola, J. F. (1969), *Perception and Psychophysics*, vol. 6, pp. 321–6

Attneave, F. (1950), *American Journal of Psychology*, vol. 63, pp. 516–56

Attneave, F. (1959), *Applications of Information Theory to Psychology*, New York: Holt, Rinehart and Winston

Audley, R. J. (1960), *Psychological Review*, vol. 67, pp. 1–15

Audley, R. J. (1973), in S. Kornblum (ed.), *Attention and Performance*, vol. 4, London: Academic Press

Audley, R. J., Caudrey, D. J., Howell, P., and Powell, D. J. (1975), in P. M. A. Rabbitt and S. Dornic (eds.), *Attention and Performance* vol. 5, London: Academic Press

Audley, R. J., and Pike, A. R. (1965), *British Journal of Mathematical and Statistical Psychology*, vol. 18, pp. 207–25

Ayllon, T., and Sommer, R. (1956), *Journal of Psychology*, vol. 41, pp. 163–76

Baddeley, A. D., and Hitch, G. (1974), in G. H. Bower (ed.), *The Psychology of Learning and Motivation*, vol. 8, New York: Academic Press

Bamber, D. (1969), *Perception and Psychophysics*, vol. 6, pp. 169–74

Banks, M. S., Aslin, R. N., and Letson, R. D. (1975), *Science*, vol. 190, pp. 675–7

Baron, J. (1973), *Quarterly Journal of Experimental Psychology*, vol. 25, pp. 241–6

Bastian, J., Eimas, P. D., and Liberman, A. M. (1961), *Journal of the Acoustical Society of America*, vol. 33, p. 842

Becker, C. A. (1979), *Journal of Experimental Psychology: Human Perception and Performance*, vol. 5, pp. 252–9

Becker, C. A., and Killion, T. H. (1977), *Journal of Experimental Psychology: Human Perception and Performance*, vol. 3, pp. 389–401

Beller, H. K. (1970), *Journal of Experimental Psychology*, vol. 84, pp. 213–19

Benson, D. F. (1981), in F. J. Pirozzolo and M. C. Wittrock (eds.), *Neuropsychological and Cognitive Processes in Reading*, New York: Academic Press

Berko, J. (1958), *Word*, vol. 14, pp. 150–77

Berlin, B., and Kay, P. (1969), *Basic Colour Terms: Their Universality and Evolution*, Berkeley: University of California Press

Bernstein, I. H., and Reese, C. (1965), *Psychonomic Science*, vol. 3, pp. 259–60

Bertelson, P. (1966), *Quarterly Journal of Experimental Psychology*, vol. 18, pp. 153–64

Bertelson, P., and Tisseyre, F. (1966), *Nature*, vol. 212, pp. 1069–70

Beveridge, W. M. (1935), *British Journal of Psychology*, vol. 26, pp. 59–62

Beyrl, R. (1926), *Zeitschrift für Psychologie*, vol. 100, pp. 344–71

Biederman, I., Mezzanotte, R. J., Rabinowitz, J. C., Francolini, C. M., and Plude, D. (1981), *Human Factors*, vol. 23, pp. 153–64

Biederman, I., Mezzanotte, R. J., and Rabinowitz, J. C. (1982), *Cognitive Psychology*, vol. 14, pp. 143–77

Birch, H. G., and Belmont, L. (1964), *American Journal of Orthopsychiatry*, vol. 34, pp. 852–61

Blakemore, C. (1970), *Journal of Physiology*, vol. 209, pp. 155–78

Blakemore, C. (1973), in R. A. Hinde and J. Stevenson-Hinde, (eds.), *Constraints on Learning*, London: Academic Press

Blakemore, C. (1975), in M. S. Gazzaniga and C. Blakemore (eds.), *Handbook of Psychobiology*, New York: Academic Press

Blakemore, C., and Campbell, F. W. (1969), *Journal of Physiology*, vol. 203, pp. 237–60

Bootzin, R. R., and Natsoulas, T. (1965), *Journal of Personality and Social Psychology*, vol. 1, pp. 461–8

Bower, T. G. R. (1964), *Psychonomic Science*, vol. 1, p. 368

Bower, T. G. R. (1965), *Science*, vol. 149, pp. 88–9

Bower, T. G. R. (1966a), *Science*, vol. 151, pp. 832–4

Bower, T. G. R. (1966b), *Scientific American*, vol. 215 (6), pp. 60–92

Bower, T. G. R. (1974), *Development in Infancy*, San Francisco: Freeman

Bower, T. G. R., Broughton, J. M., and Moore, M. K. (1970a), *Perception and Psychophysics*, vol. 8, pp. 51–3

Bower, T. G. R., Broughton, J. M., and Moore, M. K. (1970b), *Nature*, vol. 228, pp. 679–81

Bower, T. G. R., Broughton, J. M. and Moore, M. K. (1970c), *Perception and Psychophysics*, vol. 9, pp. 193–6

Bower, T. G. R., Broughton, J. M., and Moore, M. K. (1971), *Journal of Experimental Child Psychology*, vol. 11, pp. 182–93

Bower, T. G. R. and Wishart, J. G. (1972), *Cognition*, vol. 1, pp. 165–72

Bowerman, M. (1977), in P. N. Johnson-Laird and P. Wason (eds.), *Thinking: Readings in Cognitive Science*, Cambridge: Cambridge University Press

Brebner, J., and Gordon, J. (1962), *Quarterly Journal of Experimental Psychology*, vol. 14, pp. 113–16

Broadbent, D. E. (1958), *Perception and Communication*, London: Pergamon

Broadbent, D. E. (1962), *Scientific American*, vol. 206 (4), p. 143–51

Broadbent, D. E. (1971), *Decision and Stress*, London: Academic Press

Broadbent, D. E., and Gregory, M. (1962), *Nature*, vol. 193, pp. 1315–16

Broadbent, D. E., and Gregory, M. (1967), *Nature*, vol. 215, pp. 581–4

Broadbent, D. E., Ladefoged, P., and Lawrence, W. (1956), *Nature*, vol. 178, pp. 815–16

Brown, D. R. (1953), *American Journal of Psychology*, vol. 66, pp. 199–214

Brown, R. W. (1965), *Social Psychology*, Glencoe, Illinois: Free Press

Brown, R. W. (1976), *Cognition*, vol. 4, pp. 125–53

Brown, R. W., and Lenneberg, E. (1956), *Journal of Abnormal and Social Psychology*, vol. 49, pp. 454–62

Bruce, D. J. (1964), *British Journal of Educational Psychology*, vol. 34, pp. 158–70

Bruner, J. S., and Goodman, C. C. (1947), *Journal of Abnormal and Social Psychology*, vol. 42, pp. 33–44

Bruner, J. S., Goodnow, J. J., and Austin, G. A. (1956), *A Study of Thinking*, New York: Wiley

Bruner, J. S., and Kenney, H. (1966), in J. S. Bruner, R. R. Olver and P. M. Greenfield (eds.), *Studies in Cognitive Growth*, New York: Wiley

Bruner, J. S., and Olver, R. R. (1963), *Monographs of the Society for Research in Child Development*, vol. 28, whole no. 86, pp. 125–41

Bruner, J. S., and Postman, L. (1946), *Journal of Personality*, vol. 15, pp. 300–8

Bruner, J. S., and Postman, L. (1949), *Journal of Personality*, vol. 18, pp. 206–23

Bryant, P. E., Jones, P., Claxton, V., and Perkins, G. M. (1972), *Nature*, vol. 240, pp. 303–4

Byrne, D. (1961), *Journal of Personality*, vol. 29, pp. 334–49

Calfee, R. C. (1976), in D. Klahr (ed.), *Cognition and Instruction*, Hillsdale, NJ: Erlbaum

Calfee, R. C., and Spector, J. E. (1981), in F. J. Pirozzolo and M. C. Wittrock (eds.), *Neuropsychological and Cognitive Processes in Reading*, New York: Academic Press

Carey, S., and Diamond, R. (1977), *Science*, vol. 195, pp. 312–14

Carmichael, L., Hogan, H. P., and Walter, A. A. (1932), *Journal of Experimental Psychology*, vol. 15, pp. 73–86

Carpenter, B., Wiener, M., and Carpenter, J. J. (1956), *Journal of Abnormal and Social Psychology*, vol. 52, pp. 380–3

Carroll, J. B., and Casagrande, J. B. (1958), in E. Maccoby, T. M. Newcomb and E. L. Hartley (eds.), *Readings in Social Psychology*, 3rd edn, New York: Holt, Rinehart and Winston

Carter, L., and Schooler, E. (1949), *Psychological Review*, vol. 56, pp. 200–8

Chapman, C. R., and Feather, B. W. (1972), *Journal of Experimental Psychology*, vol. 93, pp. 338–42

Chase, W. G., and Posner, M. I. (1965), paper presented to the Midwestern Psychological Association, Chicago, Illinois

Chase, W. G., and Simon, H. (1973), *Cognitive Psychology*, vol. 4, pp. 55–81

Cherry, E. C. (1953), *Journal of the Acoustical Society of America*, vol. 25, pp. 975–9

Clark, H. H., and Clark, E. V. (1977), *Psychology and Language: An Introduction to Psycholinguistics*, New York: Harcourt, Brace, Jovanovich

Clark, M. M. (1970), *Reading Difficulties in Schools*, Harmondsworth: Penguin

Clark, S. E. (1969), *Journal of Experimental Psychology*, vol. 82, pp. 263–6

Cole, M., and Scribner, S. (1974), *Culture and Thought: A Psychological Introduction*, London: Wiley

Cole, R. A., Coltheart, M., and Allard, F. (1974), *Quarterly Journal of Experimental Psychology*, vol. 26, pp. 1–7

Cole, R. A., and Scott, B. (1974), *Psychological Review*, vol. 81, pp. 348–74

Coltheart, M., Davelaar, E., Jonasson, J. T., and Besner, D. (1977), in S. Dornic (ed.), *Attention and Performance*, vol. 6, Hillsdale, NJ: Erlbaum

Connor, J. M. (1972), *Perception and Psychophysics*, vol. 12. pp. 121–8

Cornsweet, J. N. (1970), *Visual Perception*, New York: Academic Press

Corteen, R. S., and Wood, B. (1972), *Journal of Experimental Psychology*, vol. 94, pp. 308–13

Cowen, E. L., and Beier, E. G. (1954), *Journal of Abnormal and Social Psychology*, vol. 49, pp. 178–82

Craft, J. L., and Hinrichs, J. V. (1975), *Perceptual and Motor Skills*, vol, 41, pp. 323–6

Craik, F. I. M., and Kirsner, K. (1974), *Quarterly Journal of Experimental Psychology*, vol. 26, pp. 274–84

Craik, F. I. M., and Lockhart, R. S. (1972), *Journal of Verbal Learning and Verbal Behaviour*, vol. 11, pp. 671–84

Crane, N. L., and Ross, L. E. (1967), *Journal of Experimental Child Psychology*, vol. 5, pp. 1–15

Crossman, E. R. F. W. (1955), *Quarterly Journal of Experimental Psychology*, vol. 7, pp. 176–95

Darwin, C. J. (1981), *Quarterly Journal of Experimental Psychology*, vol. 33A, pp. 185–207

Delattre, P. C., Liberman, A. M., and Cooper, F. S. (1955), *Journal of the Acoustical Society of America*, vol. 27, pp. 769–73

Deregowski, J. B. (1980), *Illusions, Patterns and Pictures*, London: Academic Press

Deregowski, J. B., Muldrow, E. S., and Muldrow, W. F. (1972), *Perception*, vol. 1, pp. 417–25

Deutsch, J. A., and Deutsch, D. (1967), *Quarterly Journal of Experimental Psychology*, vol. 19, pp. 362–3

Devalois, R. L., and Devalois, K. K. (1975), in E. C. Carterette and M. P. Friedman (eds.), *Handbook of Perception*, vol. 5, New York: Academic Press

Dews, P. B., and Wiesel, J. N. (1970), *Journal of Physiology*, vol. 206, pp. 437–55

Diehl, R. L. (1981), *Psychological Bulletin*, vol. 89, pp. 1–18

Dixon, N. F. (1958), *Quarterly Journal of Experimental Psychology*, vol. 10, pp. 211–19

Dixon, N. F. (1971), *Subliminal Perception: The Nature of a Controversy*, London: McGraw-Hill

Dixon, N. F. (1981), *Preconscious Processing*, Chichester: Wiley

Dixon, N. F., and Henley, S. H. A. (1980), in M. A. Jeeves (ed.), *Psychology Survey III*, London: George Allen and Unwin

Donaldson, M. (1976), in V. Hamilton and M. D. Vernon (eds.), *The Development of Cognitive Processes*, London: Academic Press

Donders, F. C. (1868), translation in *Acta Psychologica*, vol. 30 (1969) pp. 412–31; also published as: W. G. Koster, (ed.), *Attention and Performance*, vol. 2, Amsterdam: North Holland Publishing Co.

Dorfman, D. D. (1970), *Journal of Personality and Social Psychology*, vol. 7, pp. 1–10

Dorfman, D. D., Grossberg, J. M., and Kroeker, L. (1965), *Journal of Personality and Social Psychology*, vol. 2, pp. 552–62

Dowling, J. E., and Boycott, B. B. (1966), *Proceedings of the Royal Society of London*, series B, vol. 166, pp. 80–111

Doyle, A. B. (1973), *Journal of Experimental Child Psychology*, vol. 15, pp. 100–15

Drever, J. (1955), *American Journal of Psychology*, vol. 68, pp. 605–14

Dulany, D. E. (1957), *Journal of Abnormal and Social Psychology*, vol. 55, pp. 333–8

Dumas, J. (1972), *Perception and Psychophysics*, vol. 11, pp. 209–12

Egeth, H., Ionides, J., and Wall, S. (1972), *Cognitive Psychology*, vol. 3, pp. 674–98

Eimas, P. D., and Corbit, J. D. (1973), *Cognitive Psychology*, vol. 4, pp. 99–109

Eimas, P. D., Siqueland, E. R., Jusczyk, P., and Vigorito, P. (1971), *Science*, vol. 171, pp. 303–6

Elkind, D. (1969), in L. P. Lipsitt, and H. W. Reese, (eds.), *Advances in Child Development and Behaviour*, vol. 4, New York: Academic Press

Epstein, W. (1967), *Varieties of Perceptual Learning*, New York: McGraw-Hill

Erdelyi, M. H. (1974), *Psychological Review*, vol. 81, pp. 1–25

Eriksen, C. W. (1951), *Journal of Abnormal and Social Psychology*, vol. 46, pp. 557–64

Eriksen, C. W., and Collins, J. F. (1969), *Journal of Experimental Psychology*, vol. 80, pp. 489–92

Eriksen, C. W., and Johnson, H. J. (1964), *Journal of Experimental Psychology*, vol. 68, pp. 28–36

Erwin, D. E. (1976), *Journal of Experimental Psychology: Human Perception and Performance*, vol. 2, pp. 191–209

Esposito, N. J. (1975), *Psychological Bulletin*, vol. 82, pp. 432–55

Estes, W. K. (1972), *Perception and Psychophysics*, vol. 12, pp. 278–86

Ettlinger, G. (1967), in W. Wathen-Dunn (ed.), *Models for the Perception of Speech and Visual Form*, Cambridge, Mass.: MIT Press

Fantz, R. L. (1961), *Scientific American*, vol. 204 (5), pp. 66–72

Fantz, R. L. (1963), *Science*, vol. 140, pp. 296–7

Fantz, R. L., and Ordy, J. M. (1959), *Psychological Research*, vol. 9, pp. 159–64

Fitts, P. M., and Switzer, G. (1962), *Journal of Experimental Psychology*, vol. 63, pp. 321–9

Fletcher, B. C. (1981), *Quarterly Journal of Experimental Psychology*, vol. 33A, pp. 167–76

Foley, J. P. (1940), *Journal of Genetic Psychology*, vol. 56, pp. 21–51

Forsman, A. (1967), *Journal of Experimental Child Psychology*, vol. 5, pp. 406–29

Forster, D. M., and Grierson, A. T. (1978), *British Journal of Psychology*, vol. 69, pp. 489–98

Fourcin, A. J. (1980), in H. A. Beagley (ed.) *Auditory Investigation: The Scientific and Technological Basis*, Oxford: Clarendon Press

Frisby, J. P. (1979), *Seeing*, Oxford: Oxford University Press

Fry, D. B. (1964), *Phonetica*, vol. 11, pp. 164–74

Fulkerson, S. C. (1957), *Journal of Experimental Psychology*, vol. 54, pp. 188–94

Garner, W. R. (1970), *American Psychologist*, vol. 25, pp. 350–8

Garner, W. R. (1974), *The Processing of Information and Structure*, New York: Wiley

Gazzaniga, M. S., and Sperry, R. W. (1967), *Brain*, vol. 90, pp. 131–48

Georgeson, M. (1979), in N. S. Sutherland (ed.), *Tutorial Essays in Psychology*, vol. 2, Hillsdale, NJ: Erlbaum

Geschwind, N., Quadfasel, F. A., and Segarra, F. (1968), *Neuropsychologia*, vol. 6, pp. 327–40

Geyer, L. H., and Dewald, C. G. (1973), *Perception and Psychophysics*, vol. 14, pp. 471–82

Gholson, B., and Hohle, R. H. (1969), *Journal of Experimental Psychology*, vol. 82, pp. 581–3

Gibson, E. J. (1969), *Principles of Perceptual Learning and Development*, New York: Appleton-Century-Crofts

Gibson, E. J., and Bergman, R. (1954), *Journal of Experimental Psychology*, vol. 48, pp. 473–82

Gibson, E. J., Bergman, R., and Purdy, J. (1955), *Journal of Experimental Psychology*, vol. 50, pp. 97–105

Gibson, E. J., and Levin, H. (1975), *The Psychology of Reading*, Cambridge, Mass.: MIT Press

Gibson, E. J., Shurcliff, A., and Yonas, A. (1970), in H. Levin and J. P. Williams (eds.), *Basic Studies in Reading*, New York: Basic Books

Gibson, E. J. and Walk, R. D. (1960), *Scientific American*, vol. 202 (4), pp. 64–71

Gibson, E. J., Walk, R. D., Pick, H. L., and Tighe, T. J. (1958), *Journal of Comparative and Physiological Psychology*, vol. 51, pp. 584–7

Gibson, E. J., and Yonas, A. (1966), *Perception and Psychophysics*, vol. 1, pp. 169–71

Gibson, J. J. (1950), *The Perception of the Visual World*, Boston: Houghton Mifflin

Gibson, J. J. (1959), in S. Koch (ed.), *Psychology: A Study of a Science*, vol. 1, New York: McGraw-Hill

Gibson, J. J. (1966), *The Senses Considered as Perceptual Systems*, Boston: Houghton Mifflin

Gibson, J. J. (1979), *The Ecological Approach to Perception*, Boston: Houghton Mifflin

Gibson, J. J., and Gibson, E. J. (1955), *Psychological Review*, vol. 62, pp. 32–41

Gilchrist, A. L. (1977), *Science*, vol. 195, pp. 185–7

Gilchrist, J. C., Ludeman, J. F., and Lysak, W. (1954), *Journal of Abnormal and Social Psychology*, vol. 49, pp. 423–6

Gilchrist, J. C., and Nesberg, L. S. (1952), *Journal of Experimental Psychology*, vol. 44, pp. 369–76

Gilinsky, A. S., and Cohen, H. H. (1972), *Perception and Psychophysics*, vol. 11, pp. 129–34

Gleitman, L. R., and Rozin, P. (1977), in A. S. Reber and D. L. Scarborough, (eds.), *Toward a Psychology of Reading: The Proceedings of the CUNY Conference*, Hillsdale, NJ: Erlbaum

Goldiamond, I., and Hawkins, W. T. (1958), *Journal of Experimental Psychology*, vol. 56, pp. 457–63

Gough, P. B. (1972), in J. K. Kavanagh and I. G. Mattingley (eds.), *Language by Eye and Ear*, Cambridge, Mass.: MIT Press

Gray, J. A., and Wedderburn, A. A. (1960), *Quarterly Journal of Experimental Psychology*, vol. 12, pp. 180–4

Green, D. M. (1956), in J. A. Swets (ed.), *Signal Detection and Recognition by Human Observers: Contemporary Readings*, New York: Wiley

Gregory, R. L. (1969), *Eye and Brain*, New York: McGraw-Hill

Gregory, R. L. (1970), *The Intelligent Eye*, New York: McGraw-Hill

Gregory, R. L., and Wallace, J. G. (1963), *Experimental Psychology Society*, Monographs no. 2

Griffiths, P., and Atkinson, M. (1976), 'A door to verbs', paper presented at the third International Child Language Symposium

Gross, C. G., Rocha-Miranda, C. E., and Bender, D. B. (1972), *Journal of Neurophysiology*, vol. 35, pp. 96-111

Guzman, A. (1969), in A. Grasselli (ed.), *Automatic Interpretation and Classification of Images*, New York: Academic Press

Haber, L. R., and Haber, R. N. (1981), in F. J. Pirozzolo and M. C. Wittrock (eds.), *Neuropsychological and Cognitive Processes in Reading*, New York: Academic Press

Hagen, M. A., and Jones, R. K. (1978), in R. Walk and H. Pick (eds.), *Perception and Experience*, New York: Plenum

Haith, M. M., Morrison, F. J., Sheingold, K., and Mindes, P. (1973), *Journal of Experimental Child Psychology*, vol. 15, pp. 454–69

Hale, D. J. (1967), *Quarterly Journal of Experimental Psychology*, vol. 19, pp. 133–41

Hale, G. A. (1979), in G. A. Hale and M. Lewis (eds.), *Attention and Cognitive Development*, New York: Plenum

Hardy, G. R., and Legge, D. (1968), *Quarterly Journal of Experimental Psychology*, vol. 20, pp. 20–9

Hardyck, C. D., and Petrinovich, L. F. (1970), *Journal of Verbal Learning and Verbal Behaviour*, vol. 9, pp. 647–52

Harm, O. J., and Lappin, J. S. (1973), *Journal of Experimental Psychology*, vol. 100, pp. 416–18

Harper, R. S. (1953), *American Journal of Psychology*, vol. 66, pp. 86–9

Harway, N. I. (1963), *Journal of Experimental Psychology*, vol. 65, pp. 385–90

Hatano, G., Miyake, Y., and Binks, M. G. (1977), *Cognition*, vol. 5, pp. 57–71

Hebb, D. O. (1949), *The Organization of Behaviour*, New York: Wiley

Held, R., Birch, E., and Gwiazda, J. (1980), *Proceedings of the National Academy of Sciences*, vol. 77, pp. 55–72

Held, R., and Hein, A. (1963), *Journal of Comparative and Physiological Psychology*, vol. 56, pp. 872–6

Held, R., and Rekosh, J. (1963), *Science*, vol. 141, pp. 722–3

Helmholz, H. von (1850), *Physiological Optics*, ed. J. P. C. Southall, New York: Dover (1964)

Helson, H. (1959), in S. Koch (ed.), *Psychology: A Study of a Science*, vol. 1, New York: McGraw-Hill

Henderson, L. (1977), in N. S. Sutherland (ed.), *Tutorial Essays in Psychology*, vol. 1, Hillsdale, NJ: Erlbaum

Hering, E. (1877), *Outlines of a Theory of the Light Sense*, trans. L. M. Hurvich and D. Jameson, Cambridge, Mass: Harvard University Press (1964)

Hess, E. (1956), *Scientific American*, vol. 195 (1), pp. 71–80

Hess, E. (1965), *Scientific American*, vol. 212 (4), pp. 46–54

Hick, W. E. (1952), *Quarterly Journal of Experimental Psychology*, vol. 4, pp. 11–26

Hinrichs, J. V. (1970), *Psychonomic Science*, vol. 21, pp. 227–8

Hinrichs, J. V., and Krainz, P. L. (1970), *Journal of Experimental Psychology*, vol. 85, pp. 330–4

Hochberg, J. (1968), in R. N. Haber (ed.), *Contemporary Theory and Research in Visual Perception*, New York: Holt, Rinehart and Winston

Hochberg, J. (1972), in J. W. Kling and L. A. Riggs, *Woodworth and Schlosberg's Experimental Psychology*, revised edn, London: Methuen

Hochberg, J. (1978), *Perception*, 2nd edn, Englewood Cliffs, NJ: Prentice-Hall

Hochberg, J., and Beck, J. (1954), *Journal of Experimental Psychology*, vol. 47, pp. 263–6

Hochberg, J., and Brooks, V. (1958), *Journal of Experimental Psychology*, vol. 55, pp. 490–1

Hochberg, J., and Brooks, V. (1962), *American Journal of Psychology*, vol. 75, pp. 624–8

Hochberg, J., and McAlister, E. (1953), *Journal of Experimental Psychology*, vol. 46, pp. 361–4

Hochberg, J., Triebel, W., and Seaman, G. (1951), *Journal of Experimental Psychology*, vol. 41, pp. 153–9

Hockey, G. R. J. (1970), *Quarterly Journal of Experimental Psychology*, vol. 22, pp. 37–42

Hohle, R. H. (1965), *Journal of Experimental Psychology*, vol. 69, pp. 382–6

Hohle, R. H. (1967), in L. P. Lipsitt and C. C. Spiker (eds.), *Advances in Child Development and Behaviour*, vol. 3, New York: Academic Press

Holding, D. H. (1979), in N. S. Sutherland (ed.), *Tutorial Essays in Psychology*, vol. 2, Hillsdale, NJ: Erlbaum

Hubel, D. H., and Wiesel, T. N. (1962), *Journal of Physiology*, vol. 160, pp. 106–54

Hubel, D. H., and Wiesel, T. N. (1963), *Journal of Neurophysiology*, vol. 26, pp. 994–1002

Hubel, D. H., and Wiesel, T. N. (1968), *Journal of Physiology*, vol. 195, pp. 215–43

Hubel, D. H., and Wiesel, T. N. (1970), *Journal of Physiology*, vol. 206, pp. 419–36

Hyman, R. (1953), *Journal of Experimental Psychology*, vol. 45, pp. 188–96

Ionides, J., and Gleitman, H. (1972), *Perception and Psychophysics*, vol. 12, pp. 457–60

Ittelson, W. H., and Kilpatrick, F. P. (1951), *Scientific American*, vol. 185 (2), pp. 50–5

Jackson, D. N. (1954), *Journal of Psychology*, vol. 38, pp. 339–57

Jahoda, G. (1979), *British Journal of Psychology*, vol. 70, pp. 351–63

Jahoda, G., and McGurk, H. (1974), *British Journal of Psychology*, vol. 65, pp. 141–9

Jakobson, R., Fant, G. G. M., and Halle, M. (1961), *Preliminaries to Speech Analysis: The Distinctive Features and their Correlates*, Cambridge, Mass.: MIT Press

Johnson, J. C., and McClelland, J. L. (1973), *Perception and Psychophysics*, vol. 14, pp. 365–70

Johnson, N. F. (1975), *Journal of Verbal Learning and Verbal Behaviour*, vol. 14, pp. 17–29

Jones, B. (1974), *Bulletin of the Psychonomic Society*, vol. 3, pp. 163–5

Juel, C. L. (1977), 'An independent-process model of reading for beginning readers', unpublished doctoral dissertation, Stanford University

Julesz, B. (1964), *Science*, vol. 145, pp. 356–62

Juola, J. F., Schadler, M., Chabot, R., McCaughey, M., and Wait, J. (1979), in L. B. Reznick and P. A. Weaver (eds.), *Theory and Practice of Early Reading*, Hillsdale, NJ: Erlbaum

Just, M. A., and Carpenter, P. A. (1980), *Psychological Review*, vol. 87, pp. 329–54

Kahneman, D. (1966), *Journal of Experimental Psychology*, vol. 71, pp. 543–9

Kahneman, D. (1973), *Attention and Effort*, New York: Prentice-Hall

Kanizsa, G. (1955), *Rivista di Psicologia*, vol. 49, pp. 7–30

Kantowitz, B. H. (1974), in B. H. Kantowitz (ed.), *Human Information Processing*, Hillsdale, NJ: Erlbaum

Kemler, D., and Smith, L. (1979), *Journal of Experimental Psychology: General*, vol. 108, pp. 133–50

Kendler, H. H., and Kendler, J. S. (1962), *Psychological Review*, vol. 69, pp. 1–16

Kinsbourne, M., and Warrington, E. K. (1964), *Journal of Neurology, Neurosurgery and Psychiatry*, vol. 27, pp. 296–9

Klatzky, R., and Thompson, A. (1975), paper presented at sixteenth meeting of the Psychonomic Society, Denver, Colorado

Kleiman, G. M. (1975), *Journal of Verbal Learning and Verbal Behaviour*, vol. 14, pp. 323–39

Kohler, I. (1964), *Psychological Issues*, vol. 3, pp. 1–173

Koffka, K. (1935), *Principles of Gestalt Psychology*, New York: Harcourt Brace

Kornblum, S. (1975), in P. M. A. Rabbitt and S. Dornic (eds.), *Attention and Performance*, vol. 5, London: Academic Press

Laberge, D. (1975), in P. M. A. Rabbitt and S. Dornic (eds.), *Attention and Performance*, vol. 5, London: Academic Press

Lambert, W. W., Solomon, R. L., and Watson, P. D. (1949), *Journal of Experimental Psychology*, vol. 37, pp. 637–41

Lappin, J. S. (1967), *Journal of Experimental Psychology*, vol. 75, pp. 321–8

Lappin, J. S., and Disch, K. (1972a), *Journal of Experimental Psychology*, vol. 92; pp. 419–27

Lappin, J. S., and Disch, K. (1972b), *Journal of Experimental Psychology*, vol. 93, pp. 367–72

Lappin, J. S., and Disch, K. (1973), *Journal of Experimental Psychology*, vol. 98, pp. 279–85

Lazarus, R. S., and McCleary, R. A. (1951), *Psychological Review*, vol. 58, pp. 171–9

Lazarus, R. S., Yousem, H., and Arenberg, D. (1953), *Journal of Personality*, vol. 21, pp. 312–28

Leibowitz, H. W., and Judish, J. M. (1967), *American Journal of Psychology*, vol. 80, pp. 105–9

Leibowitz, H. W., Shiina, K., and Hennessy, R. J. (1972), *Perception and Psychophysics*, vol. 12, pp. 497–500

Lettvin, J. Y., Maturana, H. R., Pitts, W. H., and McCulloch, W. S. (1959), *Proceedings of the Institute of Radio Engineering*, vol. 47, pp. 1940–51

Leventhal, A. G., and Hirsch, H. V. B. (1975), *Science*, vol. 190, pp. 902–4

Levin, H., and Turner, A. (1968), in H. Levin, E. J. Gibson, and J. J. Gibson (eds.), *The Analysis of Reading Skill*, Washington, DC: US Department of Health, Education and Welfare

Levine, R., Chein, E., and Murphy, G. (1942), *Journal of Psychology*, vol. 13, pp. 283–93

Levy, B. A. (1977), *Journal of Verbal Learning and Verbal Behaviour*, vol. 16, pp. 623–38

Lewis, J. L. (1970), *Journal of Experimental Psychology*, vol. 85, pp. 225–8

Liberman, A. M., Cooper, F. S., Harris, K. S., and MacNeilage, P. F. (1962), in *Proceedings of the Speech Communication Seminar*, vol. 2, Stockholm: Royal Institute of Technology

Liberman, I. Y., and Shankweiler, P. (1979), in L. B. Reznick and P. A. Weaver (eds.), *Theory and Practice of Early Reading*, vol. 2, Hillsdale, NJ: Erlbaum

Lindsay, P. H., and Norman, D. A. (1977), *Human Information Processing*, 2nd edn, London: Academic Press

Lockhead, G. R. (1966), *Journal of Experimental Psychology*, vol. 72, pp. 95–104

Lockhead, G. R. (1972), *Psychological Review*, vol. 79, pp. 410–19

Lockhead, G. R. (1979), *Journal of Experimental Psychology: Human Perception and Performance*, vol. 5, pp. 746–55

Lysak, W. (1954), *Journal of Experimental Psychology*, vol. 47, pp. 343–50

McClelland, D. C., and Liberman, A. M. (1949), *Journal of Personality*, vol. 18, pp. 236–51

McClelland, J. L. (1976), *Journal of Experimental Psychology, Human Perception and Performance*, vol. 2, pp. 80–91

McClelland, J. L., and Rumelhart, D. E. (1981), *Psychological Review*, vol. 88, pp. 375–407

Maccoby, E. E., and Konrad, K. W. (1966), *Journal of Experimental Child Psychology*, vol. 3, pp. 113–22

McGinnies, E. M. (1949), *Psychological Review*, vol. 56, pp. 244–51

McGinnies, E. M., and Sherman, H. (1952), *Journal of Abnormal and Social Psychology*, vol. 47, pp. 81–5

Mackay, D. M. (1973), *Quarterly Journal of Experimental Psychology*, vol. 25, pp. 22–40

McKenzie, B. E., and Day, R. H. (1972), *Science*, vol. 178, pp. 1108–10

McLeod, P. (1978), *Quarterly Journal of Experimental Psychology*, vol. 30, pp. 83–9

McNamara, H. J. (1959), *Perceptual and Motor Skills*, vol. 9, pp. 67–80

McNamara, H. J., Solley, C. M., and Long, J. (1958), *Journal of Abnormal and Social Psychology*, vol. 57, pp. 91–8

MacNeilage, P. F. (1970), *Psychological Review*, vol. 77, pp. 182–96

McNeill, D., and Lindig, K. (1973), *Journal of Verbal Learning and Verbal Behaviour*, vol. 12, pp. 419–30

MacNicol, D. (1972), *A Primer of Signal Detection Theory*, London: George Allen and Unwin

Mackworth, N. H., and Bruner, J. S. (1970), *Human Development*, vol. 13, pp. 149–77

Marcel, A. J. (1970), in A. F. Sanders (ed.), *Attention and Performance*, vol. 3, Amsterdam: North Holland Publishing Co.

Marcel, A. J. (1976), 'Unconscious reading: experiments on people who do not know that they are reading', paper presented to the British Association for the Advancement of Science

Marg, E., Adams, J. E., and Rutkin, B. (1968), *Experientia*, vol. 24, pp. 348–50

Marr, D. (1976), *Philosophical Transactions of the Royal Society of London*, series B, vol. 275, pp. 483–519

Marr, D. (1980), *Philosophical Transactions of the Royal Society of London*, series B, vol. 290, pp. 199–218

Marr, D., and Nisihara, H. K. (1978), *Proceedings of the Royal Society of London*, series B, vol. 200, pp. 269–94

Marr, D. and Poggio, T. (1979), *Proceedings of the Royal Society of London*, series B, vol. 204, pp. 301–28

Martin, M. (1979), *Neuropsychologia*, vol. 17, pp. 33-40

Massaro, D. W. (1975), (ed.), *Understanding Language: An Information Processing Analysis of Speech Perception, Reading and Psycholinguistics*, New York: Academic Press

Mattis, S. (1981), in F. J. Pirozzolo and M. C. Wittrock (eds.), *Neuropsychological and Cognitive Processes in Reading*, New York: Academic Press

Mayhew, J. E., Frisby, J. P., and Gale, P. (1977), *Perception*, vol. 6, pp. 207–8

Mayzner, M. S., and Tresselt, M. E. (1969), *Psychonomic Science*, vol. 17, pp. 77–8

Merkel, J. (1885), *Philosophische Studien*, vol. 2, pp. 73–127

Meyer, D. E., Schvaneveldt, R. W., and Ruddy, M. G. (1975), in P. M. A. Rabbitt and S. Dornic, (eds.), *Attention and Performance*, vol. 5, New York: Academic Press

Mezrich, J. J. (1973), *Perception and Psychophysics*, vol. 13, pp. 45–8

Miller, D. R., and Walk, R. D. (1975), 'Self-produced movement is unnecessary for the development of visually-guided depth discrimination', paper presented at Eastern Psychological Association Meeting, New York

Miller, G. A., and Johnson-Laird, P. N. (1975), *Language and Perception*, Cambridge: Cambridge University Press

Miller, G. A., and Nicely, P. (1955), *Journal of the Acoustical Society of America*, vol. 27, pp. 338–52

Miller, J. O., and Pachella, R. G. (1973), *Journal of Experimental Psychology*, vol. 101, pp. 227–31

Miller, L. (1969), *Perceptual and Motor Skills*, vol. 28, pp. 631–9

Miller, N. E., and Dollard, J. (1941), *Social Learning and Imitation*, New Haven: Yale University Press

Moray, N. (1969), *Listening and Attention*, Harmondsworth: Penguin

Morton, J. (1969), *British Journal of Psychology*, vol. 60, pp. 329–46

Mueller, J. H. (1976), in M. Zuckerman and C. D. Spielberger (eds.), *Emotions and Anxiety: New Concepts, Methods and Applications*, Hillsdale, NJ: Erlbaum

Mundy Castle, A. C., and Nelson, G. K. (1962), *Psychologica Africana*, vol. 9, pp. 240–71

Neisser, U. (1963), *American Journal of Psychology*, vol. 76, pp. 376–85

Neisser, U. (1966), *Cognitive Psychology*, New York: Appleton-Century-Crofts

Nelson, K. (1977), in P. N. Johnson-Laird and P. C. Wason (eds.), *Thinking: Readings in Cognitive Science*, Cambridge: Cambridge University Press

Newbigging, P. L. (1961), *Canadian Journal of Psychology*, vol. 15, pp. 123–32 and 133–42

Newell, A., and Simon, H. A. (1972), *Human Problem Solving*, Englewood Cliffs, NJ: Prentice-Hall

Newstead, S. E., and Dennis, I. (1979), *Quarterly Journal of Experimental Psychology*, vol. 31, pp. 477–88

Norman, D. A. (1968), *Psychological Review*, vol. 75, pp. 522–36

Norman, D. A. (1969), *Quarterly Journal of Experimental Psychology*, vol. 21, pp. 85–93

Norman, D. A., and Bobrow, D. G. (1975), *Cognitive Psychology*, vol. 7, pp. 44–64

Pachella, R. G. (1974), in B. H. Kantowitz (ed.), *Human Information Processing*, Hillsdale, NJ: Erlbaum

Pachella, R. G., and Miller, J. O. (1976), *Perception and Psychophysics*, vol. 19, pp. 29–34

Palmer, S. E. (1975), in D. A. Norman, D. E. Rumelhart, and LNR Research Group (eds.), *Explorations in Cognition*, San Francisco: Freeman

Parks, T. E. (1965), *American Journal of Psychology*, vol. 76, pp. 145–7

Patterson, K. E. (1981), *British Journal of Psychology*, vol. 72, pp. 151–74
Penfield, W. (1952), *Archives of Neurology and Psychiatry*, vol. 67, pp. 178–98
Perrin, S., and Spencer, C. (1980), *Bulletin of the British Psychological Society*, vol. 32, pp. 405–6
Peterson, L. R. (1969), *Psychological Review*, vol. 76, pp. 376–86
Pettigrew, T. F., Allport, G. W., and Barnett, E. O. (1958), *British Journal of Psychology*, vol 49, pp. 265–78
Pew, R. W. (1969), *Acta Psychologica*, vol. 30, pp. 16–26; also published as W. G. Koster (ed.), *Attention and Performance*, vol. 2, Amsterdam: North Holland Publishing Co.
Pew, R. W., and Rupp, G. (1971), *Journal of Experimental Psychology*, vol. 90, pp. 1–7
Philpott, A., and Wilding, J. (1979), *British Journal of Psychology*, vol. 70, pp. 559–64
Piaget, J. (1955), *The Child's Construction of Reality*, London: Routledge and Kegan Paul
Pick, A. D. (1965), *Journal of Experimental Psychology*, vol. 69, pp. 331–9
Pirozzolo, F. J. (1978), in E. C. Carterette and M. P. Friedman (eds.), *Handbook of Perception*, vol. 9, New York: Academic Press
Pollack, I., and Pickett, J. M. (1964), *Journal of Verbal Learning and Verbal Behaviour*, vol. 3, pp. 79–84
Pomerantz, J. R., and Garner, W. R. (1973), *Perception and Psychophysics*, vol. 14, pp. 565–9
Pomerantz, J. R., and Schwaitzberg, S. D. (1975), *Perception and Psychophysics*, vol. 18, pp. 355–61
Poppel, E., Held, R., and Frost, D. (1973), *Nature*, vol. 243, pp. 295–6
Posner, M. I. (1973), *Cognition: An Introduction*, Glenview, Ill.: Scott, Foresman and Co.
Posner, M. I., and Boies, S. J. (1971), *Psychological Review*, vol. 78, pp. 376–86
Posner, M. I., and Mitchell, R. F. (1967), *Psychological Review*, vol. 74, pp. 392–409
Postman, L., and Schneider, B. (1951), *Psychological Review*, vol. 58, pp. 271–84
Postman, L., Bronson, W. C., and Gropper, G. L. (1953), *Journal of Abnormal and Social Psychology*, vol. 48, pp. 215–24
Postman, L., Bruner, J. S., and McGinnies, E. M. (1948), *Journal of Abnormal and Social Psychology*, vol 43, pp. 142–54
Potter, M. C. (1966), in J. S. Bruner, R. C. Olver and P. M. Greenfield, (eds.), *Studies in Cognitive Growth*, New York: Wiley
Proshansky, H., and Murphy, G. (1942), *Journal of Psychology*, vol. 13, pp. 295–305
Pustell, T. E. (1957), *Journal of Personality*, vol. 25, pp. 425–38

Ratliff, F. (1961), in W. A. Rosenblith (ed.), *Sensory Communication*, Cambridge, Mass.: MIT Press

Rauschecher, J. P., and Harris, L. H. (1981), *Neuroscience Letters*, Supplement 7, abstracts of the fifth European Neuroscience Congress, Liège

Rayner, K., and McConkie, G. W. (1977), in A. S. Reber and D. L. Scarborough (eds.), *Toward a Psychology of Reading: Proceedings of the CUNY Conference*, Hillsdale, NJ: Erlbaum

Reddy, D. R., and Erman, L. D. (1975), in D. R. Reddy (ed.), *Speech Recognition*, New York: Academic Press

Reece, M. M. (1954), *Journal of Abnormal and Social Psychology*, vol. 49, pp. 165–72

Reed, S. (1972), *Cognitive Psychology*, vol. 3, pp. 382–407

Reicher, G. M. (1969), *Journal of Experimental Psychology*, vol. 81, pp. 275–80

Riding, R. J. (1979), *British Journal of Educational Psychology*, vol. 49. pp. 297–303

Rigby, W. K., and Rigby, M. K. (1956), *Perceptual and Motor Skills*, vol. 6. pp. 29–35

Roberts, L. G. (1965), in J. T. Tippet *et al.* (eds.), *Optical and Electro-optical Information Processing*, Cambridge, Mass.: MIT Press

Rock, I. (1966), *The Nature of Perceptual Adaptation*, New York: Basic Books

Rock, I., and Ebenholz, S. (1959), *Psychological Review*, vol. 66, pp. 387–401

Rock, I., and Fleck, F. (1950), *Journal of Experimental Psychology*, vol. 40, pp. 766–76

Rosch, E. (1975), *Journal of Experimental Psychology: General*, vol. 104, pp. 192–233

Rosch, E., and Mervis, C. B. (1975), *Cognitive Psychology*, vol. 7, pp. 573–605

Rosch, E., Mervis, C. B., Gray, W. D., Johnson, D. M., and Boyes–Braem, P. (1976), *Cognitive Psychology*, vol. 8, pp. 382–439

Rozin, P., and Gleitman, L. R. (1977), in A. S. Reber and D. L. Scarborough (eds.), *Toward a Psychology of Reading: Proceedings of the CUNY Conference*, Hillsdale, NJ: Erlbaum

Rozin, P., Puritsky, S., and Sotsky, R. (1971), *Science*, vol. 171, pp. 1264–7

Rubens, A. B., and Benson, D. F. (1971), *Archives of Neurology*, vol. 24, pp. 305–16

Rubenstein, H., Lewis, S. S., and Rubenstein, M. A. (1971), *Journal of Verbal Learning and Verbal Behaviour*, vol. 10, pp. 647–57

Rudishill, M. (1956), *Journal of Psychology*, vol. 42, pp. 317–28

Rumelhart, D. E., and Siple, P. (1974), *Psychological Review*, vol. 81, pp. 99–118

Salapatek, P., and Kessen, W. (1966), *Journal of Experimental Child Psychology*, vol. 3, pp. 155–67

Sales, B. D., and Haber, R. N. (1968), *Perception and Psychophysics*, vol. 3, pp. 156–60

Samuels, S. J., Laberge, D., and Bremer, C. D. (1978), *Journal of Verbal Learning and Verbal Behaviour*, vol. 17, pp. 715–20

Sapir, E. (1929), *Language*, vol. 5, pp. 207–14

Saraga, E., and Shallice, T. (1973), *Perception and Psychophysics*, vol. 13, pp. 261–70

Sasanuma, S., and Fujimura, O. (1971), *Cortex*, vol. 7, pp. 1–18

Satz, P. and Morris, R. (1981), in F. J. Pirozzolo and M. C. Wittrock (eds.), *Neuropsychological and Cognitive Processes in Reading*, New York: Academic Press

Schachter, S., and Singer, J. E. (1962), *Psychological Review*, vol. 69, pp. 379–99

Schafer, R., and Murphy, G. (1943), *Journal of Experimental Psychology*, vol. 32, pp. 335–43

Schatz, C. D. (1954), *Language*, vol. 30, pp. 47–56

Schlodtmann, W. (1902), *Archive für Ophthalmologie*, vol. 54, pp. 256–67

Schneider, W., and Shiffrin, R. M. (1977), *Psychological Review*, vol. 84, pp. 1–66

Schuck, J. R. (1973), *Perception and Psychophysics*, vol. 13, pp. 382–90

Schwartz, S. P., Pomerantz, J. R., and Egeth, H. E. (1977), *Journal of Experimental Psychology: Human Perception and Performance*, vol. 3, pp. 402–10

Secord, P. F., Bevan, W., and Katz, B. (1956), *Journal of Abnormal and Social Psychology*, 53, pp. 78–83

Seeleman, V. (1940), *Archives of Psychology*, New York, no. 258

Selfridge, O. G. (1959), in *The Mechanization of Thought Processes*, London: HMSO

Serpell, R. (1979), *British Journal of Psychology*, vol. 70, pp. 365–80

Seymour, P. H. K. (1979), *Human visual cognition*, New York: Collier Macmillan

Shaffer, L. H. (1975), *Quarterly Journal of Experimental Psychology*, vol. 27, pp. 419–32

Shepard, R. N. (1964), *Journal of Mathematical Psychology*, vol. 1, pp. 54–87

Shepard, R. N., and Metzler, J. (1971), *Science*, vol. 171, pp. 701–3

Shepp, B. E., and Swartz, K. B. (1976), *Journal of Experimental Child Psychology*, vol. 22, pp. 73–85

Shiffrin, R. M., and Schneider, W. (1977), *Psychological Review*, vol. 84, pp. 67–190

Siegel, A. W., and Stevenson, H. W. (1966), *Child Development*, vol. 37, pp. 811–17

Smith, D. C. (1981), *Science*, vol. 213, pp. 1137–9

Smith, D. E. P., and Hochberg, J. E. (1954), *Journal of Psychology*, vol. 38, pp. 83–7

Smith, E. E. (1968), *Psychological Bulletin*, vol. 69, pp. 77–110

Smith, E. E., and Haviland, S. E. (1972), *Journal of Experimental Psychology*, vol. 92, pp. 59–64

Smith, J. A. (1974), 'The relationship between phonemic sensitivity and the effectiveness of phonemic retrieval cues in preliterate children', unpublished doctoral dissertation, University of Pennsylvania

Smith, L., and Kemler, D. (1977), *Journal of Experimental Child Psychology*, vol. 24, pp. 279–98

Smith, L., and Kemler, D. (1978), *Cognitive Psychology*, vol. 10, pp. 502–32

Smith, N. V. (1973), *The Acquisition of Phonology: A Case Study*, Cambridge: Cambridge University Press

Snyder, C. R. R. (1972), *Journal of Experimental Psychology*, vol. 92, pp. 428–31

Snyder, F. W. and Snyder, C. W. (1956), *Journal of Psychology*, vol. 41, pp. 177–84

Solley, C. M. and Engel, M. (1960), *Journal of Genetic Psychology*, vol. 97, pp. 77–91

Solley, C. M. and Long, J. (1958), *Perceptual and Motor Skills*, vol. 8, pp. 235–40

Solley, C. M., and Sommer, R. (1957), *Journal of General Psychology*, vol. 56, pp. 3–11

Solomon, R. L., and Howes, D. H. (1951), *Psychological Review*, vol. 58, pp. 256–70

Somekh, D. E., and Wilding, J. M. (1973), *British Journal of Psychology*, vol. 64, pp. 339–49

Sommer, R. (1956a), *Journal of Psychology*, vol. 42, pp. 143–8

Sommer, R. (1956b), *Journal of Personality*, vol. 25, pp. 550–9

Spelke, E., Hirst, W., and Neisser, U. (1976), *Cognition*, vol. 4, pp. 215–30

Spencer, T. J. (1969), *Journal of Experimental Psychology*, vol. 81, pp. 132–40

Sperling, G. (1960), *Psychological Monographs*, vol. 74 (11, whole no. 498), pp. 1–29

Sperling, G., Budiansky, J., Spivak, J. G., and Johnson, M. C. (1971), *Science*, vol. 174, pp. 307–11

Sperry, R. W. (1951), in S. S. Stevens (ed.), *Handbook of Experimental Psychology*, New York: Wiley

Spreen, O., Benton, A. L., and Fincham, R. W. (1965), *Archives of Neurology*, vol. 13, pp. 84–92

Stanners, R. F., Jastrzembski, J. E., and Westbrook, A. (1975), *Journal of Verbal Learning and Verbal Behaviour*, vol. 14, pp. 259–64

Stanovich, K. E., and Pachella, R. G. (1977), *Journal of Experimental Psychology: Human Perception and Performance*, vol. 3, pp. 411–21

Sternberg, S. (1966), *Science*, vol. 153, pp. 652–4

Sternberg, S. (1969), *Acta Psychologica*, vol. 30, pp. 276–315; also published as W. G. Koster (ed.), *Attention and Performance*, vol. 2, Amsterdam: North Holland Publishing Co.

Stevens, K. N., and Halle, M. (1967), in W. Wathen-Dunn (ed.), *Models for the Perception of Speech and Visual Form*, Cambridge, Mass.: MIT Press

Stewart, V. M. (1973), *International Journal of Psychology*, vol. 8, pp. 83–94

Stratton, G. M. (1896), *Psychological Review*, vol. 3, pp. 611–17

Stratton, G. M. (1897), *Psychological Review*, vol. 4, pp. 182–7

Stryker, M. P., and Sherk, H. (1975), *Science*, vol. 190, pp. 904–6

Studdert-Kennedy, M., and Shankweiler, D. (1970), *Journal of the Acoustical Society of America*, vol. 48, pp. 579–91

Sutherland, N. S. (1961), *Experimental Psychology Society Monographs*, no. 1

Swensson, R. G. (1972), *Perception and Psychophysics*, vol. 12, pp. 16–32

Tajfel, H., and Wilkes, A. L. (1963), *British Journal of Psychology*, vol. 44, pp. 101–14

Taylor, D. A. (1976), *Perception and Psychophysics*, vol. 20, pp. 187–90

Teichner, W. H., and Krebs, M. J. (1974), *Psychological Review*, vol. 81, pp. 75–98

Theios, J. (1975), in P. M. A. Rabbitt and S. Dornic (eds.), *Attention and Performance*, vol. 5, London: Academic Press

Thomas, L. F. (1962), *Ergonomics*, vol. 5, pp. 429–34

Thomas, W. I. (1937), *Primitive Behaviour*, New York: McGraw-Hill

Thouless, R. H. (1933), *Journal of Social Psychology*, vol. 4, pp. 330–9

Tierney, M. (1973), reported in D. A. Allport (1980), p. 140

Townsend, J. T. (1974), in B. H. Kantowitz (ed.), *Human Information Processing*, Hillsdale, NJ: Erlbaum

Treisman, A. (1964a), *American Journal of Psychology*, vol. 77, pp. 533–46

Treisman, A. (1964b), *British Medical Bulletin*, vol. 20, pp. 12–16

Treisman, A. (1964c), *American Journal of Psychology*, vol. 77, pp. 206–19

Treisman, A. (1969), *Psychological Review*, vol. 76, pp. 282–9

Treisman, A. (1977), *Perception and Psychophysics*, vol. 22, pp. 1–14

Treisman, A., and Geffen, G. (1967), *Quarterly Journal of Experimental Psychology*, vol. 19, pp. 1–17

Treisman, A., Squire, R., and Green, J. (1974), *Memory and Cognition*, vol. 2, pp. 641–6

Treisman, A., Russell, R., and Green, J. (1975), in P. M. A. Rabbitt and S. Dornic (eds.), *Attention and Performance*, vol. 5, London: Academic Press

Turnbull, C. (1961), *The Forest People: A Study of Pygmies in the Congo*, New York: Simon and Schuster

Turvey, M. T. (1973), *Psychological Review*, vol. 80, pp. 1–52

Turvey, M. T. (1977), *Psychological Review*, vol. 84, pp. 67–88

Turvey, M. T., and Kravetz, S. (1970), *Perception and Psychophysics*, vol. 8, pp. 171–2

Tversky, A. (1977), *Psychological Review*, vol. 84, pp. 327–50

Uhr, L., and Vossler, C. (1966), in L. Uhr (ed.), *Pattern Recognition*, New York: Wiley

Underwood, G. (1974), *Quarterly Journal of Experimental Psychology*, vol. 26, pp. 368–72

Underwood, G. (1976), *British Journal of Psychology*, vol. 67, pp. 327–38

Updyke, B. V. (1974), *Journal of Neurophysiology*, vol. 37, pp. 896–909

Uttal, W. R., Bunnell, L. M., and Corwin, S. (1970), *Perception and Psychophysics*, vol. 8, pp. 385–8

Vernon, M. D. (1952), *A Further Study of Visual Perception*, Cambridge: Cambridge University Press

Vickers, D. (1979), *Decision Processes in Visual Perception*, London: Academic Press

Vickers, D., Caudrey, D., and Willson, R. (1971), *Acta Psychologica*, vol. 35, pp. 151–72

Vickers, D., Nettelbeck, J., and Willson, R. J. (1972), *Perception*, vol. 1, pp. 263–95

Vurpillot, E. (1976a), *The Visual World of the Child*, London: George Allen and Unwin

Vurpillot, E. (1976b), in V. Hamilton and M. D. Vernon (eds.), *The Development of Cognitive Processes*, London: Academic Press

Vygotsky, L. S. (1962), *Thought and Language*, Cambridge, Mass.: MIT Press

Walk, R. D. (1976), in V. Hamilton and M. D. Vernon (eds.), *The Development of Cognitive Processes*, London: Academic Press

Walk, R. D., and Gibson, E. J. (1961), *Psychological Monographs*, vol. 75, (15, whole no. 519), pp. 1–44

Wallach, H. (1963), *Scientific American*, vol. 208 (1), pp. 107–16

Warren, R. M. (1970), *Science*, vol. 167, pp. 392–3

Warren, R. M. (1971), *Perception and Psychophysics*, vol. 9, pp. 345–9

Warrington, E. K., and Taylor, A. M. (1973), *Cortex*, vol. 9, pp. 152–64

Warrington, E. K., and Taylor, A. M. (1978), *Perception*, vol. 7, pp. 695–705

Weiskrantz, L., Warrington, E. K., Sanders, M. D., and Marshall, J. (1974), *Brain*, vol. 97, pp. 709–28

Weisstein, N., and Harris, C. S. (1974), *Science*, vol. 186, pp. 752–5

Werner, H. (1961), *Comparative Psychology of Mental Development*, New York: Science Editions

Wertheimer, M. (1961), *Science*, vol. 134, p. 1692

Wheeler, D. (1970), *Cognitive Psychology*, vol. 1, pp. 59–85

Whitman, C. P., and Geller, E. S. (1971), *Journal of Experimental Psychology*, vol. 91, pp. 299–304

Whorf, B. L. (1956), *Language, Thought and Reality: Selected Writings of Benjamin Lee Whorf*, ed. J. B. Carroll, New York: Wiley

Wickelgren, W. A. (1977), *Acta Psychologica*, vol. 41, pp. 67–85

Wickens, C. D. (1974), *Psychological Bulletin*, vol. 81, pp. 739–55

Wiesel, T. N., and Hubel, D. H. (1965), *Journal of Neurophysiology*, vol. 28, pp. 1029–40

Wilcox, L., and Wilding, J. M. (1970), *Nature*, vol. 227, pp. 1152–3

Wilding, J. M. (1971a), *Acta Psychologica*, vol. 35, pp. 378–98

Wilding, J. M. (1971b), *Acta Psychologica*, vol. 35, pp. 399–413

Wilding, J. M. (1974), *Acta Psychologica*, vol. 38, pp. 483–500

Wilding, J. M. (1978a), *Acta Psychologica*, vol. 42, pp. 231–51

Wilding, J. M. (1978b), in A. Burton and J. Radford (eds.), *Thinking in Perspective*, London: Methuen

Wilding, J. M., and Farrell, J. M. (1970), *Psychonomic Science*, vol. 19, pp. 123–4

Williams, J. A. (1966), *Journal of Experimental Psychology*, vol. 71, pp. 665–72

Winter, W. (1967), *Psychologica Africana*, vol. 12, pp. 42–8

Wispe, L. G., and Drambarean, N. C. (1953), *Journal of Experimental Psychology*, vol. 46, pp. 25–31

Wohlwill, J. F. (1963), in L. P. Lipsitt and C. C. Spiker (eds.), *Advances in Child Development and Behaviour*, vol. 1, New York: Academic Press

Wohlwill, J. F. (1964), *Perceptual and Motor Skills*, vol. 19, pp. 403–13

Wohlwill, J. F. (1965), *Journal of Experimental Child Psychology*, vol. 2, pp. 163–77

Wood, C. C., and Jennings, J. R. (1976), *Perception and Psychophysics*, vol. 19, pp. 92–101

Yamadori, A. (1975), *Brain*, vol. 98, pp. 231–8

Yntema, D. B., and Torgerson, W. S. (1967), in W. Edwards and A. Tversky (eds.), *Decision Making*, Harmondsworth: Penguin

Yntema, D. B., and Trask, F. P. (1963), *Journal of Verbal Learning and Verbal Behaviour*, vol. 2, pp. 65–74

Yonas, A., and Hagen, M. A. (1973), *Journal of Experimental Child Psychology*, vol. 15, pp. 254–65

Zajonc, R. B., and Dorfman, D. D. (1965), *Psychological Review*, vol. 71, pp. 273–90

Zaporozhets, A. V. (1965), *Monographs of the Society for Research in Child Development*, vol. 30 (2), pp. 82–101

Zeigler, H. P., and Leibowitz, H. (1957), *American Journal of Psychology*, vol. 70, pp. 106–9

Zeki, S. (1973), *Brain Research*, vol. 53, pp. 422–7

Zelniker, J., and Jeffrey, W. E. (1976), *Monographs of the Society for Research in Child Development*, vol. 41 (5, whole no.168), pp. 1–59

Zingg, R. M. (1940), *American Journal of Psychology*, vol. 53, pp. 487–517

Index